RUNNING BETWEEN THE WICKETS

Also by the author

A Biography of Rahul Dravid: The Nice Guy Who Finished First

Cricket World Cup: Cherish and Relish

SMG: A Biography of Sunil Manohar Gavaskar

Hero: A Biography of Sachin Ramesh Tendulkar

Winning Like Sachin: Think & Win Like Tendulkar

The Trail of Cricket's Holy Grail: The World Cup, from 1975 to 2019

RUNNING BETWEEN THE WICKETS

THE STORY OF
THE INDIAN MEN'S CRICKET TEAM

DEVENDRA PRABHUDESAI

Published by
Rupa Publications India Pvt. Ltd 2025
161-B/4, Gulmohar House,
Yusuf Sarai Community Centre,
New Delhi 110049

Sales centres:
Bengaluru Chennai
Hyderabad Kolkata Mumbai

Copyright © Devendra Prabhudesai 2025

Cover photographs: Srenik Sett, Ashutosh Sharma, Madhav Apte's collection, Madhav Mantri's collection, Gopal Bhat, Prof. R.S. Shetty's collection

The views and opinions expressed in this book are the author's own and the facts are as reported by him; these have been verified to the extent possible, and the publishers are not in any way liable for the same.

All rights reserved.
No part of this publication may be reproduced, transmitted, or stored in a retrieval system, in any form or by any means, electronic, mechanical, photocopying, recording or otherwise, without the prior permission of the publisher.

P-ISBN: 978-93-7003-393-1
E-ISBN: 978-93-7003-582-9

First impression 2025

10 9 8 7 6 5 4 3 2 1

The moral right of the author has been asserted.

Printed in India

This book is sold subject to the condition that it shall not, by way of trade or otherwise, be lent, resold, hired out or otherwise circulated, without the publisher's prior consent, in any form of binding or cover other than that in which it is published.

Dedicated to

Sumedh Shah, pioneer of sport management in India
Dear Mr Shah,
Thank you for introducing me to a whole new world. Thank you for everything.

Neela Satyanarayana, state election commissioner, administrator, author, poet, composer and mother-in-law
Dear Neela mavshi,
This book was written on your desk.

Sandeep Gandhi, schoolmate and one of the finest human beings I have known
Dear Sandeep,
Miss you, my friend.

CONTENTS

Prologue ix

1. Institution 1
2. Catalyst 7
3. Forerunners 11
4. The Centurion and the Championship 17
5. 'Vizard' of Woes 22
6. Transition-I 27
7. Domestic Duels 32
8. Undivided No More 37
9. Fire and Ice 43
10. Versatile Virtuoso 48
11. Template 53
12. Musical Chairs 58
13. Resurgence 63
14. Pitchforked 69
15. Quartet 75
16. Success Overseas 80
17. 'Casting' Coup 85
18. Khadoos! 90
19. Twin Triumphs 96
20. Stagnancy 103
21. Fall and Rise 107
22. Gladiators 112
23. Transition-II 118
24. From Gavaskar To Gavaskar 124

25. All in the Mind	129
26. The Win of the Tortoise	135
27. Generation-L	140
28. 'Jimmy, Jimmy'	146
29. Ruling the World	151
30. Turbulence	156
31. Sequel	162
32. Second-Best	167
33. A Season of Two Chases	172
34. Mistrust	177
35. Boy Wonder	184
36. Spin Returns	190
37. Revolutions	196
38. Birth of the Middle Order	204
39. The Last Captaincies	211
40. Silver Linings	218
41. Larger Than Life	223
42. Team-Rebuilding	228
43. Tigers Overseas	234
44. Forward and Back	239
45. Resurrection	245
46. The League and Extraordinary Gentlemen	251
47. Ascent	256
48. Zenith	262
49. Sunsets	267
50. Boys in Blue, Men in Black	272
51. Walking the Talk	278
52. Victors Down Under	283
53. Champs Again	288
Epilogue	294
Acknowledgements	300
Bibliography	301
Index	309

PROLOGUE

Hum hain Team India! Hum pe na chalega zor! Umeedon ka suraj nikla hain chaaron ore! Iraadey hain fauladi himmatti har kadam! Apne haathon kismat likhne aaj nikal chaley hain hum! (We are Team India! We shall not be intimidated! Our spirit is as indomitable as the rising sun! Every step of ours reflects our courage and determination! To shape our own destiny is our mission!)

—Vivek Razdan, 19 January 2021

The Gabba, Brisbane, 2 December 1977

Sunil Gavaskar, India's vice-captain, was fuming on his way back to the dressing-room. Moments earlier, a delivery by Wayne Clarke, Australia's debutant paceman, had ricocheted off the inside-edge of his bat, onto the chest-guard underneath his shirt. From there, it had rebounded to the fielder at short leg. He reckoned that had he not worn a chest-guard, the ball would have hit him and dropped at his feet. For Gavaskar, pain was preferable to an early dismissal any day.

Pahlanji 'Polly' Umrigar, the manager of the Indian team, had the players' well-being in mind when he insisted that they wore chest-guards to shield themselves from the blows that they were bound to cop on the lively Australian wickets. Gavaskar had missed a couple of games before the first Test and was therefore not used to wearing a chest-guard. He wanted the freedom to decide whether to wear one, but was overruled.

The Indian team's third full tour of Australia had begun at a time when the sport was battling a crisis. Kerry Packer, Australian media magnate, had signed over fifty cricketers from across the globe to play in the World Series Cricket (WSC), his brainchild. While the International Cricket Conference (ICC) and its member-nations were aghast at the creation of a parallel institution, Packer's recruits were defiant. They were frustrated with the condescending attitude of the 'establishment' and delighted when Packer promised to pay them what they believed they deserved. Top Australian cricketers of the time signed up with WSC, as did their counterparts from the West Indies. Packer's recruits also included cricketers from England, Pakistan and South Africa, a country that was facing a sporting boycott at the time.

When the establishment slapped bans on the signatories, Packer went to court on behalf of the latter. The ICC and the Test and County Cricket Board (TCCB)[1], which ran cricket in England, were reprimanded for 'unreasonable restraint of trade'. However, that did not deter the establishment from doing what was within its control.

The TCCB sacked Tony Greig, England captain and a Packer signatory. The Australian Cricket Board decided not to consider WSC's Australian recruits for selection in international and domestic cricket. Packer retaliated by scheduling WSC matches on the same dates as Test matches in Australia. When they were denied access to traditional cricket grounds, the WSC booked arenas that were used for other sports and pioneered the concept of 'drop-in' pitches, which were created externally and then installed in the middle of the arena with the help of cranes.

Bishan Bedi's Indians knew that the exodus to the WSC would prevent the Australians from putting together a competitive team.

---

[1] The TCCB was subsumed within the ECB—England and Wales Cricket Board—in 1997.

The visitors' egos were also bruised. The fact that the WSC had not signed Indian cricketers suggested that they were not considered good enough. The team was therefore eager to make a statement on the field.

The visitors beat four Australian states outright before the first Test in Brisbane, in which the home team's XI comprised six debutants. Three others had played less than ten Tests each.

One of the two seniors was Jeff Thomson, the fastest bowler on earth at that point. He too had signed up with WSC but was forced to withdraw due to an existing contract with a radio station, which made it mandatory for him to represent the state of Queensland in domestic cricket. The other senior in the XI was the 41-year-old Robert 'Bob' Simpson, former Australia captain and icon.

Simpson was assigned the captaincy and the responsibility of hand-holding a bunch of youngsters. He had retired from international cricket a decade ago, but had been playing Grade (club) cricket in Sydney. Of course, an international series was a different proposition altogether, but Simpson's apprehensions were dispelled by no less a figure than Sir Don Bradman, who reminded him of his own return at 38, after an eight-year hiatus from cricket due to World War II.

Shortly after Simpson won the toss and elected to bat at the Gabba, the hosts floundered against the genius of Bishan Bedi, who took five wickets and hastened Australia's dismissal at 166.

All the Indians had to do was negotiate Thomson and accumulate a lead—or so it seemed. However, Gavaskar's chest-guard let him down and Mohinder Amarnath fell soon after. Gundappa Viswanath engineered a recovery in the company of Dilip Vengsarkar, but the former's dismissal triggered a collapse and India conceded a 13-run lead. Not for the first or last time, the Indian batters had let their bowlers down.

Australia got off to another poor start in the second innings. However, David Ogilvie and Peter Toohey batted well in the company of Simpson, who scored 89. Madan Lal and Mohinder made inroads with the second new ball, but the Indians allowed an old jinx to reassert itself. The bowlers failed to dislodge the tail-enders and Australia's last two wickets added 81. India needed 341 to win.

Vengsarkar departed early. Mohinder, Viswanath and Ashok Mankad got off to strong starts, but could not consolidate. Gavaskar, however, was in the zone. His drives were gorgeous and his horizontal bat strokes, emphatic. His footwork was as adept at responding to Thomson's pace as it was against the leg-spin of Simpson and Tony Mann. He was batting without the encumbrance of a chest-guard, Umrigar having relented.

In Syed Kirmani, who came in at 196-5, Gavaskar found the partner he had been looking for. Both batted well in tandem and took the score along. The spectators rose to Gavaskar when he drove an attempted yorker by Alan Hurst through the covers to complete his eleventh Test century.

India were 98 runs away when Gavaskar fished at a Wayne Clarke delivery in the 'corridor of uncertainty' and was caught behind. Madan Lal and Erapalli Prasanna came and went, but Kirmani refused to surrender. Bedi supported him ably.

Kirmani completed his fifty but mistimed a hook soon after and was caught. Now, it was all up to Bedi. He took a single to mid-wicket and hoped that Bhagwat Chandrasekhar would last the last two balls of a Thomson over. He didn't. Australia won by 17 runs.

While it was not the first or last time India had lost the first Test of a series overseas, a loss to a 'third XI' hurt. But then, they had only themselves to blame. The batters should have clicked in the first innings. The new-ball bowlers should have been given more overs with the second new ball in Australia's second innings.

Sunil Gavaskar marshalled his team's pursuit of a target on the last day of a Test on several occasions before and after this match. It was also not the only time India was set a target in excess of 300 at the Gabba.

Prologue

The Gabba, Brisbane, 15 January 2021

As Mohammed Siraj stood at the top of his run-up, waiting for David Warner to get ready for the first ball of the Test, the paceman from Hyderabad reflected on what had happened in the last two months.

The Indian team had begun its thirteenth full tour of Australia at a time when the planet was combating a catastrophe. COVID-19 had infected millions, killed thousands and crippled economies. The Indian players had gone into a two-week quarantine after flying to Australia from the United Arab Emirates, where they had been playing in the Indian Premier League (IPL).

Shortly after the team reached Australia, Siraj, a new entrant into the national squad, received news of his father's demise. He considered returning home, but his mother convinced him to keep pursuing his father's dreams. He stayed back and made an impressive debut in the second Test in Melbourne. The fourth and final Test was played at Brisbane, a city that usually hosted the first Test of a series in Australia.

Siraj, three Tests old, was India's most experienced bowler in the playing XI at the Gabba. India had lost as many as eight players—all of whom were certainties in the XI at the start of the Test series—to either injury or paternal leave, by the time the fourth Test began. The casualties comprised the entire first-choice bowling line-up—Jasprit Bumrah, Mohammed Shami, Umesh Yadav, Ravichandran Ashwin and Ravindra Jadeja. Ironically, the pandemic came to the visitors' rescue. Their squad was larger than usual, as flying replacements from India at short notice was out of the question.

Siraj's colleagues in Brisbane comprised the Tamil Nadu duo of Thangarasu Natarajan, a left-arm paceman, and Washington Sundar, an off-spinning all-rounder. Both had been a part of the squad for the limited-overs games and had stayed back for the Tests as net bowlers. However, the surfeit of injuries in the camp meant that both were handed Test caps at the Gabba. Navdeep Saini and Shardul Thakur, the other two members of the bowling line-up, had played one Test each.

The full-strength Australian XI scored 369 against India's third XI in the first innings. Saini strained his groin, adding to the list of casualties. However, Natarajan, Thakur and Sundar struck thrice each. Siraj, who was disappointed about finishing with a solitary wicket, was reassured by Bharat Arun, India's bowling coach, that he had bowled so well that the batsmen had tried to break free against his colleagues and paid the price. The bowlers had hunted in a pack.

When India batted, five of their top six bats crossed 20, but Pat Cummins, Mitchell Starc, Josh Hazlewood and Nathan Lyon, who together constituted the most formidable bowling attack in the world, kept pegging away. India were 186-6 when Sundar was joined by Thakur. For Australia, who had not lost a Test at the Gabba since November 1988, a massive first-innings lead beckoned.

Thakur and Sundar were not specialist batters, but both epitomized India's traditional schools of batting. Thakur displayed the grit and gumption that had been the hallmark of batters from Mumbai, his hometown. The left-handed Sundar, who had started life as an opening batter before off-spin got the better of him, rekindled memories of India's batting artists down the decades, with his penchant for finding the gaps. The duo added 123 and India were dismissed for 336.

Thakur was not done yet. Both Siraj and he had taken four wickets each by the time Australia's last pair came together in the second innings. It was Siraj who completed a 'five-for' when Hazlewood skied him to Thakur at third-man. He was India's highest wicket-taker of the series, with 13 scalps. India needed 328 to win.

Rohit Sharma, who had joined the Indian team for the last two Tests, nicked Cummins to Tim Paine, Australia's keeper-captain, with only 18 on the board. His dismissal did not ruffle his partner, Shubman Gill.

As Gill drove and punched with panache, Cheteshwar Pujara, who had faced over 700 balls in the series already, blocked and nudged. His propensity to take his eyes off deliveries that reared awkwardly off a length, resulted in his being hit several times. India were 83-1 at lunch.

Pujara took more blows, including one on the ribs, after the resumption. In the 46th over of the innings, bowled by Starc, Gill followed an audacious hook for six with an uppercut over third-man for four. Starc dug the next delivery short, only to be pulled for another boundary. The batsmen then crossed and Pujara added insult to injury with a cut for four. Gill had moved to 91 when he nicked Lyon to slip. 132-2.

Concern levels rose in the Indian camp when Pujara's ring finger got jammed between a Hazlewood delivery and the handle of his bat. There was some concern as he had injured it in an earlier game as well. Fortunately, he was able to carry on. A little later, Hazlewood hit him again, this time on the side of the helmet. Luckily, there was no damage on either occasion. Ajinkya Rahane, the Indian captain, hit Lyon into the stands beyond mid-wicket and appeared to be in control until a delivery from Cummins, which he attempted to cut over the slips, kissed his gloves and was devoured by Paine. 167-3.

Rahane's 24 in 22 cameo left no one in any doubt as to what was on his mind. As they crossed, the captain instructed Rishabh Pant, the incoming batter, to hold on till tea, which was 15 minutes away. He could do whatever he wanted after the resumption, Rahane advised. At tea, India were 145 runs away, with at least 37 overs left.

Shortly after tea, Pant charged down the track at Lyon and swung but missed. Thankfully for him, so did Paine, adding four byes to the Indian total. The ball was turning square. Those who expected Pant to exercise caution after the reprieve were stunned when he advanced to Lyon again and this time, connected. That six over long-on, hit against the turn, meant India crossed the

200-run mark. To emphasize that he knew what he was doing, Pant then cut Starc resoundingly for four. At the other end, Pujara late-cut Marcus Labuschagne for four to bring up his fifty.

The second new ball worked for Australia. India were a hundred runs away when Cummins won a leg-before shout against Pujara. The batter's 56 off 211 balls was worth its weight in gold. Pant retaliated by thrashing Hazlewood through the covers for four. Cummins was then subjected to similar treatment.

Mayank Agarwal, an opener now batting in the middle order, played a couple of good strokes before being caught in the covers. 265-5. Washington Sundar began his innings with a stunning off-drive off Cummins, but the Australians then pulled things back. With eight overs left, India needed 50.

Only one run came off the first four balls of the next over, bowled by Cummins. Sundar's eyes lit up when Cummins pitched the fifth ball short. The batter swung at it with a horizontal bat, both feet off the ground when he made contact, and the ball flew into the stands. It was followed by another audacious stroke. Sundar opened the face of his bat to a delivery pitched outside the off-stump, and dispatched it over the slips for a boundary. 39 needed off 42.

Pant's response to his partner's audacity was a 'falling scoop' off Lyon that hurried to the fine-leg boundary. He followed it with a slog-sweep for another four. In a sign that the momentum was with the visitors, the Australians ended up conceding byes and leg-byes.

Only ten runs were needed off the remaining 26 deliveries when Sundar tried to reverse-sweep Lyon. He missed and was bowled.

The first ball of the next over, bowled by Hazlewood, reared off a length. Pant leaped and slapped it while airborne. The roars of the Indian supporters when he was lying flat on the ground alerted him to the fact that the ball had gone for a four.

Only three runs were needed off 21 deliveries when Thakur holed out to short mid-wicket. However, Pant had crossed. He then drove Hazlewood and ran. As the cherry sped past him, Navdeep Saini, the non-striker, forgot his groin injury and sprinted, but he did not have to exert himself too much. The ball raced to the rope.

Considering everything that the Indians had been through on the tour, it was the greatest-ever series victory in 144 years of Test cricket.

The Indian cricketers, some of whom could not have imagined at the start of the series that not only would they play in it but also influence its outcome, had stared down all the jinxes of Indian cricket and made them blink. In what was a bizarre coincidence, their captain, Ajinkya Rahane, was called 'Jinks' by his teammates.

A lot happened between those two Tests at the Gabba. And before and after.

1
INSTITUTION

Throughout the season, I had tried in different ways to assist the Indian players because I felt it was part of our responsibility to encourage and improve their standard.

Test cricket between England and Australia is still supreme, but it cannot remain in isolation, and will be materially strengthened if other countries can match their skill.

That day undoubtedly will come; as the mother country founded and nurtured her colonies, so should we assist the less mature cricketing countries to the highest standard of play.

—Sir Don Bradman, referring to the 1947-48 series between India and Australia, *Farewell to Cricket*[1]

The earliest recorded reference to cricket being played on Indian soil can be traced back to 1721. A British sailor named Downing, whose ship was anchored off the coast of Cambay (Khambhat) in what is modern-day Gujarat, wrote about him and his colleagues 'diverting themselves with playing cricket and other exercises.'

Members of India's civilian population started playing cricket in the first half of the nineteenth century. The Parsis of Bombay

---

[1]Bradman, Don, *Farewell to Cricket*, Hodder & Stoughton, London, 1950.

(officially renamed Mumbai in 1995), pioneers in the fields of law, industry and politics, took the lead in cricket as well. They were followed by the Hindus and Muslims.

The performances of the Parsi cricketers on what was their second tour of England in 1888 (they first toured in 1886) earned them a match against G.F. Vernon's XI that toured India in 1889-90 to play Britons who were posted on the subcontinent. The Parsis won that match, played at Bombay's Esplanade Maidan, by four wickets. They defeated another team from England in 1892.

There was a fortuitous development for Indian cricket in 1891. Lord George Robert Canning Harris, the former England captain, was appointed Governor of the Bombay Presidency—spanning most of modern-day Maharashtra, Gujarat, Karnataka, Sind (now in Pakistan) and even Aden across the Arabian Sea. The cricketer in him grasped the potential of the Parsis, and he convinced the Bombay Gymkhana, a British institution that prohibited entry to 'dogs and Indians', to institute annual Presidency matches between the Europeans and the Parsis.

The first Presidency match was played in 1892. The Bombay Gymkhana complied with Lord Harris' suggestion that it be represented by a strong team, comprising players from all over the Bombay Presidency. The rulers were wary of losing to the ruled, of course.

Bombay, the gateway to the Raj, had a head-start over other cities of British India on the cricketing front, equipped as it was from the very beginning with grounds and turf pitches that helped yield quality cricketers. The annual Presidency match became a Triangular in 1907 and a Quadrangular in 1912, with the entry of the Hindus and Muslims respectively.

This communal model was replicated in other cities, but the Bombay Quadrangular retained its eminence. The best cricketers from across the country started coming to Bombay annually to represent their respective communities in the Quadrangular, in much the same way that cricketers from across the world fly to India annually to play the IPL in the 21st century. The final squads were picked by the Bombay Gymkhana (Europeans), Parsi Gymkhana, Hindu Gymkhana and Islam Gymkhana.

The 1890s also witnessed the advent of two greats. Kumar Sri Ranjitsinhji, prince of Nawanagar, captured the imagination of cricket-lovers in England with his batting when he was studying at Cambridge. He later represented England and scored a century on his Test debut. At the other end of the spectrum was Baloo Palwankar, a left-arm spinner from Poona (renamed Pune in 1978). The Hindus were reluctant to play him because he belonged to the social strata that had been classified as untouchable. However, merit eventually prevailed. Three of Baloo's brothers followed in his footsteps. In fact, one of them—Vithal Palwankar—even captained the Hindus in the Quadrangular.

The pinnacle of Baloo's career was the tour of England by an All-India team, funded by the Tatas—the premier industrial house. The lineup comprised five Hindus, three Muslims and six Parsis, drawn from across the subcontinent. The Indians won only two (and lost 10) of their 14 first-class matches, but Baloo took scores of wickets.

Framji Patel, the organizer of the tour, tried to convince Ranjitsinhji, who by then had been crowned Jam Saheb of Nawanagar, to lead the team, but in vain. The first Indian to make waves as a cricketer at the international level gave the impression of being indifferent to Indian cricket. Bhupinder Singh, the Maharaja of Patiala, was then designated captain, but he played in only a couple of games.

Sixteen years later, a significant meeting took place at Delhi's Roshanara Club, after the conclusion of a match between northern India and the Marylebone Cricket Club (MCC), cricket's most venerated institution, whose team was touring the subcontinent in 1926–27. The attendees were Bhupinder Singh, Arthur Gilligan, the MCC captain and a former England captain, Grant Govan, an English businessman, and Anthony De Mello, his Indian employee. It was during this meeting that Gilligan pronounced that he had seen enough on the tour to conclude that India was 'ready for Test cricket'.

The next step for the Indians was to create an apex body, which would represent them at the ICC[2] and manage first-class cricket in the land.

Bhupinder Singh, Govan and De Mello convened a meeting in Delhi in November 1927, which was attended by representatives of Sind, Punjab, Patiala, Delhi, the United Provinces, Rajputana, Alwar, Bhopal, Gwalior, Baroda, Kathiawar and Central India. There was consensus that a Board of Cricket Control was necessary to ensure the following:

- Advance and control the game throughout India.
- Arrange and control inter-territorial, foreign and other cricket matches.
- Make arrangements incidental to visits of teams to India.
- Manage and control all-India representatives playing within and outside India.
- If necessary, control and help resolve all or any inter-territorial disputes.
- Settle disputes or differences between associations affiliated to the Board and appeals referred to it by any such associations.
- Adopt, if desirable, all rules and amendments passed by the MCC.

At a subsequent meeting in December 1927, it was unanimously decided that a provisional Board of Control would be formed, to be replaced by a permanent body as soon as eight territorial associations were created. Govan and De Mello then travelled

---

[2]Cricket's apex body was called the Imperial Cricket Conference from its inception in 1909 till 1965, when it was rechristened the International Cricket Conference. It was re-rechristened the International Cricket Council in 1989.

to England to propose India's inclusion in the ICC. The ICC responded positively, but the duo was dismayed to discover after its return to India that only six associations had been created.

Keen as they were about India hosting South Africa in 1929 and touring England in 1931, Govan and De Mello insisted at the next meeting of the provisional board in December 1928 that a permanent board be formed, even though the target of eight associations had not been achieved.

Thus was born the Board of Control for Cricket in India, of which Govan and De Mello were elected president and secretary, respectively. Five months later, the ICC granted the BCCI full membership.

At this time, the subcontinent was in tumult, with the freedom movement gaining momentum. The series against South Africa did not materialize and the tour of England was postponed by a year.

At an emergency meeting of the BCCI in September 1931, Gajapatairaj Vijaya Ananda, the Maharajkumar of Vizianagaram, offered the board INR 50,000, inclusive of INR 40,000 to cover the expenses of the tour of England in 1932. Vizzy, as he came to be known, was seen to be ingratiating himself with Willingdon, India's viceroy, in what was clearly an attempt to capitalize on the latter's disdain for Bhupinder Singh.

The Maharaja of Patiala did not appreciate Vizzy's bid to oust him as Indian cricket's premier patron. At the BCCI's annual meeting in November 1931, Bhupinder Singh offered to host the selection trials for the England tour and indemnify the expenses that would be incurred on the trip. Elated by the offer, the BCCI snubbed Vizzy.

Sixty-five years after Govan and De Mello met the ICC in London to submit the BCCI's request for admission, another seminal meeting took place in the same city. This was after the BCCI teamed up with its Pakistani and Sri Lankan counterparts to bid for the hosting rights of the 1996 World Cup. Up against them were England, whose attempts to tinker with the process did not go down very well with one of the Asian representatives. This individual supposedly stated, 'I did my schooling in British India. Our teachers would say, "Brittania rules the waves." I did not know that Brittania also waives the rules.' After fourteen hours of deliberations, the subcontinent won by 27 votes to England's ten.

2
CATALYST

One of the 26 first-class matches that Arthur Gilligan's MCC side played on its 1926–27 India tour was a two-day affair against the Hindus at the Bombay Gymkhana, which began on 30 November 1926. MCC batted first and scored 363. The Hindus were 67-2 on the second day when C.K. Nayudu joined L.P. Jai in the middle.

Gilligan, who had taken the game off and was seated in the clubhouse, saw Nayudu open his account with a two off George Boyes, the left-arm spinner from Hampshire. It was the proverbial lull before the storm. A little later, Nayudu stepped down the wicket to hit a Boyes delivery over the clubhouse. In Boyes' next over, Nayudu swung him for another six, the ball landing in a tent next to the clubhouse. It was followed by another. The spectators found their voice and clapped. Joining them in the applause were the umpires.

Nayudu then targeted the other bowlers, even as his teammates struggled against them. He had a close shave at 33 when Ewart Astill, the seamer, deceived him with a slower ball. Nayudu mistimed and skied it, but the bowler spilt the catch. At lunch, the Hindus were 154-6 with Nayudu on 50.

Every vantage point, be it the branches of the trees that lined the periphery of the ground or the rooftops of the adjoining buildings, was occupied by the time play resumed.

Nayudu added insult to injury by hitting Astill for four more sixes, thus making a mockery of the opposition's attempt to curb the scoring by placing all the fielders on the boundary. Maurice Tate, England's fast-bowling hero of the 1924–25 Ashes, had troubled the Indian batters in the earlier games, but he could not subdue Nayudu. The crowds rejoiced when their hero completed his century in only 65 minutes.

Bob Wyatt, who replaced Tate in the attack, began with a maiden over, but was hit for four and six in his second over. In his third over, Nayudu hit him for 22. Jack Mercer, the paceman, was reintroduced into the attack, but Nayudu did not spare him either. His innings finally ended when he went for another big hit off paceman George Geary and was caught by Astill.

Nayudu's 153 in 116 minutes featured 49 scoring strokes, including 14 boundaries and 11 sixes. It was the highest number of sixes ever hit in a first-class innings at that stage. When stumps were drawn that evening, the spectators gathered outside the Bombay Gymkhana to catch a glimpse of Nayudu. He was showered with gifts, including a silver bat and a Triumph motorcycle.

Among those fascinated by Nayudu's innings was a 15-year-old boy named Vijay Merchant. His surname was actually Thakersay, but the principal of his school had rechristened him Merchant at the time of admission, when the boy told him that his was a family of cloth merchants and traders.

L.R. Tairsee, the president of Bombay's Hindu Gymkhana, referred to his institution's successful endeavour to initiate social reforms in his welcome address at a dinner in honour of the MCC team, a few days after Nayudu's innings. The audience, which comprised Ranjitsinhji among others, did not take too long to figure out where he was coming from; he was basically implying that it was time for the British to follow in the footsteps of the upper-caste Hindus, who had reached out to the marginalized sections. Vithal, Baloo's brother, was the captain of their cricket team, after all.

It could be contended that Tairsee was emboldened to make a subtle appeal to the British to start treating their Indian subjects fairly only because of the way Nayudu had batted against a team representing the rulers.

Nayudu was born in Nagpur in 1895 and introduced to cricket by his father and uncle, both of whom had studied in England. There are stories of them being close to Ranjitsinhji, as well as claims that the prince relayed the following tips to the young Nayudu through them:

- Keep the bat straight.
- Hit the ball hard.
- Don't be scared.

Since his formative years, Nayudu swore by the dictum that 'cricket ought to be played in harmony with its inherent genius, with wild and free abandon.' His first scoring stroke on his debut for the Hindus in the 1916 Quadrangular was a six. His consistency in the Bombay Quadrangular and other tournaments in the years that followed had made him the most popular cricketer in the land. His batting apart, he was an outstanding fielder and an underrated off-break bowler. Underperformance and admitting to physical pain were his pet peeves.

A fortnight after Nayudu's innings at the Bombay Gymkhana, Gilligan led the MCC in an unofficial Test against an All-India side at the same venue. Dinkar Balwant Deodhar, a classy batter from Poona who was added to the XI after Vithal withdrew due to injury, scored 148. Nayudu, who led in Vithal's absence, scored 18. Two other players who made an impact were Janardhan Navle, the wicketkeeper who opened the batting and scored 74, and Nazir Ali, a fast-bowling all-rounder who took four wickets. Wazir Ali, the latter's elder brother and a top-order batter, scored 48 to add to his three centuries in the other games that he played against the MCC.

However, the one performance that impressed Gilligan the

most was the one that he had watched at the Bombay Gymkhana on 1 December 1926. Subsequently, he had assured Bhupinder, Govan and De Mello that he would do his bit to ensure that India attained Test status.

Another prominent supporter of Indian cricket was Lord Harris. As governor of Bombay Presidency in the 1890s, he had encouraged the inception of the annual Presidency match and allotted land on the Bombay seafront to the Parsis, Hindus and Muslims to create their own gymkhanas. In the same year in which Nayudu scored that 153, Lord Harris had presided over an ICC meeting in London where it was decided to extend membership of the latter to countries within the British empire where cricket was being played. That was how the West Indies, New Zealand and eventually India entered the fold.

Like Nayudu in the 1930s, Sachin Tendulkar in the 1990s often made watchers believe that the match was being played on two different wickets. Tendulkar opened the batting for India for the first time in a one-day international against New Zealand in Auckland in March 1994. When he was dismissed after scoring 82 off 49 balls, the spectators, the opposition and his teammates were joined in the applause by the umpires.

Some six decades before Tendulkar became the first minor to be allowed entry into the clubhouse of the Cricket Club of India (CCI), Ardeshir Furdorji Sohrabji Talyarkhan, the pioneer of live sports commentary in India, declined All-India Radio's invitation to do the ball-by-ball cricket broadcast of a Quadrangular game at the Bombay Gymkhana, because he would have to wear an identification card. He was Indian and the Bombay Gymkhana was out of bounds for dogs and Indians, after all. His British friends then convinced Joseph Kay, the Bombay Gymkhana president, to invite him as a 'guest', so that he could do the commentary. That made Talyarkhan the first Indian to be invited as a guest by the Bombay Gymkhana.

3
FORERUNNERS

No politics, no caste, just cricket. This is the unofficial slogan of the cricket team that has come from India after a lapse of 21 years to try its strength against England and the first class counties.

There has never been such a team of contrasts meeting on the common footing of cricket. The 18 players speak eight to ten languages among them; they belong to four or five different castes.

—*Evening Standard*, 13 April 1932

Fifty-seven players from all over the subcontinent were invited to Patiala in January 1932 to attend the selection trials for the England tour. Three batters from Bombay—including Vijay Merchant, who had watched Nayudu's innings in December 1926 and established a reputation as a batter in the years that followed—declined the invitation as a mark of protest against British rule; the Civil Disobedience movement was on, and Mahatma Gandhi was in prison.

The BCCI invited Ranjitsinhji to chair the selection committee. While Dr H.D. Kanga and Alexander Hosie, both former cricketers, refused the invitation to join the panel, Ahsan-ul-Haq, who had played first-class cricket in England at the turn of the century and later represented the Muslims in the Quadrangular, came on board. Ranji's other co-panellists were Prince Gyanashyamsinhji of Limbdi and Vizzy. Duleepsinhji, the nephew of Ranjitsinhji, and Iftikar Ali Khan, the Nawab of Pataudi, were co-opted onto the panel. Both princes were quality cricketers, who had learnt the sport while pursuing academics in England. In fact, they had even been touted as likely captains of India. But here they were, watching the trials instead of running them.

Notwithstanding the presence of multiple selectors, there was never any doubt as to who was calling the shots. Bhupinder Singh was in charge.

The final squad was announced on 4 February 1932. Bhupinder himself was named captain, Gyanashyamsinhji vice-captain and Vizzy, the deputy vice-captain. Thus, two of the selectors picked themselves. Major E.W.C. Ricketts, who had spent many years in military service in India, was named manager.

The remainder of the squad was as follows:

- **Batters:** Wazir Ali, Sorabji Colah, Naoomal Jeoomal, Nariman Marshall, Joginder Singh and Lall Singh
- **Wicketkeepers:** Janardhan Navle and Bahadur Kapadia
- **Fast/medium-pace bowlers:** Mohammed Nissar, Amar Singh, Ghulam Mohammed and Shankarrao Godambe
- **Fast bowling all-rounder:** Nazir Ali
- **Slow-bowling all-rounders:** C.K. Nayudu and Phiroze Palia

The team comprised seven Hindus, four Muslims, four Parsis and three Sikhs. Not much was known about two of the Sikhs. Joginder Singh was a member of Bhupinder Singh's personal retinue and apparently a versatile sportsperson, and Lall Singh, who hailed from Malaysia, was said to be an outstanding fielder.

Ranji recommended the inclusion of Amar Singh, his subject at Nawanagar. Although Amar Singh was primarily a bowler, it was his batting—specifically, a six hit by him that struck a horse-carriage driver—in a trial game in Delhi which caught the Jam Saheb's attention.

A couple of weeks after the team was announced, Bhupinder dropped out. It was later contended that he had never intended to tour and got himself named captain only to stave Vizzy off. The BCCI then chose Natwarsinhji Bhavsinhji—the Maharaja of Porbandar and husband of Gyanashyamsinhji's sister—to lead the squad. Natwarsinhji could hardly put bat to ball, but he could be counted upon to deliver after-dinner speeches. In 1932, royalty mattered.

Vizzy himself did not appreciate being named deputy vice-captain and withdrew as well. His replacement was Jahangir Khan, a fast-bowling all-rounder from Lahore.

Not all the players who travelled to England by the RMS *Strathnaver* were strangers to the country. Nayudu had gone to England the year before and represented the Indian Gymkhana in the leagues to familiarize himself with the conditions.

The Indians won four, drew five and lost one of their ten first-class games before the solitary Test. Natwarsinhji, fed up with the criticism of his cricketing skills, declared himself unavailable as a player after leading the visitors to victory against Cambridge.

Nayudu, who had led India to victory against Northamptonshire in an earlier game, helmed the squad against Lancashire and Worcestershire, drawing the first game and winning the second. He was in form as well, having scored a century against the MCC at Lord's. With Gyanashyamsinhji struggling due to a back injury that he had sustained while scoring a century against the Eastern Counties, Natwarsinhji nominated C.K. Nayudu as captain for the Test.

While it might seem appropriate that India's top cricketer of 1932 was the nation's first Test captain, it was not perceived that way 93 years ago.

India's inaugural Test, a three-day game that commenced at the Lord's Cricket Ground, the home of the MCC, on

25 June 1932, got off to a dramatic start, first off and then on the field. Natwarsinhji was woken up in the early hours by players who expressed their reluctance to play under Nayudu, who they claimed was too dictatorial. Natwarsinhji shot off a cable, not to the BCCI president or secretary, but to Bhupinder, who responded with another cable, in which he instructed the team to accept Nayudu as captain and get on with it.

The players were introduced to King George V, the titular head of the British empire, before the start. Douglas Jardine, England's Bombay-born captain, won the toss and elected to bat.

Nayudu welcomed Herbert Sutcliffe and Percy Holmes, England's openers, who had put on a record 555 for their county Yorkshire just a few days ago, with three slips and the same number of short-legs. The score was 8 when Mohammed Nissar induced Sutcliffe to play on to his stumps. The paceman proceeded to uproot Holmes' off-stump with the last ball of the same over. A little later, Frank Woolley took on Lall Singh's throwing arm, only to be run out. England were 19-3.

However, the debutants could not capitalize on the start. Half-centuries by Jardine and Les Ames enabled England to score 259. India's first innings showcased the team's inexperience. Seven of the top eight batters entered double figures, but no one crossed 40 and they conceded a first-innings lead of 70. Jardine then scored 85 and declared his team's second innings at 275-8 on the final morning. Amar Singh bowled brilliantly in England's second innings, but without luck.

Up against a target of 346, India's only option was to play it safe, but that wasn't something the stroke-makers in the side were used to doing. Amar Singh delayed the inevitable with a belligerent 51. He owed his fifty, the first by an Indian in Tests, to Phiroze Palia, who batted at number eleven due to an injured thigh. A doctor had advised him against taking the field, but Nayudu insisted that he did and had his way. India lost by 158 runs.

The Indians played fifteen more first-class matches on the tour, of which they won five, drew four and lost six. They could well have won a fifth, but Surrey was allowed to reach 364 after being reduced to 145-7. It wasn't the last time the Indians started well with the ball, only to allow the opposition's lower order to get away.

Nayudu topped the batting averages for the tour, with 1,618 runs. His batting average of 46.4 was the best by an Indian and a commendable performance in an age of uncovered wickets. Amar Singh headed the bowling honours with 111 wickets at an average of 20.78.

The animosity between Nayudu and some of his teammates outlasted the trip. Sorabji Colah even threatened to throw him overboard on the voyage back to India. It was Natwarsinhji's presence that prevented the bitterness from spilling over during the tour.

Fatehsinghrao Gaekwad, the erstwhile Maharaja of Baroda, made a similar impact on India's tour of Pakistan in 1978–79. Although the princes were stripped of their titles by the Government of India in the early 1970s, they continued to be revered in both India and Pakistan. Given the tenuous political relationship between the countries, the Indian view was that the team needed a diplomat as manager. Gaekwad's appointment was a masterstroke. Many of the Pakistanis who flocked to see a king during the tour were his former subjects who had migrated across the border after Partition.

WHAT MIGHT HAVE BEEN

Just before playing their inaugural Test in 1932, the Indians beat Worcestershire by three wickets. Iftikar Ali Khan, the Nawab of Pataudi, scored 83 for the county. Around the same time, K.S. Duleepsinhji, who had already represented England in 12 Tests from 1929 to 1931, scored 128 in a trial game prior to the selection of the England team for the Ashes series later that year.

Tuberculosis prevented him from touring Australia, but Iftikar was picked.

For the BCCI, requesting either or both these exceptional cricketers to nurture the Indian cricket team was a no-brainer. However, Duleep was advised by Ranji himself to opt for England, as that was where he had learnt all his cricket. Ranji had given the impression of being indifferent to Indian cricket all along, although he did try to help Govan and De Mello organize a tour by Australia in 1930–31, after England declined to visit that season.

What if Duleep and Iftikar, the two co-opted members of the selection committee that picked the Indian team for the tour of England in 1932, had been part of the team itself? Iftikar did lead in one of the trial games before declaring himself unavailable for the tour. He went on to represent Worcestershire against his compatriots when they were in England.

There is no doubt that the Indian team would have fared a lot better with either or both princes in the squad. One of them would have been named captain. There would have been no man-management issues, with the commoners in the squad happily playing under princes who were outstanding cricketers themselves. Natwarsinhji would never have entered the picture. Batters of the ilk of Duleep and Iftikar, with their knowledge of English conditions, could well have given Nissar, Amar Singh and Jahangir Khan, who excelled in the inaugural Test anyway, a lot more runs to bowl with.

Had Iftikar represented India in June 1932, he would not have represented England in the acrimonious 'Bodyline series' against Australia which followed. He scored a century on his Test debut in Sydney but played only one more Test in the series, as he refused to field in the Bodyline 'leg-trap'. Douglas Jardine, the England captain, was not someone who brooked dissent.

Indian cricket fans could have hailed a Pataudi for his leadership four decades before they actually did so, had Iftikar Ali Khan captained India in 1932.

4
THE CENTURION AND THE CHAMPIONSHIP

Vizzy ensured that the cricket stadium in Delhi, whose construction he financed, comprised a pavilion that bore the name of Willingdon, the viceroy. The arena, which shared its name with the Ferozeshah Kotla fort that stood next to it, hosted a match between the team that had toured England in 1932 and a Rest of India side led by Vizzy, in February 1933. Vizzy's team applauded C.K. Nayudu when the latter went in to bat, ostensibly to acknowledge his performance in England. However, Nayudu was abused by some of his own teammates from the pavilion. These were the players who had objected to his allegedly dictatorial style of functioning in England.

Nayudu, unflustered as always, scored 102. The fissures within his team were not apparent when it bowled. Amar Singh, who did not get along with him, took 12 wickets to seal victory by an innings and 109 runs.

Ranji passed away in April 1933 and was succeeded as Chancellor of the Chamber of Princes by Bhupinder, much to Willingdon's chagrin. The anti-Bhupinder camp hit back at an emergency BCCI meeting in May 1933, when the British heads of the affiliated associations got the subcontinent divided into three zones—East, North and West—with each of them nominating a member for the selection panel that would pick the Indian team for the Test series against England in 1933–34. Two of the selectors—Alec Hosie (East) and S.E.L. West (North)—were British. The lone Indian was Dr H.D. Kanga (West). He had declined the invitation in 1932 but was persuaded to take up the assignment this time around.

Bombay, the cricket capital of the subcontinent, had neither hosted a significant game of cricket nor had it had any say in cricket administration since 1929, when the Quadrangular was suspended due to political turbulence. The Hindu Gymkhana had even gone so far as to question the creation of the BCCI itself. However, the England tour of 1932 had prompted a rethink. A lot was happening and Bombay did not want to be left behind. The Hindu Gymkhana joined the Bombay Presidency Cricket Association, a BCCI affiliate, in October 1932.

Bombay was also assigned one of the three Tests against England. The metropolis alone possessed the financial means to pay the BCCI the guarantee fee of ₹26,000. Representatives of Calcutta (renamed Kolkata in 2001) and Madras (renamed Chennai in 1996) were reluctant to host the other two Tests, but they fell in line after hearing that Nawab Moin-ud-Dowla was trying to get a Test allotted to Secunderabad, his bastion.

Apart from Jardine, the captain, and Hedley Verity, the left-arm spinner, the England squad did not comprise a single player who had figured in the 'Bodyline' series in Australia, the year before. Even Jardine may not have toured, had his connection with India not run deep. Shortly after the announcement of the team, the MCC received a cable[3], ostensibly from the BCCI, alleging that it had insulted Indian cricket by selecting a second-string side. It was later discovered that the cable had been sent by a

---

[3]From 1903–04 to 1976–77, the MCC organized Test match tours by England cricket teams.

clerk who worked in the telegraph office[4].

C.K. Nayudu was named India's captain for the Test series just before the visitors played the viceroy's XI in Delhi. This time around, Nayudu was not backed by the Bhupinder Singh camp. Yadavindra Singh, the crown prince of Patiala, who had scored 66 for Southern Punjab against the visitors, had emerged as a contender for the captaincy, after all.

Even as all this was happening, the Bombay Gymkhana was being readied for the first-ever Test on Indian soil. A makeshift double-tiered stand was erected for the four-day game that was to begin on 15 December 1933.

The Indian team was selected after three trial games. Merchant and L.P. Jai, both of whom had refused to tour England in 1932, were picked. L. Ramji, Amar Singh's brother and a fast bowler, also made it. So did R. Jamshedji, a 41-year-old left-arm spinner from Bombay. India's fifth debutant in the first Test was Amarnath Nanik Bharadwaj[5], who had scored 109 for southern Punjab against the visitors.

Amarnath opened in the first two trial games but failed. He then explained to the selectors that although he had scored a century for southern Punjab as an opener, he wasn't used to that role. He requested an opportunity to bat one-down in the last trial game. The selectors agreed and he scored 50 and 78.

Over 10,000 spectators watched the start of the first Test on Indian soil. Mohammed Nissar's second consecutive 'five-for' in Tests could not prevent the MCC from totalling 438 in response to India's 219. The hosts were 21-2 in their second innings, when Nayudu joined Amarnath in the middle. A partnership ensued.

Amarnath scattered the fielders with his strokes. He had

---

[4]Docker, Edward Wyberth, *History of Indian Cricket*, Macmillan Company of India, 1976.
[5]Amarnath prefixed Lala to his name to distinguish himself from a contemporary cricketer who was his namesake.

eleven boundaries in his fifty and he carried on in the same vein. Even Nayudu was overwhelmed when Amarnath completed a single to become India's first Test centurion. The captain forgot that the ball was still in play and left the crease to congratulate his partner. He could have been run out, but Jardine signalled to Harry Elliott, the wicketkeeper, to let things be. Like Nayudu in 1926, Amarnath was swamped by gifts, from cash to ornaments.

India was at 159-2 at stumps on day three. However, the innings caved in on the fourth morning after Nayudu fell for 67 and Amarnath was brilliantly caught by Stan Nichols for 118. England needed only 40 to win which they achieved easily.

India drew the second Test in Calcutta, thanks to Dilawar Hussain, the debutant wicketkeeper-batter. He scored 59 in the first innings despite a blow to the head, and 57 in the second. C.S. Nayudu, a leg-spinner and the captain's younger brother, supported Hussain in a seventh-wicket stand of 52 in the second innings. Amar Singh took 7-86 in the first innings of the final Test in Madras and Yadavindra Singh scored 60 on his Test debut. However, the Indian batters were uncomfortable against spin. Verity took eleven wickets in the match and England won by 202 runs.

Jardine's suggestion that the BCCI institute an annual domestic competition was taken on board by Anthony De Mello and Sikandar Hayat Khan, who had succeeded Govan as president. When De Mello displayed the design of the trophy for the proposed national championship during a board meeting at Shimla in July 1934, Bhupinder announced that he would have a gold trophy worth 500 pounds made out of the design, provided that it was named after the late Ranjitsinhji.

However, Vizzy prevailed upon the board members to convene another meeting in October 1934, where the majority voted in favour of a trophy named for Willingdon, who Vizzy argued had done a lot more for Indian cricket than Ranji. *The Times of India* even carried a picture of the Willingdon Trophy on 20 November 1934. The national championship was already two matches old by then.

The 17 participants in the inaugural edition of the national championship were divided into four zones. Every game was to be a knockout and the winner in each zone was to qualify for the semi-finals. The teams were as follows:

- **East:** Bengal, United Provinces, CP and Berar, Rajputana and Central Indian states
- **West:** Bombay, Gujarat, Sind, western Indian states and Maharashtra
- **North:** North India, southern Punjab, Delhi and Army
- **South:** Madras, Hyderabad and Mysore

The start of the championship was dramatic, with Madras beating Mysore in a single day. Bombay, led by L.P. Jai, went on to beat northern India in the final. The mystery over the name of the championship ended after the winners played a festival game against the Cricket Club of India in Delhi, which they lost. It was here that Willingdon of all people presented the Ranji Trophy to Homi Vajifdar, who led Bombay in the festival game in Jai's absence.

The BCCI never explained why it overturned its decision of October 1934. With the national championship attracting sparse crowds, the board probably realized that it needed Bhupinder Singh and his financial muscle to stay afloat.

5

'VIZARD' OF WOES

Massive crowds turned up for the Bombay Quadrangular in 1934, the first in five years. With a tour of England in 1936 on the anvil, Bhupinder Singh thought of inviting a team from Australia to give the top Indian cricketers quality match practice. Frank Tarrant, Bhupinder's aide, went over to Australia and assembled a team led by Jack Ryder, who had captained Australia in the 1928–29 Ashes. It was christened 'The Maharaja of Patiala's team of Australian cricketers'.

A week before the visitors played their first game, the BCCI announced the appointment of Iftikar Ali Khan Pataudi as the captain for the England tour, which was more than six months away. Iftikar had attended a tournament organized by Vizzy to celebrate the silver jubilee of King George V's reign and impressed watchers with his batting in the nets. Vizzy also replaced the ailing Duleep on the selection panel. Nayudu contested against Iftikar, but he got only four votes to his rival's 13.

The 24 matches—inclusive of four unofficial Tests—played by the Australians over a period of 13 weeks were interspersed with some bizarre happenings off the field. Those who were pleased with Iftikar's appointment for the England tour, given his familiarity with English conditions, were flummoxed when the prince withdrew from the first two Tests on grounds of ill-health.

He ended up missing all four. Before the first Test, the selection panel that comprised Iftikar, Vizzy and Dr Kanga declared that it intended to examine vice-captaincy options for the England tour. However, Dr Kanga resigned soon after this announcement.

Yadavindra Singh was assigned the captaincy for the first Test, which was to be played in Bombay—the same city he had been heckled in for being named captain of the Hindus ahead of Nayudu just the year before. Nayudu declared his support for Yadavindra, but India lost by nine wickets. Nayudu then led in the second Test in Calcutta, which was also lost. Wazir Ali took over for the third and fourth Tests at Lahore and Madras respectively, both of which India won.

Something interesting happened between the last two Tests. A newspaper carried a story of the acrimony on the 1932 tour. The same story also attributed the defeats of the Indian team in the first two Tests against the Australians to the fractious relationship between the players. That the team needed a *unifier* was emphasized.

A few days later, Vizzy led a Moin-ud-Dowla XI to an innings victory over the visitors. Simultaneously, Vizzy courted the affiliated units of the board, promising spots for their players in the squad for England. Then came Iftikar's announcement that he was opting out of the 1936 tour altogether. Apparently, 'reasons of state' were to blame. There is every reason to believe that Willingdon may have ensured that Iftikar stayed occupied.

Vizzy's PR campaign was planned as meticulously as one from the early 2020s, when every attempt—ranging from subtle to direct—was made by some quarters to credit a certain player for a series win, although he was not with the team when it created history. The player who had actually led India to victory in the series was mentioned almost as an afterthought.

Bhupinder Singh, who had organized the tour by the Australians in the 1935–36 season, which had not only given the Indian cricketers exposure but also yielded revenue for the BCCI, was understandably upset by the developments that preceded the

England tour. He declared Yadavindra's unavailability for the tour and withdrew his invitation to the Indian team to train in Patiala. Nayudu contested for the captaincy and lost again, this time by four votes to Vizzy's ten.

Vizzy, the worst cricketer in a team of twenty, arrived in England in April 1936 with 36 items of personal luggage and two servants. S.M. Hadi from Hyderabad was the team's treasurer and Major Brittain-Jones, an aide of Willingdon's, was the manager. There was no designated vice-captain.

Amarnath was a marked man after he expressed his displeasure for not being assigned the field he wanted for his brand of brisk medium-pace, during the game against Leicestershire. He apologized when told to do so by the manager and scored two centuries in the next match against Essex. He then hurt his shin and sprained his back in subsequent games, but Vizzy refused to give him a break.

By the time the Indians played the Minor Counties in their twelfth first-class game of the tour, Amarnath had to his credit 591 runs and 32 wickets. He had been slotted to bat at number four in the game, but Vizzy held him back and ultimately sent him in at number seven, just before stumps. A livid Amarnath stormed into the dressing-room, unbeaten on 1, and let it be known in colourful Punjabi that he was not used to being treated so disrespectfully.

After the Indians completed a victory by an innings and 74 runs on the evening of 19 June 1936, Amarnath was informed by the manager that he was being sent back to India on disciplinary grounds. Senior members of the team intervened and spoke to Vizzy, who agreed to reconsider the decision after Amarnath submitted an apology. However, Brittain-Jones did not budge.

Amarnath was welcomed warmly at the Bombay docks on 9 July 1936. The Nawab of Bhopal, who had been elected president of the BCCI the year before, pushed for the all-rounder's return to England. It was then that Vizzy and Brittain-Jones, the Viceroy's aide, played their trump-card. Amarnath was about to board a flight for London when the Nawab of Bhopal received a cable from a higher-up, threatening him with 'consequences' if he did not back down. The Nawab, a British vassal, had no choice.

Vizzy was incensed when some players, including Merchant, suggested that he hand over the captaincy to Nayudu for the Tests at least. India lost the first Test at Lord's despite some fine bowling by Nissar and Amar Singh.

The captain's sycophancy to the British yielded him a knighthood. He skipped a three-day game against Lancashire to attend his investiture ceremony, but the story went that when he learnt that the Indians, who were being led by C.K. Nayudu, were in a dominant position, he sent a cable to the Indian dressing-room, instructing Nissar to bowl full-tosses in the second innings to jeopardize a likely victory. However, Nayudu had the last laugh. He took up bowling duties himself and finished with 6-46. India's 84-run win was their first over a county on the tour.

The second Test, which was played in Manchester, was made memorable by India's seventh opening combination in six Tests. Both Merchant and Syed Mushtaq Ali were *converted* openers. Merchant had started off as a middle-order batter, while Mushtaq had begun as a left-arm spinner who could bat. The pair's 215-run second-wicket partnership against Minor Counties was likely on Vizzy's mind when he asked Mushtaq to partner with Merchant at Manchester after Dattaram Hindlekar, who had opened with Merchant at Lord's, was ruled out due to injury.

India were 368 runs in arrears when Merchant and Mushtaq arrived at the wicket in the second innings. Mushtaq, with his propensity to essay strokes that were not to be found in the coaching manual, turned out to be the perfect foil to Merchant, an epitome of technical perfection, who believed in wearing the bowlers down. Mushtaq became India's first Test cricketer to score a century overseas and India were 190-0 at stumps on the penultimate evening.

He (Vizzy) called me to his room that evening and presented me a gold watch. After praising my batting, he reminded me that just as Merchant had run me out in the first innings, I now had an opportunity to run him out. I was shocked. I told the captain that we were representing the country and there was no way I was going to do anything like that. I left his room immediately. Just before we resumed the next day, I told Vijay that he better be careful, as I had been instructed to run him out.

—Syed Mushtaq Ali, *Indian Cricketer of the Millennium*[6]

The openers ignored their captain's blatant attempt to pit a Muslim against a Hindu. Merchant also completed his century and India drew the Test.

India lost the last Test at The Oval, but not before a Nayudu special. Asked to follow on after being bowled out for 222 in response to England's 471-8, India were 159-4 when the 41-year-old made his way to the middle. The outgoing batter was Baqa Jilani, who had been rewarded with a Test cap only because he had abused Nayudu in front of the team.

Nayudu was hit on the heart by Gubby Allen, the England captain, early in his innings. However, he hit the next ball for a boundary. His 81 enabled India to avoid an innings defeat.

There were shades of 1936 on India's tour of England in 1996. A prominent member of the team returned to India before the Test series began, after claiming that he had been insulted by the captain. Like Merchant and Mushtaq in 1936, two youngsters excelled with the bat in 1996 and went on to have glorious careers.

---

[6]This was a television series produced by Professional Management Group in 1999.

6

TRANSITION-I

Your Excellency, what would you prefer to accept from sportsmen? Money for your government or immortality for yourself?

In early 1935, the Cricket Club of India, which had been established in Delhi in 1933 with Bhupinder Singh as president and De Mello as secretary, was looking for a permanent address in Bombay. The CCI had been conceptualized as India's equivalent of the MCC and was expected to take on the responsibility of raising funds for Indian cricket through subscriptions, organizing domestic tournaments and promoting the game across the land. Concurrently, the BCCI was to play an advisory role, organize international series and represent India in the ICC.

De Mello had identified Sub-block No. 2, a reclaimed plot on Bombay's southern tip, as a probable location for a clubhouse and stadium. However, there was a problem. Although the CCI was making remarkable progress in terms of subscriptions and life-memberships, the price of the plot was astronomical. After several unsuccessful attempts to convince the government to slash the price, De Mello sought a meeting with Lord Brabourne, the governor of the Bombay Presidency.

The governor chose immortality over money.

The CCI acquired 90,000 square yards of land at the rate of 1 pound per yard, in what was a heist for all practical purposes. Work commenced on the construction of a clubhouse and stadium, courtesy of donations by corporates and members of the royalty. De Mello drove the process off the field, while Frank Tarrant handled the preparation of the arena. The Brabourne Stadium was formally inaugurated in the presence of Lord Brabourne, Bhupinder Singh, and a sea of celebrities in December 1937, with a game between CCI XI and a team from England, led by Lord Lionel Tennyson, a former England captain.

The BCCI failed in its attempts to secure an official Test series against either South Africa or the West Indies in 1937–38, and the Indians therefore had to settle for a series of unofficial Tests against Tennyson's team, which was a combination of retired cricketers and future prospects.

Likewise, Vizzy failed to prevent the setting up of a committee to look into the issues that had plagued the 1936 tour. The committee, comprising Sir John Beaumont, Chief Justice of the Bombay Court, Dr P. Subbaroyan, president of the Madras Cricket Association, and Sikandar Hayat Khan, indicted not only the captain for his poor cricketing and leadership skills, but also Nayudu for 'not cooperating with the captain and being aloof from the team.' Strangely, the committee had not interacted with Nayudu at all before drawing this conclusion. The fact was that a professional like Nayudu would have put his personal differences aside and cooperated with the captain, had the latter approached him in the first place.

The appointment of the 26-year-old Vijay Merchant as captain for the series against Tennyson's team indicated that the selectors had the future in mind. Nayudu missed the first unofficial Test in Lahore—which India lost—as he was travelling. However, he declared his availability for the second Test in Bombay. Merchant also gave the impression that he wanted Nayudu in the team. When he reached Bombay for the game, Nayudu was allegedly asked to meet an influential individual,[7] who questioned him about the happenings in England in 1936.

The following morning, Nayudu learnt from the papers that he had not been included in the playing XI. His replacement was Mohammed Saeed, a player from Patiala. The very least Merchant, a Nayudu fan, could have done, was inform his idol himself, but that was not to be. History repeated itself six decades later, when the player who had led India in the calendar year of 1997, was informed by the media on the second day of 1998 that he had lost the job.

Nayudu withdrew from the series in disgust. To assuage his fans who were seething after India lost the Bombay Test to go 0-2 down in the series, the board declared that an additional Test would be played in the city, with Nayudu leading India. That led to more trouble. Digvijaysinhji, the Jam Saheb of Nawanagar and the then president of the BCCI, voiced his objection to the additional Test, but he was overruled by De Mello, the secretary, who got the member units of the board on his side. Digvijaysinhji resigned in protest.

The Indians won the next two Tests to level the series. A fifth Test was played in Bombay, but without Nayudu. In fact, he was also invited to play the fourth Test in Madras after protests by his fans, but he declined. India lost the fifth Test by 156 runs, thus losing the series 2-3. Merchant, who had a poor series by his standards with only 98 runs from nine innings, later apologized to Nayudu for what the latter had been through.

On the bright side, the series witnessed the advent of two stars. One was Vijay Hazare from Maharashtra and the other was Mulvantrai Mankad, a left-arm spinner and right-handed batter, whose all-round heroics had enabled Nawanagar to win the Ranji Trophy in 1936–37.

---

[7]There is reason to believe that it was Bhupinder Singh. Edward Wybergh Docker writes in *History of Indian Cricket* (1976, Macmillan) that Nayudu was told to report to a certain personage's address.

While serving with the Maharaja of Dewas, one of India's princely states, Hazare met Clarrie Grimmett, the legendary Australian leg-spinner. Grimmett, who had come to India to coach the Raja of Jath, the brother-in-law of Hazare's employer, honed Hazare's batting and encouraged him to continue bowling medium-pace.

Mankad, who had grown up idolizing Nissar and local hero Amar Singh, was mentored by Albert Wensley, a fast bowler from England who represented Nawanagar in the Ranji Trophy. Wensley shaped the man, whom the world would address as Vinoo, into a left-arm finger spinner adept at flight, turn and deception. Mankad was only 20 when he was picked against Tennyson's team. He missed the first Test, but his performances with bat and ball in the next four were extraordinary:

- 38, 2-6, 88 and 0-38 in Bombay
- 55, 0-2, 25 and 4-47 in Calcutta
- 113, 3-18 and 3-55 in Madras
- 0-3, 0, 3-49 and 57 in Bombay

Mankad would bowl India to a much more significant victory in Madras, 14 years later.

Bhupinder Singh passed away on 23 March 1938, six days after Anthony De Mello put in his papers as secretary of the BCCI and CCI. Indian cricket would always be indebted to the Maharaja of Patiala for his patronage in its fledgling years. There was another tragedy, a couple of years later. Amar Singh succumbed to pneumonia. He was only 29. It took Indian cricket a long time to recover from the loss.

Fortunately for India, domestic cricket continued to be played even during World War II. Amar Singh's demise, Mankad's success and the suspension of international cricket from 1939 to 1945 due to the war, set into motion a process of transition.

Till that point, Indian cricket had revolved around aggressive batting, as epitomized by Nayudu, and fast bowling, as personified by Nissar and Amar Singh. However, Mankad ensured that spin, which the Indians had not taken seriously till then, came into prominence. Around the same time, C.S. Nayudu came of age as a leg-spinner and Ghulam Ahmed, a Hyderabad resident, made an impression with his off-spin in the Ranji Trophy. Spin displaced pace as the cornerstone of Indian bowling in the years that followed.

The pendulum swung the other way after a Test series against Pakistan in 1978. India's senior spinners were taken to the cleaners by the Pakistani batters, but a fast bowler who made his debut in the series impressed with both ball and bat.

7
DOMESTIC DUELS

The Bombay Quadrangular became a Pentangular in 1937 with the addition of the Rest team, comprising Catholics, Jews and Anglo-Indians. The tournament also shifted from the Bombay Gymkhana to the Brabourne Stadium.

Ironically, the first season of the Pentangular featured four teams. The Hindu Gymkhana objected to the number of seats that was assigned to its members by the CCI and dropped out. The matter was resolved before the start of the next season.

As it would be revealed in the years to come, this was not the last time the CCI would incur the wrath of another body over the distribution of seats.

The Rest's star player was Vijay Hazare. He was also a member of the Maharashtra team that won the Ranji Trophy in 1939–40 and 1940–41 under the captaincy of D.B. Deodhar, who was still going strong in his late 40s, nearly a decade after he had been deemed too old for Test cricket and was therefore not considered for the 1932 tour of England. Hazare's 316 against Baroda in the 1939–40 season was the first triple century in the Ranji Trophy.

The two Vijays—Merchant and Hazare—were at the forefront of another transition in Indian cricket. They were a lot more consistent than the dashers of the time, which prompted youngsters to imbibe their mantra: 'Give the bowler the first hour and then take the next five.' The consequent proliferation of batters who invested in technique and patience also resulted in many youngsters taking up spin. It seemed pointless to expend one's energy in the heat and humidity of the subcontinent to bowl fast to batters who took and gave no chances.

This was also the time some people started criticizing the Pentangular for being communal. It was claimed that the Hindu Gymkhana had withdrawn from the tournament in 1940 because Mahatma Gandhi had voiced his opposition of communalism in all aspects of life. However, the fact was that the Hindu Gymkhana participated in the Pentangular in the following year and won!

The Bombay Cricket Association, which ran the Pentangular, was convinced that the criticism stemmed from envy. While the Pentangular was attracting huge crowds, the decade-old Ranji Trophy was still struggling to do so. The format's supporters also pointed out that its detractors were targeting only Bombay. They were not panning communal cricket tournaments that were being played in other cities of the subcontinent.

Dr Subbarayan, who succeeded Digvijaysinhji as BCCI president in 1937, even threatened to resign if the Pentangular was not scrapped. However, the BCA held its own. Eventually, the BCCI realized that it could not arm-twist the BCA, which was financially stable and not dependent on the parent body.

The fallout of the Quit India movement and the gathering of war clouds on India's eastern borders resulted in the cancellation of the Pentangular in 1942–43. However, it was resumed in the next season. Hazare scored 248 for Rest against the Muslims. Merchant scored 250 for the Hindus in the final against Rest. He then declared at 581-5 and his bowlers dismissed Rest for 133. Following on, Rest was at 62-5 when Hazare was joined by Vivek, his younger brother. The match was long gone, but Vivek stayed, and Vijay kept going. By the time Vijay Hazare was last out, he had scored 309 out of his team's total of 387.

Merchant later scored 359 for Bombay against Maharashtra in the Ranji Trophy. His season's aggregate of 865 was overhauled by Hazare, who became the first batter to score 1,000 first-class runs in an Indian season.

There was an encore to the Merchant-Hazare duel in the new millennium. Amol Muzumdar surpassed Amarjit Kaypee's tally of 7,623 to become the highest scorer in the Ranji Trophy, in November 2009. He held the record till December 2011, when Wasim Jaffer, his old Mumbai teammate, surpassed him. Muzumdar then overtook Jaffer in the next season, in which he was leading Andhra. However, Jaffer caught up in the Ranji Trophy final between Mumbai and Saurashtra a couple of months later—and this time, held on to the lead.

The 1944–45 season witnessed two epic finals at the Brabourne Stadium. Bombay took on Holkar, led by Nayudu, in the Ranji final. Holkar was a rebooted version of the Central India team, which had participated in the Ranji Trophy before it was dissolved due to financial issues. Nayudu's stint with Holkar, which began in 1941–42, marked his return to the tournament after six years. He had led Central India in their inaugural game of the competition but pulled out after being replaced as captain by the prince of Alirajpur for the next game. Nayudu was not one to suffer fools gladly. Years later, he was given a free hand by the Maharaja of Holkar to build a team.

Bombay scored 462 and then dismissed Holkar for 360. In the second innings, Bombay amassed 764, of which Merchant's contribution was 278. Needing 867 to win, Holkar were all out for 492. England maestro Denis Compton, who had been posted in Mhow[8] on war service and was persuaded by Nayudu to play for Holkar, scored a double century. The game was called on All India Radio by AFS Talyarkhan, whose refusal to share the microphone with anybody else was as firm as his conviction

---

[8]Mhow was renamed the town Dr Ambedkar Nagar by the Government of Madhya Pradesh in 2003. Ambedkar, one of India's greatest social and political reformers, was born here.

that the Pentangular's time had come. On the other side were individuals like De Mello, who declared that there was nothing communal about the Pentangular, and Nayudu, who called it the 'greatest tournament in the world'.

However, other influential voices from beyond the boundary had the final say.

The Pentangular's last hurrah was a pulsating final between the Hindus and Muslims in November 1944. During the game, the footmarks of the bowlers created a depression in the bowling crease at one end of the Brabourne pitch. Vijay Merchant, the Hindu captain, requested the umpires to have the depression levelled, to ensure that the approach of his bowlers was not affected. He was told by the umpires that Mushtaq Ali, his opposite number, would have to agree to the same.

> Placing my hand on his shoulders, I said to him, 'You have my permission, Vijay.' I still remember how Merchant's face beamed with joy [...] Had we lost the match on account of the concession made, I would never have regretted my decision. But as it happens, the guardian angel of cricket kept a benign watch over us ...
>
> —Syed Mushtaq Ali, *Cricket Delightful*[9]

The Muslims needed 298 to win. Mushtaq, who had been hit on the ribs in the first innings, came in to bat in the second after the loss of three early wickets. He was still in pain, but stirring words by C.K. Nayudu did the trick. Mushtaq scored only 36, but his knock gave the innings an impetus. K.C. Ibrahim, the opener, essayed an outstanding hand and the Muslims won by one wicket.

With the war drawing to a close, Merchant led an Indian team comprising Amarnath, Mushtaq Ali, Hazare and Mankad, among others, on a tour of Ceylon[10]. This was followed by a series

---

[9] Ali, Syed Mushtaq, *Cricket Delightful*, Rupa & Co., Calcutta, 1967.
[10] As Sri Lanka was known at the time.

against an Australian Services team, which had stopped over on its way home from England.

In the first unofficial Test in Bombay, the Australians scored 531 and then bundled India out for 339. Following on, the hosts scored 304, leaving the Australians to score 113 to win with 20 minutes of play left. It was an impossible ask, but Merchant still placed eight fielders around the leg-side boundary and instructed his bowlers to bowl outside the leg-stump. These tactics did not impress Duleepsinhji, now the chairman of selectors, who reproached the captain publicly.

Mushtaq Ali, who had scored 103 for a Princes XI against the visitors, missed the Bombay Test as he was unwell, but his message regarding his indisposition did not reach the selectors. They left him out for the second Test in Calcutta on disciplinary grounds, only to reinstate him after protests by fans. Keith Miller, who would go on to become one of the most popular cricketers of the 1950s, scored 82 in a drawn game.

India broke the sequence of draws in the third Test in Madras, in which Merchant and Mushtaq opened together for India for the first time since 1936. Shute Banerjee, the paceman from Bengal, and Chandu Sarwate, the spinner from Holkar, shared 16 of the 20 opposition wickets. Their performance, along with a double century by Rusi Modi, an elegant batter from Bombay, and a century by Amarnath, ensured that Mankad, who had skipped the game due to his wedding, was not missed. India won by six wickets.

The appointment of Merchant—who had scored 155 in Calcutta—as captain for the official tour of England in 1946 seemed a foregone conclusion.

8

UNDIVIDED NO MORE

The end of the World War induced uncertainty amongst the rulers of India's 565 princely states. With independence imminent, they were wondering whether they would regain control of their respective kingdoms or be required to merge with the Union of India.

The Nawab of Bhopal, who headed the chamber of princes and was Iftikar Ali Khan's father-in-law, sensed an opportunity to make a statement when the BCCI convened a meeting in Madras on 26 January 1946 to pick the captain and manager for the England tour and appoint selectors to pick the rest of the squad.

The Nawab planned assiduously. Both Iftikar and Yadavindra, who was now the Maharaja of Patiala, represented southern Punjab against Delhi in a Ranji Trophy match, a fortnight before the meeting. Iftikar scored only seven in what was his first and, as it turned out, only Ranji appearance, but it was good enough.

The meeting in Madras was not christened the Madras Mad-Hatters' Tea Party for nothing. Homi Contractor from Bombay, who managed the team on the Ceylon tour, was outvoted by Pankaj Gupta, a hockey administrator from Delhi who had now decided to try his hand at cricket administration.

The Bombay Cricket Association had expected a 9-9 tie in the election for the captain and Dr Subbarayan, the BCCI president, to then exercise his prerogative of the casting vote in Merchant's favour, despite the spat between the two men during the previous year's Ranji final against Holkar, wherein the board president had protested against some umpiring decisions awarded against Holkar and was asked to leave the Bombay dressing-room by Merchant. However, Baroda and Maharashtra, two associations Bombay had been banking on, shifted loyalties and Iftikar won by ten votes to Merchant's eight.

It was unlikely that the Nawab of Pataudi would withdraw from the tour like he did a decade previously, as that would have embarrassed his father-in-law. His victory thrilled his fellow princes, who viewed it as an opportunity to show the world that only one of them could keep a team representing as diverse a land as India together.

At the same meeting, Duleepsinhji was voted out of the selection committee and Nayudu and Deodhar were voted into it. A couple of months later, Holkar scored a record 912-8 against Mysore in the Ranji semi-final. They won and went on to beat Baroda in the final, where their top performer was the fifty-year-old national selector, who scored a double century and a fifty.

Merchant's disappointment at being passed over for the captaincy did not reflect in his preparations for the tour. He batted on the maidans of Bombay early in the mornings, when there would be some dew on the pitches, to attune himself to the damp tracks he expected to encounter in England.

The 1946 Indian line-up was the first one to fly, rather than sail, for a series. Banerjee and Chandu Sarwate, India's heroes against the Australian Services team in 1945–46, created history in the third tour game against Surrey with a last-wicket stand of 249. It was the first instance of numbers ten and eleven scoring centuries in a first-class innings. (Sarwate and Banerjee were to be later emulated by Mumbai's Tanush Kotian and Tushar Deshpande, who scored centuries against Baroda in a Ranji Trophy match in 2023–24.)

However, Banerjee failed to strike bowling form, and he was therefore not picked for the first Test at Lord's, which featured nine debutants, six of whom were Indian, including Mankad and Hazare. Both had to wait for nearly a decade to play an official Test because of World War II. India's XI also comprised Amarnath, who was playing his first Test on English soil. Hazare and he were to share the new ball, in addition to leading the batting.

Amarnath took five wickets, but as had been the case in 1932, the Indians let their opponents get away. The visitors batted and fielded poorly and lost by ten wickets. Alec Bedser, one of England's three debutants, had match figures of 11-145. Bedser had the Indians in trouble in the second Test as well, but the last pair of Hindlekar and Ranga Sohoni managed to hang on for a draw.

The start of the third Test at The Oval on 17 August 1946 was preceded by a pogrom unleashed by the Muslim League against the Hindu community in Calcutta.

After the tragedy, Anthony De Mello, BCCI's new president, took the position that it was not advisable to indulge in anything that could potentially compound the situation. This was a blow to the Pentangular, as he had been one of its most vocal supporters. The Bombay Cricket Association smelt the coffee and the journey of the Pentangular, which had begun with the Presidency matches in 1892, came to an end.

On the eve of The Oval Test, Merchant told Rusi Modi, his India and Bombay teammate, that he wanted to have a good night's sleep as he wished to score a hundred the next day. He scored 128.

A similar conversation took place on the eve of the last Test of another Indian tour of England, 33 years later. The captain of the home team asked the foremost batter of the visiting side, if there was anything he planned to do in London before returning home. 'Yes, there is one thing I came here for but haven't yet got. A century,' he said. Like Merchant in 1946, Sunil Gavaskar kept his word. His 221 nearly took India to victory.

Merchant averaged a stupendous 74 in the first-class matches on the 1946 tour. Iftikar struggled with the bat and his health, but he ensured harmony in the Indian dressing-room, which was an achievement in itself after the events of 1932 and 1936. The tour could be termed a success, with the Indians winning 11 and losing only four of 29 first-class games.

The most dramatic win was achieved against South of England at Hastings. Merchant, who was leading India in Iftikar's absence, scored 82 and 39, but he strained his groin. Amarnath took over and surprised even his own teammates by declaring the second innings and setting the opposition a target of 277 in three hours. Indian captains were not known to take such risks. South of England started well, but they were not allowed to get away and the Indians won by 10 runs. Amarnath finished with 4-96.

The Indian cricketers got involved in the 1946–47 edition of the Ranji Trophy after their return from England. Baroda beat Holkar in the final, thanks to a world record fourth-wicket partnership of 577 between Vijay Hazare and Gul Mohammad[11]. Hazare's 288 gave him an aggregate of 561 runs from only four Ranji games. He also took 38 wickets in the season. Gul Mohammad, who like Hazare had represented India against England in 1946, scored 319.

By the time Baroda won the Ranji Trophy, India's independence was imminent. The Indians had waged their first war of independence against the British in 1857, when sepoys in the Indian army had revolted against their British superiors. Attempts to initiate another armed revolution in the early years of the 20th century were complemented by the rise of a non-violent mass movement headed by M.K. Gandhi. Both approaches were disparate, but they fed off each other, much to the discomfiture

---

[11] The record for the highest partnership in first-class cricket was broken by Sri Lankans Kumar Sangakkara and Mahela Jayawardene, who added 624 for the third wicket in a Test match against South Africa at Colombo in 2006.

of the rulers. The final nails in the coffin of the British Raj were hammered in the mid-1940s, when Netaji Subhas Chandra Bose and his Indian National Army gave the British a tough time on India's eastern borders. The INA failed to realize its objective, but its officers and soldiers became national heroes. The last straw for the British was the naval mutiny of 1946. They did not have it in them to tackle a repetition of 1857.

However, the British were determined not to leave without delivering a final body-blow to a land they had plundered for two centuries.

WHAT MIGHT HAVE BEEN

India paid a heavy price for independence. A new country called Pakistan, which comprised Muslim-majority areas of the Punjab in the west and Bengal in the east, came into being. Partition resulted in violence and the biggest exodus in the history of mankind.

Cricket was not immune to the turmoil. Amarnath was nearly attacked by a mob on a train from Patiala to Ambala, soon after Partition. Fazal Mahmood, a paceman from Lahore, would have been assaulted on a train from Pune to Bombay, had it not been for Nayudu, who drove the mobsters away with a cricket bat. Mahmood was on his way back home after attending a preparatory camp for India's tour of Australia, in Pune. He flew to Karachi from Bombay and went on to become Pakistan's first cricketing icon.

In the years that followed, many people from both sides speculated on what might have been had Partition not happened.

For starters, India would have had an embarrassment of cricketing riches. The thought of contemporaries like Vinoo Mankad and Fazal Mahmood, Sunil Gavaskar and Imran Khan, Kapil Dev and Abdul Qadir, Sachin Tendulkar and Wasim Akram, Rahul Dravid and Inzamam-ul-Haq, and Virat Kohli and Mohammed Amir representing the same team is mind-boggling.

India would have become a cricketing powerhouse years before it actually did. Those who represented India in later years would have handled the batting and those who represented Pakistan would have managed the bowling. Players like Jasprit Bumrah and Javed Miandad would have been exceptions to this rule. Had undivided India, at any point, felt that it was getting a raw deal from the ICC, the country could well have gone solo, crippling international cricket in the process. The IPL could have appeared much earlier as well.

However, there is another side to the story. Would people of diverse faiths have been allowed to co-exist harmoniously by religious extremists who thrive on hate? Had there been disharmony and strife, would India be where it is today? With the supply of exceptional cricketers exceeding the demand, wouldn't there have been conflicts over selection and accusations of parochialism?

We shall never know the answers to these questions.

9
FIRE AND ICE

The appointment of Lala Amarnath, a commoner, as independent India's first cricket captain, eleven years after his banishment from England, mirrored India's evolution from a British colony into a democracy.

Vijay Merchant, the original choice as captain for India's first tour of Australia, withdrew due to injury. Mushtaq Ali, the vice-captain, was reluctant to tour because of a bereavement in the family, but he was persuaded by the Maharaja of Holkar to change his mind. Accordingly, he reached out to the BCCI, only to be informed by De Mello that he was not required anymore.

It wasn't the last instance of a cricket administrator letting his ego supersede common-sense.

De Mello's insistence on joining the selectors to pick the team prompted Deodhar to resign from the committee. The president was also an uninvited attendee at an interaction between Amarnath and the Calcutta media, where he prevented the captain from answering questions and wrote down the replies on sheets of paper. He left after telling the journalists to carry his replies, only to learn later that Amarnath had torn the sheets.

The Indians had agreed to play on uncovered pitches in Australia, but they were let down by the weather-gods. They had the worst of the batting conditions in the first Test in Brisbane. Australia declared at 382-8 and then bowled India out for 58 and 98. India took a 140-run lead in the second innings in the second Test in Sydney, but the game was washed out.

In the third Test in Melbourne, Amarnath declared 103 runs behind Australia's first-innings total, in a bid to capitalize on a rain-battered wicket. However, his teammates dropped multiple catches.

> I got out to (Ray) Lindwall seven times out of nine. I asked him if I was doing anything wrong. He said that I am coming down late on the yorker and possibly if I (reduce the swing), then it will be all right. I thanked him and made 116 the next day
>
> —Vinoo Mankad (Films Division, 1973)

Mankad scored another hundred in the fifth Test, and was also successful with the ball. He made news for warning and then running out Bill Brown, the Australian opener, for backing up too far at the non-striker's end, first in a game against an Australian XI and then again in the second Test in Sydney.

Dattu Phadkar, a pace-bowling all-rounder who made his debut in Sydney, scored 123 in the fourth Test in Adelaide. Vijay Hazare scored a century in each innings of the same game. These performances notwithstanding, India lost 0-4. The biggest disappointment was their captain. Lala Amarnath scored 1,162 runs on the tour, but his highest score in the five Tests was 36. This failure was inexplicable since he had performed quite well in the state games. In a similar way, his son's rapid descent in the 1983–84 season after a rapid ascent in the previous one also left many scratching their heads.

De Mello was not amused when the affiliated units of the board voted in favour of Amarnath captaining India in the series against the West Indies in 1948–49. When the captain refused to reveal the batting order to him during the second Test in Bombay, the president could not take it.

After three draws, the fourth Test in Madras witnessed a bouncer war that the West Indies won. While Dattu Phadkar took 7-159 and made the West Indies batters hurry with their strokes, he had no support. On the other hand, the Windies had three bowlers—Prior Jones, John Trim and Gerry Gomez—who replied in kind.

The Indians went flat out for a win in the last Test, also played in Bombay. Shute Banerjee, who finally got a Test cap, shared new-ball duties with Phadkar and took five wickets in the game, with Phadkar and Mankad taking six each. India had six-and-a-half hours to score 361 to win.

Amarnath put the chase back on track after the early fall of the openers, with a knock of 39. Modi and Hazare batted excellently, with the latter scoring a hundred. Phadkar was enterprising, but then, the Indians were undone by a combination of gamesmanship and inept umpiring. The West Indies bowlers adopted a leg-side line, with six fielders placed on that side of the wicket. With minutes and not overs mattering in those days, the visitors wasted time by calling for drinks and having Clyde Walcott, the wicketkeeper, walk to the boundary line to retrieve the ball and then amble back to his position.

India still ought to have won, but the umpire miscounted the deliveries of what should have been the penultimate over and called the game off with one delivery left. At that stage, the cut-off time was ninety seconds away, which meant that a new over could have easily been started. Only six runs were needed at that stage.

The home team's 0-1 defeat inspired De Mello to go for the kill. In a board meeting in April 1949, he suspended Amarnath from playing any cricket in India and produced a list of 23 instances wherein the latter had displayed indiscipline, according to him. The list included a claim that the latter had accepted a financial inducement to keep a certain player in the team.

Amarnath planned his riposte meticulously. He convened a press conference in Calcutta in June 1949 to present a point-by-point rebuttal of the charges. The following month, he filed a defamation case in the Calcutta High Court, suing De Mello for one lakh rupees. He also declared that he would initiate legal action against the BCCI for suspending him without hearing his side of the story. That sent the members into a tizzy, and they agreed to expunge the portions pertaining to his suspension from the minutes of the April 1949 meeting. The charges against him were also dropped. On his part, he tendered a token apology.

However, De Mello managed to keep Amarnath out of unofficial Test series against Commonwealth teams in 1949–50 and 1950–51, which were organized after the BCCI failed to secure tours by national teams. The Commonwealth teams were an assortment of cricketers from England, Australia and the West Indies.

In the absence of the indisposed Merchant, Hazare led India to a 2-1 win against the Commonwealth side in 1949–50. His calm, collected and icy countenance was in stark contrast to Amarnath's fiery disposition. Hazare also starred in Baroda's Ranji Trophy triumph in the same season. Merchant captained India in the second series in 1950–51, which India lost 0-1.

De Mello's reign as board president ended when he won five votes to J.C. Mukherjea's 12 in the 1951 elections. It took him 13 years to realize that those who lived by the sword were destined to die by it. In his rebuttal to the suspension order passed against him, Amarnath had blamed De Mello for the resignation of Digvijaysinhji as president in 1938. In 1951, De Mello's detractors slammed him for failing to convince the MCC to send England's best team to India in 1951–52. A second-string team toured instead. Hazare defeated Merchant by the same margin as the one in the BCCI's presidential election, to be named captain of India.

Both Vijays scored centuries in the first Test in Delhi. Merchant's decision to retire after the game marked the end of the professional rivalry between the two. They had immense respect for each other and Merchant even stated that he would have withdrawn his candidature for the captaincy had he known that he would be competing against his namesake.

After completing another century in the second Test in Bombay, Hazare was hit above the eyebrow by Fred Ridgway, the paceman. He came off for repairs, but Nayudu, now the chairman of selectors, insisted that he resume his innings immediately. Hazare duly rushed back and scored 155 before he was run out. After three consecutive draws, England won the fourth Test in Kanpur by eight wickets.

The last Test in Madras was a watershed for the hosts. Centuries by Pankaj Roy and Polly Umrigar facilitated a declaration at 457-9 in response to England's 266. The visitors had no answer to Mankad's left-arm spin and Ghulam Ahmed's off-spin in their second essay and were bowled out for 183. Mankad took 12 wickets in the match, including an 8-55 run in the first innings. The Indians thus opened their account in Test cricket with a victory by an innings and eight runs, twenty years after their debut in 1932.

10

VERSATILE VIRTUOSO

The euphoria of the win in Madras evaporated when the team for the England tour in mid-1952 was announced. Vinoo Mankad, a professional cricketer at a time when there was little money in the game, had received a lucrative offer from Haslingden, a club in the Lancashire league in England. For him, the best-case scenario was to represent India in the four Tests that the visitors were scheduled to play in England and play for his club for the remainder of the season.

However, the BCCI insisted on his availability for the entire tour and the selection committee headed by Nayudu chose not to pick India's premier cricketer of the era. Fans were not amused to read that one of the selectors had claimed that India could produce a dozen spinners like Mankad.

There was a similar standoff involving two icons in the third decade of the new millennium. One of them was playing and the other had become an administrator. The former expressed his desire to step down from the captaincy in the shortest format, but he was told that the board wanted the same captain for both white-ball versions. A new white-ball captain was duly appointed. A month later, the player resigned as Test captain as well and made claims that were denied by the senior icon.

Mankad represented Bombay against Holkar in the 1951–52 Ranji Trophy final before leaving for England. The rival captains in the game were the 57-year-old Nayudu and the 30-year-old Madhav Mantri. Bombay batted first and scored 596. Holkar's innings involved a dramatic passage of play.

> A Phadkar bouncer struck Col. C.K. Nayudu on the mouth. A lot of blood spurted out. We were all concerned, but the great man waved the medics away, spat out a couple of teeth and carried on! Phadkar, who was naturally flustered, sent down the next delivery outside the off-stump, at half-pace. Col. Nayudu then turned to me and said, 'Skipper, tell your bowler to revert to his original pace!' I responded by taking Phadkar off!
>
> —Madhav Mantri, *75 Years of the Ranji Trophy*[12]

Mankad, it was claimed, was the one who told Phadkar to bowl Nayudu a bouncer. Bombay won by 531 runs, with Mankad taking six wickets.

The Indians struggled in England and Hazare and Pankaj Gupta, the manager, were unnerved enough to check Mankad's availability for the Tests at least. However, Haslingden replied that he would be released only for the first Test in Leeds.

Vijay Manjrekar, a 20-year-old Bombay batter playing his first Test overseas, scored 133 and added 222 for the fourth wicket with Hazare in the first innings in Leeds. After England took a lead of 41, the Indian captain dropped himself down to no. 6 in the second innings to tend to a throbbing thigh. However, he had to cut the treatment short after Roy, Dattajirao Gaekwad, Mantri and Manjrekar fell for ducks. Frederick Trueman, the debutant paceman, was on a hat-trick.

Hazare hit the hat-trick ball for four. He lost Umrigar at 26 and added 105 with Phadkar, before there was another collapse. England won by seven wickets.

---

[12]This was a book published by the BCCI. It was a commemorative volume that was distributed privately.

The defeat prompted the team management to resume their chase of Mankad. They then had an unexpected benefactor in the form of Sir Herbert Merrett, the president of the Glamorgan County Club, who paid Haslingden to release the all-rounder.

Back in the Indian team, Mankad opened the batting in the second Test at Lord's and scored 72. He then bowled a marathon 73 overs to finish with 5-196. He opened the batting again in the second innings and scored 184. Thereafter, he bowled 24 overs. Tragically, his was a lone battle, as England won by eight wickets.

After Lord's, the visitors were blown away for 58, 82 and 98 in consecutive Test innings, and it was only rain in the last Test at The Oval that saved India from a 0-4 rout. India's biggest disappointments were the youngsters Umrigar and Roy, who had single-digit averages in the Tests.

Amarnath, who had missed the England tour altogether, returned as captain after the series, with his candidature being supported by Vizzy of all people. As was the case in politics and the entertainment industry, there were no permanent friends or foes in Indian cricket. The view was that India needed a feisty captain for its very first Test series against Pakistan. Vizzy also teamed up with the Cricket Association of Bengal to scuttle De Mello's bid to regain the president's post.

The first-ever Test match between Asian nations was played in Delhi. This was also Pakistan's first Test. India became the first team other than England to play a country in the latter's inaugural Test.[13]

The Pakistan XI for the game comprised nine debutants, the exceptions being Abdul Hafeez Kardar, the captain, who had played all three Tests for India in England in 1946, and Amir Elahi, who had played one Test for India in Australia in 1947–48 before migrating to Pakistan. Mankad, supported by

---

[13]Zimbabwe, Bangladesh and Afghanistan also played their inaugural Tests against India in later years.

Ghulam Ahmed, spun India to victory by an innings and 70 runs. Ahmed shone with the bat as well, adding 109 runs for the last wicket with Hemu Adhikari in the first innings. However, India capitulated on a matting wicket in the second Test in Lucknow. Fazal Mahmood, who was more accustomed to matting than his Indian counterparts, took 12 wickets.

The reluctance of the police to disperse the mob that surrounded the Indian team's bus after the game forced Amarnath to take matters into his own hands, literally. Brandishing a lathi, he drove the mob away.

Hazare, Mankad and Adhikari, all of whom had missed the Lucknow Test due to fitness issues, returned for the third Test in Bombay. The moisture in the Brabourne wicket made Amarnath consider bowling if he won the toss, which wasn't something captains were known to do at the time.

The Indian captain decided to play on the sceptical mindset of his Pakistani counterpart. At the toss, he asked Kardar what he would do if he were to win it. When an unsure Kardar asked him what he would do, Amarnath said that he would bowl. He expected Kardar to do exactly the opposite, and that is exactly what happened. The Pakistani skipper won the toss and elected to bat.

Amarnath proceeded to exploit the moisture in the wicket. His 4-40, coupled with excellent bowling by Mankad and Subhash Gupte, a leg-spinner from Bombay, ensured Pakistan's dismissal for 186. Centuries by Hazare and Umrigar enabled India to declare 201 runs ahead. However, Pakistan came back well and were 176-3 at the end of the penultimate day. At a dinner that evening, a Pakistani player asked Amarnath what roller he would have used on the pitch the following morning, had India been batting. The Indian captain, who was as mindful of the impact that rollers of different sizes could have on wickets as he was of the Pakistani mindset, replied that he would use a light roller. As he had anticipated, Pakistan opted for a heavy roller, which roused the demons in the pitch. Mankad and Gupte did the rest and left their team with only 42 to win.

The BCCI took two significant decisions during that phase. The Bombay Cricket Association, still seething at the manner in which Vijay Merchant had been passed over for the captaincy of the Indian team for the tour of England in 1946, took the initiative in prevailing upon the board to discontinue its practice of selecting the captain of the national team at its AGM. The BCA advocated that the captain needed to be picked on merit and merit alone. Its perseverance paid off and the onus of picking the captain was assigned to the national selection committee. The board also decided that the member units of the board would nominate a representative from their respective managing committees to attend meetings. No active first-class cricketer was to be permitted to represent the affiliated units at the meetings.

C. Ramaswamy, a member of the selection committee, was appointed manager for the tour of the West Indies in early 1953. Like his co-panellist Homi Contractor, he was not too fond of Amarnath. The selectors were to decide on the captain for the West Indies tour during the fourth Test against Pakistan in Madras and the board president was to announce the name during the last Test in Calcutta.

However, secrets have seldom been kept in Indian cricket. In his speech at a function in Madras after the Test had ended in a draw, Amarnath shocked the audience, which included the board president, by congratulating Vijay Hazare on his appointment as captain for the West Indies tour. Not for the first or last time in Indian cricket there had been a leak.

Amarnath offered to stand down for the last Test, but Hazare took the game off on the grounds that he needed to prepare for the tour. Thus, India was led in Calcutta by a captain who had already been sacked. The Test was drawn, which meant that India had beaten Pakistan 2-1. However, the pettiness of some people ensured that the nation could not savour its first-ever Test series win.

11
TEMPLATE

> Cricket can only thrive in the atmosphere of English culture, English language and English rule. It will never be able to survive the shock of the disappearance of British rule from our country. With the fall of British power, it is bound to lose its place of honour and slowly grow out of date.
>
> —Balkrishna Keskar, *Blitz*, July 1946

Keskar banned cricket commentaries and film music on All India Radio during his stint as minister of information and broadcasting in the 1950s, only to back down after public outrage.

The 1950s constituted the golden age of two teams. The Indian hockey team struck gold at the 1952 and 1956 Olympics. The football team qualified for the FIFA World Cup in 1950 but could not participate because of logistical and financial issues. It then won the gold at the inaugural Asian Games in 1951 and came within a whisker of winning a bronze at the 1956 Olympics. Conversely, all that the Indian cricket team had to show in 21 years was a solitary series win against Pakistan. However, cricket was the best-managed sport of the lot, and it showed.

The founding fathers of the Board and their immediate successors were visionaries. Some of the decisions they took had a huge bearing on the evolution of the game in India. First, they decided that the BCCI would be an autonomous body and would not depend on government funding. The Board would create its own resources. Second, they worked hard at the grassroots level. They understood that it was critical to have a solid foundation. The Board often struggled to make ends meet, but never compromised on the development and promotion of cricket across the land.

—Ratnakar Shetty, *ON BOARD: My Years in BCCI*[14]

One poor batting performance in the second Test cost India their first series in the West Indies. They did well otherwise. The bowlers held their own against a batting line-up comprising the three Ws—Frank Worrell, Clyde Walcott, and Everton Weekes—and would have fared even better had Ghulam Ahmed not pulled out of the tour. Hazare focused on what he could control. He gave Subhash Gupte the fields he wanted, and the leggie responded with 27 wickets in the series.

A template was created on that tour. Henceforth, India would rely on their spinners to win matches and on the batters—mostly from Bombay—to save them. The country was facing a dearth of quicks in any case. Phadkar's new-ball partner in the series was Gulabrai Ramchand, a cricketer in the Amarnath mould, in that he was primarily a batter who doubled up as a medium-pacer. Hazare also bowled a lot in the series.

Polly Umrigar, Vijay Manjrekar and the opener Madhav Apte—all Bombay boys—scored heavily. Pankaj Roy was the only non-Bombayite to score a century in the Tests.

The Indians also fielded well. Leading the way were Chandrashekhar Gadkari, Jayasinghrao Ghorpade, Madhav Apte, Dattajirao Gaekwad, and Umrigar. Manjrekar impressed behind

---

[14]Shetty, Ratnakar, *ON BOARD: My Years in BCCI*, Rupa Publications India, New Delhi, 2025.

the stumps when he stood in for the injured Ebrahim Maka and P.G. Joshi, specialist stumpers both, in the last Test. In fact, his 118 in the game made him the first Indian wicketkeeper to score a Test hundred.

The players who toured the Caribbean missed the knockout stage of the 1952–53 edition of the Ranji Trophy. That season's final between Holkar and Bengal witnessed the end of an age. Holkar took the first-innings lead, but Bengal came back strongly in the second innings and set their opponents a target of 304. Their bowlers did their best, but Holkar's last pair hung on for 70 minutes to achieve a draw, securing the trophy on the basis of the first-innings lead.

C.K. Nayudu, the winning captain, shifted to the newly constituted Andhra Pradesh team in the next season. Holkar qualified for the next two finals as well, thus making it a total of ten appearances in Ranji finals from 1944–45 to 1954–55, but lost both times. Unfortunately, cricket in the region went downhill after Holkar merged with the Madhya Bharat Cricket Association in 1955, which in turn became the Madhya Pradesh Cricket Association in 1957.

Like Nayudu in the 1940s, Sandeep Patil took over the captaincy and mentorship of the Madhya Pradesh cricket team in the late 1980s and changed the team's fortunes. Chandrakant Pandit, another Mumbai stalwart, took on the same role at the turn of the millennium. When MP was narrowly beaten by Karnataka in the Ranji Trophy final of 1998–99, he was disconsolate. More than two decades later, Pandit was back, this time as coach, and he guided Madhya Pradesh to their first Ranji title in 2021–22.

Hazare, India's captain in the West Indies, announced his retirement from international cricket after the tour. Statistically, he was India's most successful batter at that stage, with 2,192 runs at an average of 47.65 from 30 Tests.

The BCCI failed to secure an official series in its silver jubilee season of 1953–54. Another Commonwealth team toured instead and was christened the Silver Jubilee Overseas Cricket (SJOC) team. Polly Umrigar led India in the first two unofficial Tests, Hemu Adhikari took over for the third, Ghulam led in the fourth, and Phadkar was assigned the job in the fifth. It was not the ideal way to groom a new captain.

India's 2-1 win against SJOC was followed by another twist in the tale. Vinoo Mankad, who had played in only one of the unofficial Tests, was named captain for India's first tour of Pakistan. The board, now headed by Vizzy, appointed Lala Amarnath as manager.

In 1954, Pakistan seemed to be ahead of India in most aspects, cricket included. While all India had to show after 22 years of Test cricket was three Test wins and one series win, all at home, Pakistan had won a Test in its inaugural series in India in 1952 and then squared a Test series in England.

Pakistan's economy was also healthy—a military coup in 1953 notwithstanding—thanks to generous foreign aid and the export of jute from its eastern wing, which was situated on the other side of India. India, which was larger and more heterogeneous, had opted for the more arduous path towards development, by backing its own industries, aiming to achieve self-sufficiency in the production of food-grains and the creation of industrial and educational infrastructure.

When the two teams faced off in the 1954–55 season, it appeared as if they were battling to determine which of the two was more defensive. The fear of losing overrode the desire to win.

The Pakistanis also indulged in underhand methods. The first two Tests were played on matting wickets, which the Indians were not used to playing on. However, both matches were drawn. The visitors were then denied proper hotel rooms and bathing facilities in Sind. An encore in Bahawalpur, where they were to play the second Test, forced Amarnath to threaten a boycott. That forced the hosts to fall in line. The Indian manager then had a physical altercation with Kardar, who was still leading Pakistan, before the third Test in Lahore.

Despite the tactics employed by the Pakistanis, India was in with a chance of victory in the fourth Test in Peshawar, when they gained a first-innings lead of 63 and then reduced Pakistan to 70-4 in the second innings. However, Maqsood and Imtiaz Ahmed held firm. This was where the Indians missed a trick by not crowding the batters with fielders and rotating the spinners. While Gupte and Mankad himself did most of the bowling, Ghulam was hardly used. Pakistan escaped to 182 and the Test ended in a draw.

Kardar invited Amarnath to his room for a cup of tea, ostensibly to extend an olive branch, on the eve of the last Test in Karachi. The reunion of the erstwhile teammates was gatecrashed by Idris Baig, one of the umpires nominated for the Test, who dropped in and asked the Pakistani captain for instructions. He beat a retreat when he saw Amarnath, but it was too late. The Indians refused to play unless the umpire was changed. Masood Salahuddin, one of Pakistan's selectors and a qualified umpire, replaced Baig and did a fine job.

An attempt by the hosts to tamper with the wicket on which the final Test was played also did not succeed and the series ended in a 0-0 stalemate.

The Indians adhered strictly to the tradition that was established in the Caribbean. Umrigar and Manjrekar topped the batting tables and Gupte was India's top wicket-taker with 21 scalps. Naren Tamhane, a wicketkeeper from Bombay, debuted during the series and affected 19 dismissals.

12

MUSICAL CHAIRS

> He could size up a batsman's strength and play upon his weakness. He was a master when it came to pinning down a strokeplayer. One could almost hear Umrigar's brains tick as he towered over you menacingly from his place in the slips.
>
> —Ajit Wadekar, *My Cricketing Years*[15]

Ghulam Ahmed's appointment as captain for the series against New Zealand in 1955–56, despite his not having been even the vice-captain on the Pakistan tour, raised eyebrows. His friendship with Amarnath, who was now the chairman of selectors, may have helped. However, a pulled leg muscle forced him to miss the series after the drawn first Test in Hyderabad. Umrigar, who had been the vice-captain in Pakistan, took over and led India to innings victories in Bombay and Madras.

Umrigar became India's first double centurion in Tests in Hyderabad and he was emulated by Mankad in the last Test in Madras. The opening partnership of 413 between Mankad and Pankaj Roy in that Test remained a world record till 2008. Subhash Gupte had another successful series with 34 wickets.

---

[15]Wadekar, Ajit, and K.N. Prabhu, *My Cricketing Years*, Vikas Publishing House, 1973.

The 2-0 triumph over New Zealand ensured that the Indians fancied their chances against the Australians, who had lost the Ashes and a one-off Test in Pakistan before landing in India in 1956–57.

Australia was 200-8 in response to India's 161 in the first Test in Madras, but the tailenders were allowed to add 119 and the hosts were then bowled out for 153, to lose by an innings and five runs. Australia also had the better of the drawn second Test in Bombay.

> We were at the breakfast table at the CCI when Richie (Benaud) served a plate to me with a newspaper article that said Subhash (Gupte) will have the better of me. It was then that I decided, it's either me or him.
>
> —Neil Harvey, *Sportstar*[16]

Harvey scored a magnificent 140. The scenes at the Brabourne Stadium were replicated in Chennai 42 years later, when another exceptional leg-spinner was overpowered by a batting maestro.

In the final Test in Calcutta, Umrigar became the first Indian captain to bowl after winning the toss at home. Ahmed took three early wickets, but he then left the field as he was feeling unwell. He returned to take four more wickets, but the Australians, who were 25-3 at the start, managed to get 177. The Indians were never allowed to get back by Richie Benaud, who won the battle of the leggies with 23 wickets in the series to Gupte's eight. Australia won by 94 runs.

It was an early instance of an Indian team flattering to deceive when considered the favourite.

The 1957–58 season featured a failed attempt by the BCCI to unearth fast bowlers. Alan Moss, the England paceman, was

---

[16]Viswanath, G., 'Neil Harvey's scintillating 140 at Brabourne, six decades ago', *Sportstar*, 13 February 2017, https://tinyurl.com/yeanx8fp. Accessed on 18 July 2025.

invited for this exercise, but the attendees at the camp in Bombay found his training regime too rigorous. The one bright spot was the emergence of Ramakant Desai, a paceman from Bombay.

The musical chairs over the captaincy continued. Amarnath's casting vote resulted in Ghulam Ahmed's reappointment for the series against the West Indies in 1958–59. However, a knee injury kept Ahmed out of the first Test in Bombay. Then there was an ugly fallout between Amarnath and L.P. Jai, the West Zone selector, who was accused of unilaterally naming Umrigar captain for the Bombay Test.

The first Test was drawn and Ahmed returned for the second Test in Kanpur, where Gupte finished 9-102 to bowl the Windies out for 222 in the first innings. India were 182-2 in response when Wesley Hall, the Windies paceman, found his rhythm. The last eight wickets fell for 40 runs, with Hall taking six. Rohan Kanhai and Garry Sobers then neutralized both Gupte and Ahmed in the second innings. Needing 444 to win, India plummeted from 173-2 to 240 all out.

The hosts never recovered from the thrashing. The West Indies won the next Test in Calcutta by an innings and 336 runs. In this game, Hall had for company Roy Gilchrist, who gained notoriety by unleashing a mix of bouncers and beamers. Ghulam Ahmed announced his retirement after the defeat.

Umrigar, who was named captain for the remainder of the series, wanted A.K. Sengupta, a batter, to replace the injured Manjrekar for the fourth Test in Madras. However, he was vetoed by A.N. Ghosh, the BCCI secretary, who reported that R.K. Patel, the board president, wanted Jasu Patel, an off-spinner, to play instead. The president's choice made no sense as the Indians needed to beef up their batting and that was precisely the point Umrigar made, but to no avail. He resigned hours before the game got underway, refusing to relent despite the entreaties of officials. The captaincy was then handed over to Mankad, who had missed the first three Tests due to a dispute over match fees.

The ultimate irony was that Sengupta, whom Umrigar had wanted in the team in the first place, played and Jasu Patel sat out.

Mankad took four wickets in West Indies' first innings, but he then suffered an allergy and handed over charge to Ramchand. The thoroughly dispirited Indians lost by 295 runs.

The selectors met at the end of the game and decided to make Ramchand captain for the last Test in Delhi. An official rushed to the Madras railway station to intercept Ramchand before the latter boarded the train for Bombay, but he was late. With Ramchand uncontactable, the selectors appointed Col. Hemu Adhikari, who had not played a single Test in the series, as captain.

Mercifully for Indian fans, the Delhi Test was drawn. Chandrakant 'Chandu' Borde, a protégé of Hazare, scored 109 in the first innings and was on 96 in the second when the ninth wicket fell. Manjrekar then came in with his arm in a cast, to help Borde get his second century of the game. Borde hooked Gilchrist to the boundary but lost his balance while doing so and fell on the wickets. Another notable performer was the 19-year-old Ramakant Desai, who took 4-169 on his Test debut.

India's 0-3 defeat infuriated both the public and the parliamentarians to the extent that there were demands to cancel the 1959 tour of England. The selectors reacted by queering the pitch even further. Dattajirao Gaekwad, who had led Baroda to victory in the Ranji Trophy in 1957–58 but had played only one Test against the West Indies in the following season, was appointed captain. Adhikari declared himself unavailable for the tour and Ramchand wasn't selected. Mankad was also overlooked, and he never played for India again.

The captain was happy with the appointment of Fatehsinghrao Gaekwad, the Maharaja of Baroda[17], as the manager, but unhappy with the decision of the selectors to pick only two pacemen in Desai and Surendranath. With the Indians due to play five Tests

---

[17]Gaekwad was the Maharaja's Aide-De-Camp (ADC).

plus 17 matches against the counties, it was obvious that both pacemen would be overworked.

The tour went the way of its 1952 predecessor. There were a couple of bright spots, as always. Nari Contractor, the left-handed opener, defied broken ribs to score 81 in the second Test at Lord's. Thanks to him, India reached 168, and Desai, Surendranath, and Gupte then reduced the hosts to 100-7. V.M. Muddiah, an air force officer and off-spinner from Mysore, was among the reserves.

> [Ken] Barrington was at the crease and it was just the tail that we had to get rid of. But catches were deliberately dropped off Subhash Gupte. There were some senior members in the team who were horrified that we could take the lead against England. They thought this was blasphemy and dropped the catches.
>
> —V.M. Muddiah, *Casting A Spell: The Story of Karnataka Cricket*[18]

England's last three wickets added 126 and the hosts went on to win. Needing an improbable 548 to win the fourth Test in Manchester, the visitors produced their best batting of the series. Umrigar scored a hundred, as did Abbas Ali Baig, a student at Oxford who was drafted into the side as a cover for injured players. Insult was added to injury when the manager accused Umrigar, Gupte, Manjrekar and Kripal Singh of misconduct in his report. When Pankaj Roy led India in the Lord's Test after Gaekwad went down with a bronchial infection, it meant that India had had six captains in ten Tests.

The heartening bit was that there was only one direction in which Indian cricket could have gone from that point. It could not have possibly sunk any lower.

---

[18]Jaishankar, Vedam, *Casting A Spell: The Story of Karnataka Cricket*, UBS Publisher's Distributors, 2005.

13

RESURGENCE

> During the Kanpur Test against England in 1961-62, I met Vijay Hazare, the chairman of selectors [...] I said that I wanted one assurance: If I, as the captain, report to you that a particular individual is playing for himself and not for the country, and I don't want him in the team, then the selection committee will view this in the right perspective and stand by me.
>
> —Nariman Contractor,
> *Great Moments of Indian Cricket*,[19] 1986

Australia won the first Test on their 1959–60 tour of India in Delhi, by an innings and 127 runs. Gulabrai Ramchand's appointment as captain—India's seventh since 1955—appeared to have made no difference.

The second Test was played in Kanpur. When Amarnath, the chairman of selectors, saw the loose spots on the good-length area on the ground's first-ever turf wicket[20], he recommended the inclusion of Jasu Patel, who he believed would exploit the spots with his proclivity to hit the deck. India scored only 152. When the Australian openers put on fifty, Amarnath realized that Patel

---

[19]This was a documentary film released by Grindlays Bank ahead of the ICC Men's Cricket World Cup in 1987.
[20]The previous Tests at Kanpur had been played on matting.

was operating from the wrong end and conveyed the same to Ramchand. The change of ends changed the match.

Patel befuddled the batters with a mix of deliveries, some of which turned sharply while others did not. The visitors were dismissed for 219, with Patel taking 9-69.

India scored 291 in their second innings, with Nari Contractor getting 74. Patel then took five more wickets and Umrigar took four with his off-spin to seal a win by 119 runs. It was India's first-ever Test win against Australia. The enormity of the achievement could be gauged by the fact that *The Times of India*, the country's premier newspaper, carried a sports story on its front page for the first time since its inception in 1838.

> A businessman invited us to dinner on the day we won and said, 'We'll give you Rs 1,000 each as a gift.' We were paid just Rs 250 per Test in those days, and the fifth day's allowance was cut if the game ended on the fourth day. That Rs 1,000 is still to come.
>
> —Chandu Borde, *The Cricket Monthly*, 3 April 2013

Baig was kissed on the cheek by a female fan who raided the playing arena[21], shortly after he completed his second fifty in the next Test in Bombay. The story goes that when Merchant quipped on All-India Radio that no lady had done this to him despite his tall scores at the same ground, his co-commentator retorted that his style of batting had been far too dour for any spectator to contemplate such an act.

Two decades after the two Vijays had changed the Indian approach to batting, there appeared to be another transition. The early 1960s witnessed the advent of batters who did not mind taking calculated risks while playing and seemed to enjoy themselves on and off the field—they were also good-looking.

---

[21]This incident was immortalized in a Cadbury's Dairy Milk chocolate ad in the early 1990s.

Like Baig, M.L. Jaisimha, a dasher from Hyderabad, made his debut in England in 1959. The 1959–60 series against Australia saw the arrival of Salim Durani, a left-handed batter and spinner, whose father Abdul Aziz had represented Nawanagar in the 1930s. Farokh Engineer, a flamboyant wicketkeeper-batter from Bombay, played his first match for India in the 1961–62 series against England. These individuals did not take long to capture the imagination of the masses. They were admired by the men and adored by the women. Nari Contractor also had his share of admirers, among them a future chief minister of Tamil Nadu.

Another dasher who emerged around this time was Budhi Kunderan, a wicketkeeping all-rounder. Amarnath saw him playing in a game for Railways and was so impressed that he picked Kunderan in the Indian team even before the latter had played a single Ranji match.

Although the Australians of 1959–60 won the fourth Test in Madras and took the series 2-1, the Indians were satisfied with the way they had performed in the absence of the injured Gupte, Manjrekar and Umrigar. The season ended with the inaugural Irani Cup game between the Ranji Trophy winners and a Rest of India side. This one-off first-class encounter, named after Zal Irani, BCCI treasurer since 1948, became an annual feature. Initially, it was played just after the Ranji Trophy final but it was rescheduled in later years to become the curtain-raiser to the new season, in which the previous season's Ranji Trophy winners played the Rest of India.

All five Tests against the touring Pakistanis in 1960–61 were drawn, with both teams once again playing it safe. The one consolation for Indian fans was the BCCI's decision to invest in a long-term captaincy option. The 26-year-old Contractor was named captain for the first two Tests, but his appointment was later extended to the entire series. Desai troubled the Pakistani batters, including Hanif Mohammed, the visitors' bulwark, but the visitors managed to avoid defeat.

Political tensions and two wars ensured that the neighbours did not play each other for the next 18 years.

The English did an encore of 1933–34 and 1951–52 by sending a second-string team to India in the winter of 1961–62. Ken Barrington, Tony Lock and Ted Dexter (captain) apart, their leading lights gave the tour a miss.

England's condescending attitude ensured that Indian fans never ever warmed up to them the way they did to the Australians and West Indians, who had always sent their best teams to India.

Contractor sought the support of the selectors in his bid to give some players a reality check. His insistence on having meetings and rotating roommates to familiarize every player with his colleagues were not appreciated universally, but he knew what he was doing. Unfortunately, like Merchant 24 years earlier, he was unable to prevent a messy end to the career of a legend.

Subhash Gupte was representing Rajasthan as a professional at the time. After the first Test in Bombay was drawn, he was advised by the board to skip the game that Rajasthan were to play against the visitors. Gupte retorted by requesting the board to pay him ₹500, which is what he was to earn by representing Rajasthan. The board did not respond and Gupte therefore flouted its diktat. Later, he took 5-90 in the Kanpur Test, which was drawn.

Like Amarnath in 1936 and 1948–49, Gupte was now a marked man. The board did not have to wait too long to retaliate. During the rain-affected third Test in Delhi, Gupte's roommate Kripal Singh invited the hotel receptionist for a drink. However, the lady took offence and lodged a complaint with the board. Kripal was reprimanded, but bizarre as it may sound, Gupte was also pulled up for not preventing his roommate from making the call! The leggie's defence that he was not in the room when the call was made, and that Kripal was an adult and therefore responsible for his own actions, was shot down. After he was left out of the West Indies tour that followed the England series, Gupte settled in Trinidad, the homeland of Carol, his wife, whom he had met on India's previous tour of the Caribbean in 1952–53.

After three successive draws, the teams moved to Calcutta. At lunch on day three, England was around 200 runs behind India's 380 with five wickets in hand, and the new ball was due. Contractor consulted the chairman of selectors and senior players, all of whom advised him to take the new cherry at the resumption. Desai even marked his run-up, but the captain then had a hunch and decided to continue with the old ball.

Borde triggered a collapse with his leg-spin, in partnership with Durani's left-arm spin. England were bowled out for 212 and India then set the opposition a target of 421. Another fine bowling performance by the spinners resulted in a victory by 187 runs.

Durani and Borde excelled with the ball in the final Test in Madras as well, taking ten and five wickets, respectively. Supporting them were Rameshchandra Nadkarni, a left-handed spin-bowling all-rounder like Durani, and Erapalli Prasanna, an off-spinner from Mysore. Mansoor Ali Khan, Iftikar's son and the ninth Nawab of Pataudi, then thrilled the spectators in a stand of 104 with his captain, who gave him the go-ahead to take the aerial route. Contractor himself got 86, and Mansoor scored a century in only his third Test. India won by 128 runs and in the process, secured their first-ever series win over their erstwhile rulers. The top batter of the series was Manjrekar, who scored 583 runs.

Rameshchandra Nadkarni, who played for Maharashtra before shifting to Bombay, was called Bapu by his teammates. That appellation stuck to him for life. The term Bapu is widely used in Gujarat. Decades later, India gained two left-arm spinning all-rounders in the Nadkarni mould, both of whom were from Gujarat: Ravindra Jadeja and Axar Patel. Both are called Bapu by their teammates.

The 21-year-old Mansoor was named Contractor's deputy for the West Indies tour. If the plan was to groom a future captain, then it was odd on the selectors' part to overlook Borde and Jaisimha, both of whom were older and had played a lot more international cricket than Mansoor.

But then, Mansoor was a prince. In the India of the 1960s, that still mattered.

14

PITCHFORKED

> In Barbados on March 16, 1962, I definitely thought that Griffith delivered the ball with a bent arm which he suddenly straightened, and this was confirmed late in the game when he was 'no-balled' for chucking by umpire Cortez Jordan.
>
> —M.A.K. Pataudi, *Tiger's Tale: The Nawab of Pataudi*[22]

Nariman Contractor was not supposed to play the three-day game against Barbados between the second and third Tests, but injuries to many players had left him with no option. He was also convinced that a couple of his players had faked injuries as they did not want to face Wesley Hall and Charlie Griffith.

Contractor fended the fourth ball of Griffith's first over after the lunch interval. The ball popped into the air, but Conrad Hunte, who was fielding at short leg, could not reach it in time. Griffith ran in to bowl the next ball and had almost reached the popping crease when Contractor saw a window being opened in the dressing-room in the background. There was no sight-screen. The Indian captain could have backed away, but he did not.

---

[22]Pataudi, M.A.K, *Tiger's Tale: The Nawab of Pataudi*, Hind Pocket Books, Delhi, 1969.

The delivery pitched and reared. Contractor attempted to get his head out of the way, but he was late. The ball hit him just above the right ear.

Within moments, blood was oozing out of the Indian captain's nose and ears. He was rushed to hospital, where he started throwing up and experienced paralysis on the left side of his body. An X-ray revealed a fractured skull and a blood clot that was putting pressure on the brain. Ghulam Ahmed, the manager, was told that unless an emergency operation was performed to remove or reduce the size of the clot, Contractor may not live. Ahmed gave the go-ahead and a surgery was performed, with members of both teams donating blood. A specialist from Trinidad then flew to Bridgetown for another surgery.

On the field, the mayhem continued. Griffith struck Manjrekar on the nose. The batter staggered into the dressing-room and said that he had lost his vision. Fortunately, he regained it after a few minutes and resumed his innings, going on to score a century.

Contractor was unconscious for nearly a week, by which time Dolly, his better half, had reached Barbados. The couple returned to India a couple of weeks later, and Contractor underwent a third procedure at the Christian Medical College, Vellore. A steel plate was inserted in his head, that would only be extracted 60 years later, in 2022.

Contractor returned to domestic cricket in the 1963–64 season, but his international career was over. The head injury had made the board wary of recalling him. It was an unfortunate end to a promising international career.

Four decades later, another career ended prematurely due to injury. Syed Saba Karim was hit on the right eye by an Anil Kumble delivery while keeping wicket in an ODI in 2000. Attempts to save the eye went in vain, and although Karim made his Test debut a few months later, he found it difficult to carry on and announced his retirement.

Karim had something in common with the individual who found himself pitchforked to the captaincy in 1962.

Each one of Mansoor's ten teammates in the third Test against the West Indies was his senior, in terms of age as well as Test experience. All of them backed him, but they still lost 0-5. For the umpteenth time since 1932, their fans sought solace in individual brilliance. The fourth Test in Port of Spain witnessed a spectacular century by Durani and the all-round brilliance of Umrigar, who scored 172 and took five wickets.

It was expected that the visitors would find the going tough against cricketers of the calibre of Sobers, Kanhai, Hall, and Frank Worrell, the West Indies captain. Even before they lost Contractor, their own board had pushed them onto the back foot by directing the selectors to omit Gupte, the hero of their previous tour of the Caribbean. Mansoor was later criticized for underutilizing Borde's leg-spin—he was one of the heroes of the win against England—and thereby not exploiting the susceptibility of the Windies batters to bowling of that type.

Umrigar retired at the end of the subsequent domestic season. At that point, he held the Indian records for the highest number of Tests (59), Test runs (3,631) and Test centuries (12). He served the sport with distinction even after his retirement, as administrator, team manager, mentor, selector and curator.

The highlight of that 1962–63 season, apart from Bombay's fifth consecutive Ranji Trophy triumph, was the invitation extended by the BCCI to four speedsters from the West Indies to play domestic cricket, in the hope that they would inspire locals to bowl fast. Roy Gilchrist was inducted into the Hyderabad and South Zone teams, Charlie Stayers picked for Mumbai and West Zone, Chester Watson chosen for Delhi and North Zone, and Lester King picked for Bengal and East Zone. The pacers served their teams well, but they did not trigger a fast-bowling revolution in India.

The year before, the BCCI had instituted an annual interzonal competition named after Duleepsinhji. It featured five teams, representing the North, South, East, West and Central zones, respectively.

Mansoor was named captain for a series against an England team led by Mike Smith in the 1963–64 season, just two years after their previous visit. The first three Tests were drawn, but the selectors were perturbed by the captain's low scores and asked him to get his eyes examined. He dispelled their doubts with an unbeaten 203 in the fourth Test in Delhi. However, his innings did little to dispel the tedium.

After four dull draws, Mansoor elected to bowl after winning the toss in the fifth Test in Kanpur, only because he wanted to do something different. However, he refused to accept Smith's offer of both teams declaring their first innings to increase the possibility of a result. These things happened in county matches in England, but they were unheard of in Test cricket. England declared at 559-8. India were bowled out for 266 and asked to follow on, but a century by Nadkarni, to add to his fifty in the first innings, enabled the hosts to draw the game.

Nadkarni was at his best with bat and ball in the series. His bowling analysis in the first innings of the first Test in Madras read a remarkable 32-27-5-0.

The second Test in Bombay saw the debut of an unorthodox leg-spinner. Polio in childhood had rendered Bhagwat Chandrasekhar's right arm so weak that he found it difficult to even raise it. When cricket took his fancy, he converted his weakness into a weapon, delivering the ball with a whippy action. So well did he perform for Mysore in the Ranji Trophy, with the batters struggling to cope with the bounce and turn he extracted from the flattest of wickets, that he played Test cricket in the same season and took 4-67 in his very first outing.

Having played quality pace in England, Mansoor appeared to be indifferent to the Indian pacers of the time. Rajinder Pal, who debuted in the same Test as Chandrasekhar, was given only 13 overs to the latter's 62. Vasant Ranjane, another quick, played only one Test in the series, while Desai appeared in two. The captain had worked out that his best bet was spin.

WHAT MIGHT HAVE BEEN

Mansoor excelled for Winchester College and Oxford in his teens. He emulated his father by scoring a hundred in the annual encounter between Oxford and Cambridge in 1960. With the bat, he was an aggressor, and in the field, a hawk. His reflexes were sharp and his catching brilliant. When the spinners were in operation, he would move closer to the bat to snap up half-chances.

As Oxford's captain in 1961, Mansoor was only 92 runs short of his father's record tally of 1,307 runs in a single season, when disaster struck in Brighton on 1 July. The car he was travelling in, collided with another, and a splinter of the smashed windscreen pierced his right eye. However, his determination to play cricket overrode everything else. He returned to the nets within weeks, only to discover that he could not pick the length of the ball.

It took him a fair bit of trial-and-error to figure out the ideal way in which to bat with just one good eye. He resorted to getting his bat and pad behind the line of deliveries that were pitched straight and tried to attack deliveries that were not headed for the stumps. He pulled the peak of his cap over his right eye to nullify the blurred image of the ball that he saw otherwise. He had to give up fielding close-in.

Mansoor's final Test batting average of 34.91 is a classic example of stats concealing the vital. With just one eye, he essayed some incredible innings, some of which won India matches and others that saved the team from disgrace.

Rajan Bala, the celebrated cricket writer, estimated that Mansoor saved around 30 runs in each of the 46 Tests he played, which amounted to 1,380 runs in all. Adding those to his Test tally of 2,793 yields a figure of 4,173. Mr Bala reckoned that

Mansoor would have scored that many runs with two eyes from his 46 Tests at an average close to 50, the mark that separates the great from the very good.

Had the accident not happened, Indian cricket would have gained a superstar and disruptor, a decade before it found one. As captain, Mansoor would have led from the front, as opposed to pushing the team from the back, which is what the accident forced him to do. Apart from extracting the best from the spinners, which he did anyway, Mansoor could well have had an inspirational impact on his batters. 'Stylists' like M.L. Jaisimha and the mercurial Salim Durani, as well as technicians like Borde, Manjrekar and Dilip Sardesai, would have been a lot more consistent than they were, had they played under a captain who was averaging close to 50 himself.

The Indian team of the 1960s would have won more matches and Indian cricket would have come of age a few years before it actually did.

15
QUARTET

The first time India hosted two international teams was in the 1964–65 season. The selectors were divided over the captaincy and Mansoor retained it only because of the casting vote of M. Dutta Ray, the chairman of selectors. There was an encore of sorts to this episode, six years later.

The Australians, who toured first, won the first Test in Madras by 139 runs, with paceman Graham McKenzie taking ten wickets. Mansoor's 128 in the first innings enabled India to recover from 76-5, but his knock and Nadkarni's eleven wickets went in vain.

The next Test, which was played on a re-laid surface at the Brabourne Stadium, was a thriller. Australia lost Norman O'Neill to illness after the toss and had to therefore bat with ten men. Mansoor's 86 helped India gain a first-innings lead of 21. In their second innings, Australia were 246-3 when Nadkarni and Chandrasekhar broke through and terminated the innings for 274.

Needing 254 to win, India were 122-6 when Mansoor and Manjrekar joined forces. They were batting lower because the Indians had sent in two night-watchmen in Nadkarni and Surti respectively, up the order. A partnership of 93 ensued before Manjrekar was caught. Mansoor fell just nine runs later, but Borde displayed composure, along with Indrajitsinhji, the wicketkeeper. With six needed, Borde struck Tom Veivers, the off-spinner, for two boundaries to take India home.

Borde was delighted to be carried by spectators off the ground, but not so delighted when one of them flicked his bat. In those days, cricketers were underpaid and getting hold of the best equipment was therefore a challenge. The third Test in Calcutta was ruined by rain and the series thus ended in a 1-1 stalemate.

The Australians were followed by the New Zealanders. The first two Tests of this series ended in draws, but both could have gone the distance had the two boards not decided to play four-day games. The series began with the jettisoning of a stalwart. Vijay Manjrekar had gained a bit of weight and slowed down in the field, but he was still the best batter in the country by a distance. When he heard that he was on the hit-list, he scored a hundred in the first Test in Madras. However, the selectors did not relent. Manjrekar never played for India again.

The team was also not happy with the BCCI's decision to prepare wickets that favoured pace. The players felt that if the objective was to encourage fast bowlers, then the pitches ought to have been tailored accordingly in domestic cricket and not at the highest level, where it was always prudent to play to one's strengths.

In the third Test in Bombay, which was played on 12–15 March 1965, India was dismissed for 88 in response to New Zealand's 297. A recurring tradition of Indian cricket came to the fore when New Zealand enforced the follow-on. The hosts batted a lot better in their second innings, with Dilip Sardesai scoring 200 and Borde getting 109. Only 2.5 hours were left when Mansoor declared, 254 runs ahead. The Kiwis then played some daft cricket against Chandrasekhar, Durani and Srinivas Venkataraghavan, an off-spinner who had made his debut in the first Test at Madras, his hometown. The visitors were hanging on at 80-8 when the game ended. India thus came within two wickets of becoming the second team in Test history to win a Test after being asked to follow on. Coincidentally, the Indian team performed this feat against Australia in Kolkata on

15 March 2001, exactly 37 years after the conclusion of the Bombay Test against New Zealand.

The sequence of draws was broken in the last Test in Delhi. Venkataraghavan took 8-72 to bowl the visitors out for 262. Mansoor and Sardesai then scored centuries. The declaration at 465-8 was followed by a battle against the clock. New Zealand went on the defensive, while the Indians went for broke. The hosts eventually found themselves needing 70 to win in less than an hour. They completed the chase successfully, thanks in no small measure to their opponents, who sportingly played on despite a downpour.

> In fairness to Pataudi, it must be said that he believed that as players picked to represent the country, he expected each one of us to perform to our abilities. So he saw no reason for telling us how to do our jobs. But as we were so used to being led, to a lot of us this was a new experience.
>
> —Chandu Borde, *Panther's Paces*[23]

Mansoor shifted from Delhi to Hyderabad in the 1965-66 season, in which India had no international engagements. The captain of India was happy to play under Jaisimha, who led both Hyderabad and South Zone.

India's next international assignment was in 1966–67 against the West Indies, led by Garfield Sobers, the greatest cricketer on the planet. Mansoor had captained Sussex, his county team, to victory over the West Indies on their tour of England in 1966, but then, India did not have a paceman like John Snow, who had taken eleven wickets in that game. To put things in perspective, India's bowling in the first Test in Bombay was opened by Jaisimha and a debutant named Ajit Wadekar, specialist batters both. They bowled a combined total of three and two overs, respectively, before the spinners took over.

---

[23]Borde, Chandu, *Panther's Paces*, Anubandh Prakashan, 2018.

In Bombay, the Windies took a first-innings lead of 125, and then their spinners bowled well. Needing 192 to win, the visitors lost two wickets to Chandrasekhar before the close on day four. Two more strikes by Chandrasekhar on the fifth morning brought in Sobers to join the debutant Clive Lloyd. With 102 still needed and Chandrasekhar having taken eleven wickets in the game already, any other batting side would have been cautious, but the two left-handers in the middle swung their bats and finished the game off in a hurry. Sobers later stated that he had pressed the accelerator because he wanted to attend the races at the Bombay race-course that afternoon!

On the first day of the second Test in Calcutta, the spectators spilt over from the stands onto the playing arena, a consequence of more tickets being sold than Eden Gardens' capacity. The viewers were further incensed when they saw a man being manhandled by the guardians of the law. The chaos that ensued forced the police to use tear gas. The players first locked themselves in the dressing-rooms and subsequently managed to exit the ground. Hiding in the buses that drove them to their hotel were the officials, whose blood the spectators were baying for. An entire day's play was lost, but the West Indies registered a win by an innings and 45 runs.

The last Test, played in Madras, was the first since 1952 to be played at the ground originally owned by the Madras Cricket Club (MCC), which was situated in a locality called Chepauk. The Corporation Stadium had hosted Test cricket from 1955–56 to 1964–65, but 1966–67 marked a return to the arena where the Indians had registered their first-ever Test win in 1952.

On the first day, Farokh Engineer, who had been recalled to the Indian team at the expense of Kunderan, attacked the fast bowlers and nearly completed a century before lunch. Thanks to him and Borde, who scored his second century of the series, India scored 404, a total that the visitors managed to exceed by two runs. In the second innings, Ajit Wadekar was playing for his career. After being picked in the Indian team on the strength of his performances in the Ranji trophy, he had failed in Bombay, missed the Calcutta Test and then fallen for zero in the first innings in Madras.

Wadekar received a half-volley first up, which he drove for four. That boosted his confidence, and he proceeded to score 67. The middle order enabled India to reach 323.

The spinners then took over. Bishan Bedi, the left-arm spinner from the Punjab, who was playing only his second Test, was complemented in flight, turn and guile by Erapalli Prasanna, who was playing his first Test since the tour of the West Indies in 1961–62. When the seventh West Indies wicket fell at 193, the Indians sensed victory, only for their old friend Charlie Griffith to play spoilsport. The paceman supported Sobers in a match-saving stand, exasperating the Indians by using his body to get in the way of the ball as much as he did his bat. He was lucky not to be dismissed leg-before on a couple of occasions, but the Indians also goofed up by dropping catches.

India's biggest gain of the series was the slow men. The Madras Test was the first of many that Bedi, Prasanna and Chandrasekhar would play together. Venkataraghavan's presence in the dressing-room was guaranteed to keep the trio on its toes and the fans therefore had every reason to be optimistic.

16
SUCCESS OVERSEAS

Mansoor led India on a tour of England in 1967, 21 years after his father. Unlike 1952 and 1959, this time, India was sharing the summer with Pakistan and playing only three Tests. The English did not deem it commercially viable to dedicate the entire summer to a team that had lost eight out of nine Tests on its last two visits. The Indians were playing in the first half of the English summer and the Pakistanis in the second.

Mansoor's team went into the first Test in Leeds undercooked, as most of their games against the counties were truncated due to rain. At Leeds, Geoffrey Boycott scored an unbeaten 246 and England declared at 550-4. The visitors were then shot out for 164, with Ray Illingworth's off-spin and Robin Hobbs's leg spin doing all the damage. The saving grace was Mansoor, who scored 64.

The Indian batters took a cue from their captain when they followed on. Farokh Engineer and Ajit Wadekar added 168 and later, Hanumant Singh batted attractively. But the grandest performance was that of the captain's. Mansoor smashed 148 and India finished with 510, leaving the hosts with 125 to chase for the win. England slipped to 92-4, before Basil D'Oliveira and Illingworth steered them home.

The batting flopped in the next two Tests. England won the second at Lord's by an innings and 124 runs. With both

Subroto Guha and Sadanand Mohol, the two specialist fast bowlers in the team, missing due to injury, Mansoor played all four spinners—Prasanna, Chandrasekhar, Venkataraghavan and Bedi—in the final Test in Birmingham. The new ball was entrusted to Budhi Kunderan, who was to open the batting order as well. When asked what he was going to bowl, he allegedly quipped that he needed to bowl to find out. India lost by 139 runs, their eighth successive defeat on English soil.

> ...Despite what the record books show it is my belief that the 1967 Indian touring team contained a nucleus of talent as promising as any in the world. It failed only because our players were immature and because we lacked the indispensable weapon of two good fast bowlers.
>
> —M.A.K. Pataudi, *Tiger's Tale*

When he penned these lines, Mansoor was not trying to be combative as a future India coach, who during a series that was lost 1-4, declared that the Indian team had the potential to become the 'best travelling team' in the world. Both teams gave their respective leaders reasons to smile in due course.

The success of a team of Indian schoolboys that toured England in the same season was heartening. The team, captained by Mumbai all-rounder Ajit Naik, won nine and drew eight of its 17 matches against its English counterparts. Never before had an Indian cricket team gone through a tour of England unbeaten. The highlight of the tour was the game against MCC schoolboys at Lord's. With ten needed off the last two balls, Surinder Amarnath, the eldest son of independent India's first Test captain, hit two sixes. The squad also comprised Mohinder, his younger brother.

The defeat of the seniors in England prompted some to call for a change at the top. A report then came through that Mansoor was 'considering retirement'. However, he scored a double century for South Zone against West Zone in the Duleep trophy final, which preceded the selection committee meeting to pick the team for the twin-tour of Australia and New Zealand in the 1967–68 season, and was retained as captain.

Mansoor wanted Manjrekar in the side, but he was overruled by the selectors. Hanumant, Kunderan and Jaisimha also missed out. On the other hand, Ramakant Desai and Bapu Nadkarni were recalled.

None of the Indian players had been to Australia, the previous tour having been undertaken two decades ago. However, they had plenty of time to acclimatize, with five four-day games against the Australian states scheduled before the first Test in Adelaide.

The Indians began the Test series without Mansoor, who had pulled a hamstring. Chandu Borde, the stand-in captain, scored 69 before falling to a bad decision. Rusi Surti did well with bat and ball and Syed Abid Ali, a debutant all-rounder from Hyderabad, took 6-55 with his medium pace in Australia's first innings, but India still lost by 146 runs.

The defeat prompted Mansoor to play the second Test in Melbourne despite not being fully fit. The circumstances could not have been more daunting when he arrived at the crease; it was overcast, the wicket was damp, Graham McKenzie had his tail up and India were 25-5. With one good leg, the Indian captain proceeded to score 75 in the first innings and 85 in the second. With most of the fielders stationed in attacking positions, Mansoor went aerial, deliberately and judiciously.

> It was drizzling on and off [...] Each time play resumed, Tiger came out with a different bat [...] That night ... I asked Tiger about the bats. He said to me, 'Ian, I brought along a sweater, a jumper, a pair of trousers, a pair of socks, boots and jockstrap. I did not bring pads, gloves or a bat. Hence, I just picked the bat that was nearest to the door and went in.
>
> —Ian Chappell, RSD World Cricket Summit, 2011

Mansoor's belligerence could not prevent an innings defeat.

When it was decided to send Chandrasekhar, who had sustained an ankle injury, back to India, the team management asked for a batter as a replacement. Jaisimha was chosen. He flew from Hyderabad to Brisbane, the venue of the next Test, via Madras, Singapore, Perth and Sydney, reaching hours before the start of the game. He was drafted into the XI straightaway.

India owed their first-innings total of 279 in response to Australia's 379, to Jaisimha, Mansoor and Surti. The latter two rallied the innings after the third wicket fell with only nine on the board, and Jaisimha later scored 74. He fared even better in the second innings, in which India needed 395 to win. If Bill Lawry, Australia's debutant captain, expected the Indians to wilt, he was in for a surprise. Abid Ali, who opened the innings, scored 47. Surti and Mansoor batted well for the second time in the game, as did Jaisimha, who combined elegance with authority. Borde and he joined forces at 191-5 and batted excellently, taking the total past 300. Just when something sensational seemed on the cards, Borde was sixth out at 310 and the remaining wickets fell for the addition of only 45 runs. Jaisimha was the last to be dismissed for 101.

> It seems incredible after so many batting capers from some of the other Indians to think that such a highly talented batsman, technically perfect in his methods, should not have been included in India's original touring party.
>
> —Jack Fingleton, *The Hindu*

Another defeat, this time by 144 runs, in the final Test in Sydney, meant that India had lost nine of their last ten Tests. However, there was a silver lining. The Indians were battle-hardened by the time they landed in New Zealand to play a team that was not as strong as the West Indies, England and Australia, their last three opponents.

India were in danger of conceding a substantial first-innings lead in the first Test in Dunedin, but then, Desai stayed in despite having his jaw broken by New Zealand paceman Dick Motz, to add 57 for the last wicket with Bedi and help India inch ahead.

Desai's tenacity inspired his teammates. Prasanna's 6-94 left India needing 200 to win. Wadekar piloted the chase, scoring 71 to add to his 80 in the first innings. India's five-wicket win was their first in a Test match overseas, 35 years after their debut in 1932. New Zealand levelled the series in the second Test, thanks to their captain Graham Dowling's double century, but the Indians came back in the third Test in Wellington. Wadekar's 143 enabled India to take a 141-run lead in the first-innings. That was more than enough for the Indian spinners, who bundled the opposition out and left the batters with only 59 to win. The visitors also won the last Test at Auckland by 272 runs.

Every member of the team played his part in the 3-1 triumph, the chief architects being Wadekar, who batted imperiously, and Prasanna, who took 24 wickets to add to his 25 in Australia. Nadkarni, who had played his part as well, bade farewell to international cricket on a memorable note. Not many Indian cricketers before (and indeed after) him had been able to do so.

Mansoor, the first Indian captain to win a Test match and series abroad, finally had reason to feel comfortably ensconced in the role.

17
'CASTING' COUP

Vijay Merchant, the new chairman of selectors, announced his desire to 'experiment with youth' in the 1969–70 season, which was to feature tours by New Zealand and Australia.

New Zealand began their tour with a three-day game against a Combined Universities side, in which Sunil Gavaskar, an opener from Bombay, gave a good account of himself in a knock of 25.

The Indian XI for the first Test in Bombay comprised three debutants—medium-pacer Ajit Pai, opener Chetan Chauhan and middle-order batter Ashok Mankad, the son of Vinoo Mankad. India conceded a first-innings lead of 73, but recovered and won. Erapalli Prasanna carried on from where he had left off in 1967–68 and took eight wickets. Ambar Roy, who scored a half-century for the Combined Universities, was awarded a debut in the second Test at Nagpur, where the Indian batting came a cropper against Hedley Howarth's off-spin and lost by 167 runs.

Jaisimha, who had been left out of the first two Tests, was recalled for the decider at Hyderabad. The inclusion of southpaws Eknath Solkar and Ashok Gandotra in the XI made it a total of six debutants in three Tests. The game was marred by rain, but New Zealand dominated. Dowling declared the second innings overnight on the fourth day, setting India a target of 268. The Kiwis then reduced India to 76-7 before a 20-minute downpour was followed by a farce. All the New Zealanders wanted was an hour of play to mop up the game and with it, the series. When they saw the ground-staff taking their own time to mop up the field, the visitors themselves stepped in, but the minutes kept ticking away and the match was finally abandoned. The New Zealanders had every reason to feel cheated.

Borde and Sardesai were recalled for the first Test against Australia in Bombay, but the batting still flopped. Mansoor and Mankad were exceptions and added 146 in the first innings. The Australians took a first-innings lead of 74 and their bowlers then had the Indians on the run. When Venkataraghavan was eighth out at 114, he indicated his displeasure at the caught-behind verdict, as did one of the radio commentators. This infuriated the spectators, many of whom were listening to the live commentary on transistor sets. In scenes that were reminiscent of Calcutta in 1967, stands were set ablaze, but Bill Lawry, the Australian captain, insisted on continuing. Finally, both teams were escorted off the ground and play was called off for the day. Australia needed only 64 to win on the fifth morning.

Mansoor was surprised when Merchant, for all his talk about 'youth', expressed his reluctance to pick Gundappa Viswanath, who the captain reckoned was the most talented youngster in the country, for the second Test in Kanpur. Viswanath had scored 230 for Mysore against Andhra on his Ranji Trophy debut in 1967-68. His 68 for the Board President's XI against the New Zealanders earlier in the season had earned him a place in the reserves for the Hyderabad Test. Merchant argued that he had not seen Viswanath bat, but Mansoor had his way.

Viswanath was delighted to be assigned his favourite number four slot but was devastated when he fell for a duck in his first Test innings. He was a bundle of nerves till his captain predicted that 'he would score a century' in the second innings. The debutant did exactly that, batting brilliantly to score 137. The match, however, was drawn.

The spinners excelled themselves in the third Test in Delhi. Australia took a first-innings lead of 73, but they were skittled out for 107 in their second innings by Bedi and Prasanna. Bedi then went in as night-watchman and helped Wadekar stabilize the chase of 181 after the loss of two early wickets. Wadekar, who had been told to play despite a finger injury, justified his skipper's faith with an unbeaten 91 and India won by seven wickets.

The Indian batters failed again in the next Test in Calcutta, another game that witnessed crowd trouble. In the last Test in Madras, India scored 163 in response to Australia's 258. Then came the twist. Mohinder Amarnath, Lala's second son and Test debutant, struck twice with the ball at the start of Australia's second innings, and Prasanna then dismissed four batters in quick succession, to reduce Australia to 24-6. The former then beat Ian Redpath, Australia's last recognized batter, in flight, but Engineer missed the stumping. Redpath survived and the tail helped him set India a target of 249. Wadekar and Viswanath scored fifties, but they had no support. India lost the game and with it, a series they should have squared.

Merchant was re-elected chairman of selectors and a fifth selector added as a representative of Central Zone at the BCCI's AGM in September 1970. Mansoor's fans sat up when Borde was named captain of Rest of India for the Irani Cup fixture against Wadekar's Bombay. The Indian captain's decision to skip the game did not go down well with some people, who alleged that he did not want to play under Borde. Later, Borde was leading West Zone in a Duleep Trophy game at Nagpur when Merchant asked him for his views on the composition of the team for the tour of the West Indies in 1971. Borde, taken by surprise, presumed that he was in contention for the captaincy.

Change was certainly in the air, with Venkataraghavan replacing Jaisimha as captain of South Zone.

In October 1967, Mansoor had scored a double century for

South Zone against West Zone at the Brabourne Stadium in a Duleep Trophy game, just before the selectors chose the captain for the twin-tour of Australia and New Zealand. His fans prayed for an encore when the same teams met at the same venue on 2 January 1971, six days before the captain for the West Indies tour was to be picked.

It all began as planned. Mansoor came in at 188-3 and hit a six and two boundaries off Saeed Hattea, the paceman. He had reached 19 when Hattea followed his captain Borde's advice to bowl fuller and won a shout for leg-before.

Dutta Ray, the selector from the East Zone, was missing in the meeting that took place on 8 January 1971. He had lost the elections in 1970 but had still managed to be appointed selector after entreating A.N. Ghose, the board president, to give him sixty days in the post as a face-saver of sorts. Not only did Ray not quit after two months, but he also lobbied to have Keki Tarapore, a former left-arm spinner who had played one Test for India in 1948–49, named manager for the West Indies tour despite Col. Hemu Adhikari, a former captain, being the frontrunner for the post. Upset with Ray's machinations, eleven member associations of the BCCI threatened to go to court if he was allowed to attend the selection meeting.

In Ray's absence, two selectors—C.D. Gopinath (South) and M.M. Jagdale (Central)—voted for Mansoor, while the other two—Merchant (West) and Bal Dani (North)—picked Wadekar. Merchant broke the deadlock with his casting vote. Ajit Wadekar it was.

In an age where many still believed that nobody could fill the shoes of a prince, there was outrage. Merchant was even accused of 'avenging 1946', when Mansoor's father had literally come from nowhere to be appointed captain.

> I cannot think he (Merchant) had any motive when he voted against me. He must have been convinced that as a batsman

I was not pulling my weight in the side and that is good enough to drop any player.

—M.A.K. Pataudi, *All The Beautiful Boys*

Mansoor's decision to withdraw from the West Indies tour altogether after losing the captaincy did not endear him to his detractors. He also skipped the Duleep Trophy final. Engineer, who had represented the World XI against England in 1970 and had even been spoken about as a probable captain, was not considered for selection for the West Indies tour, ostensibly because he was based in England and had not played enough domestic cricket in India. Similarly, Rusi Surti, who had been based in Australia since 1968, was also overlooked. The new faces comprised the Hyderabad contingent of paceman Devraj Govindraj, wicketkeeper Pochiah Krishnamurthy and opener Kenia Jayantilal. Sunil Gavaskar, whose tall scores for Bombay in the Ranji Trophy and Bombay University had impressed the selectors, also made it. On the other hand, Borde was not considered at all. The South Zone selectors had reason to pat themselves on the back when Venkataraghavan, whom they had named their captain earlier in the season, was appointed vice-captain.

Wadekar wanted experience on a tour of a region where India had lost 0-5 on its previous visit. Salim Durani, Jaisimha, Abid Ali and Sardesai, all of whom had done well in domestic cricket, were accordingly picked. Incidentally, Mansoor had wanted the same players in the team in the previous season but was overruled.

18

KHADOOS!

> Undoubtedly the players were talented, but it takes more than talent to maintain the standards that we had set for ourselves [...] Bombay's batting tradition has been hailed all over the world, but the fact is that we would not have been half as successful had our bowlers not taken twenty wickets on a regular basis.
>
> —Ajit Wadekar, *75 Years of the Ranji Trophy*[24]

The Ranji Trophy was a knockout tournament till 1956–57, after which a zonal league-cum-knockout format was introduced. 1957–58 onwards, every team played against the other sides in its zone for points. The team with the most points from each of the five zones—North, South, Central, East and West—qualified for the knockouts.

At the BCCI's AGM in September 1970, the Maharashtra Cricket Association proposed that the top two teams from each zone should get to qualify for the knockouts. The MCA's angst was understandable. Baroda had topped the West Zone league in 1957–58, but thereafter it had been Bombay all the way. Maharashtra had never got a look-in.

---

[24]This was a book published by the BCCI. It was a commemorative volume that was distributed privately.

To understand why Bombay and Maharashtra had separate teams despite the former becoming the capital of the latter in 1960, one needs to go back to the 1930s. The Bombay Presidency Cricket Association[25], a member of the BCCI, was officially established in 1930. It was meant to represent the entire Presidency, except Sind. However, officials from Pune and Ahmedabad—both part of the Presidency—approached the BCCI for direct affiliation, and they were granted the same in 1934, just before the start of the inaugural Ranji Trophy season. It was said that one of the catalysts for the inception of the Maharashtra and Gujarat Cricket Associations was the omission of players from outside Bombay in the squad that was meant to represent the Bombay Presidency in a three-day game against Douglas Jardine's England team, just before the first Test on Indian soil in December 1933.

Today, Maharashtra, which officially became a state on 1 May 1960, is home to three different Ranji Trophy teams, two of which (Mumbai and Maharashtra) are part of the West Zone and the third (Vidarbha) is in the Central Zone. Gujarat, which came into being on the same day as Maharashtra, is also home to three Ranji Trophy teams. Saurashtra (formerly Nawanagar and Western India) and Baroda were princely states when their respective cricket associations were created. They have their headquarters in Rajkot and Baroda, respectively. The areas in the state that are not under the jurisdiction of these two associations are managed by the Gujarat Cricket Association, which is headquartered in Ahmedabad.

The BCCI did not tinker with the associations that already existed in Maharashtra and Gujarat, but it adopted the 'one state, one Ranji team' rule for all the other states that were created after Independence. The erstwhile princely state of Hyderabad, which had fielded its own cricket team since the start of the Ranji Trophy in 1934–35, was also allowed to carry on. Andhra Pradesh,

---

[25]It was renamed the Bombay Cricket Association in 1935.

which was created in 1956 with Hyderabad as its capital, fielded a separate team in the Ranji Trophy. Today, the Hyderabad Cricket Association runs and manages the sport in Telangana, which was created in 2014.

It was but natural that a metropolis like Bombay, with its rich legacy and a robust ecosystem that encompassed grounds, turf wickets, coaches, schools, colleges, clubs, corporate houses and administrators who cared for the game, kept producing exceptional cricketers. The city won the first two editions of the Ranji Trophy and repeated the achievement seven more times until 1956–57. Bombay's eminent status in Indian cricket could be gauged from the fact that India's playing XI for the first Test of the 1954–55 series against Pakistan comprised as many as eight players from the city. The gap between Bombay and the other teams only widened after the dissolution of Holkar in the mid-1950s.

After losing out to Baroda in 1957–58, Bombay topped the West Zone league in the next season and went the distance, beating Bengal in the final. Desai established a Ranji record with 50 wickets in the season, and Wadekar scored half-centuries in the semi-final and final. They were complemented by senior players like Polly Umrigar and Madhav Apte.

That victory in 1958–59 signalled the start of a triumphant run. It was not that Bombay did not have its share of alarms during this period, but every crisis birthed a champion.

The unavailability of players who were on national duty made no difference to Bombay's fortunes in the Ranji Trophy. It was famously said back then that it was easier to get into the Indian team than to represent Bombay.

Sudhakar Adhikari, an opener of the 1960s, did not want to risk losing his place by skipping a Ranji game against Maharashtra, which was to begin on the same day as his wedding. He cracked the problem by having the rites conducted at the crack of dawn, after which he left for the game. He scored a century and then attended his wedding reception in the evening.

There are many stories that underscore Bombay's supremacy in the 1960s. They beat Rajasthan in seven of ten Ranji Trophy finals from 1960–61 to 1969–70. Bhagwat Singh Mewar, also known as Bhagwatsinhji, the ex-Maharana of Udaipur and head of the Rajasthan Cricket Association, did everything he could to build a champion team, even engaging cricketers from Bombay itself as professionals, but to no avail.

There was elation in Mysore when their team scored 341 against Bombay in the 1966–67 semi-final. With Prasanna and Chandrasekhar both playing, Mysore eyed a historic win, but Wadekar scored 323 all by himself and Bombay won by an innings and five runs. The following season, Bombay took the first-innings lead in the final against Tamil Nadu but struggled against the spin duo of Venkataraghavan and Vaman Viswanath Kumar on the final day. At lunch, Tamil Nadu needed five wickets for an outright win and Bombay needed to bat out two sessions to win on first-innings lead. The champions—Bombay—did just that, with Manohar Hardikar, the captain, and the 20-year-old Solkar proving to be impossible to dislodge.

This tradition of different generations combining with splendid effect, endured. Bombay were 174-6 in response to Karnataka's 406 in the quarter-final of 1993–94, when Ravi Shastri, the captain, and Sairaj Bahutule, a leg-spinner playing his first season, scored centuries to enable Bombay to take the first-innings lead.

A word that Bombay/Mumbai's cricketers have traditionally used to describe themselves is 'khadoos', which in the city's parlance stands for a combination of determination, perseverance and obstinacy.

Cricketers from the city were at their most 'khadoos' in the 1970–71 season.

The Indian team that toured the West Indies in 1971 comprised five Bombay players: Dilip Sardesai, Ashok Mankad, Eknath Solkar, Sunil Gavaskar and Ajit Wadekar, the captain. In their absence, the 24-year-old Sudhir Naik was appointed captain of Bombay for the knockout stage of the Ranji Trophy.

Naik scored 93 in the quarter-final against Delhi. Bombay gained a first-innings lead of 106 and went on to win by ten wickets. Padmakar Shivalkar, Bombay's left-arm spinner extraordinaire, took six wickets in the game.

For the semi-final against Bengal at Calcutta, Naik convinced the selectors to add the seasoned Vijay Bhosle to the inexperienced batting line-up. Bhosle repaid the faith with an innings of 58. Ramnath Parker and Mahesh Sampat scored hundreds, and Bombay totalled 459. Shivalkar once again ran riot, taking 5-36 as the hosts collapsed for 158. He took another 'five-for' after Bengal were asked to follow on.

Borde, the captain of a full-strength Maharashtra team that met Bombay in the final, would have reflected on the irony of it all. Maharashtra had topped the West Zone league that season with 26 points to Bombay's 25. This meant that had the Maharashtra Cricket Association not insisted on the inclusion of the top two teams from each zone in the knockouts, Bombay would not have even qualified, leave alone made the final!

Bombay seized the initiative after scoring 287. Maharashtra lost their fifth wicket at 137, but Nicky Saldanha counterattacked with a series of lofted shots.

The Bombay tradition of the old guiding the new then came to the fore. Ramakant Desai, a visitor to the dressing-room at the tea interval, reminded Naik of how he had placed the latter at deep square leg and then tempted Saldanha with a bouncer, in a game some seasons ago. Saldanha had fallen for the trap and given Naik a catch.

At the resumption, Naik instructed Abdul Ismail, Bombay's new-ball bowler, to bounce Saldanha, and stationed himself at deep square-leg. History repeated itself.

Fifties by Bhosle and Sampat, and a knock of 33 by Milind Rege, the off-spinning all-rounder, in Bombay's second innings ensured that Maharashtra needed 254 to win. Maharashtra then ran into Shivalkar at his most unrelenting. There was some hope for them as long as Borde was batting, but when he fell to an outstanding catch by Rege at slip, it was all over.

At the time of writing, Bombay/Mumbai has won the Ranji Trophy 42 times in 90 seasons. The second-most successful team is Karnataka, with eight titles. That says it all. Mumbai has produced over 70 Test cricketers, including ten men's Test captains. The city's 15-year-long winning streak in the Ranji Trophy from 1958–59 to 1972–73 has no parallels in first-class cricket.

19

TWIN TRIUMPHS

Venkataraghavan, the vice-captain, alerted Wadekar about an unprecedented opportunity to grab psychological points after the West Indies were dismissed for 217 in response to India's 387 in the first Test in Kingston. With the first day having been washed out, the Test had become a four-day game, in which a follow-on could be enforced if the difference in the first innings totals of both the teams was 150 or more. The umpires had to tell Garfield Sobers, the West Indies captain, that Wadekar was well within his rights to ask the opposition to bat again. Never before had the West Indies followed on against India.

Earlier in the game, India recovered from 75-5, thanks to Solkar, Prasanna and Sardesai, who scored a magnificent 212. The West Indies drew the game, but not before the Indians realized that their opponents were no longer the force that they had been in the 1960s.

Aware that some of his players resented Mansoor's ouster, Wadekar took on a balancing act. He made the juniors feel at home, handled his contemporaries with kid gloves and sought inputs from the senior players. Intent on ensuring that the senior players reported for meetings on time, the captain used Gavaskar and Solkar, his Bombay juniors, strategically and smartly. They would invariably reach his room early, only for one of them to be told to leave and return after a while. By the time the player would come back, the seniors would have arrived in the captain's room. Wadekar would then chide the player for being late and lacking decorum. Soon enough, the seniors got the message.

The slow and low wicket at the Queen's Park Oval in Port of Spain, Trinidad, where the second Test was to be played, was straight out of the Indian spinners' dreams. However, Wadekar was unsure of what to do if he won the toss. He was relieved when Sobers called it right and elected to bat.

The spinners bowled the West Indies out for 214 and Sardesai then scored 112, his second ton in successive innings. There were half-centuries by Solkar and the debutant Sunil Gavaskar, who had missed the first Test due to a whitlow on a finger.

India secured a first-innings lead of 138, but the West Indies batted well in their second essay. Fate intervened on the fourth morning, at which point the hosts were 150-1. Charlie Davis, one of the overnight batters, was hit by a ball in the nets and could not resume his innings. When play began, Roy Fredericks, the other overnight batter, was run out.

The night before, Durani had requested Jaisimha, the senior pro, to have a word with the captain. The former was confident of dismissing both Sobers and Clive Lloyd, the mainstays of the opposition. Jaisimha then had a word with Wadekar, who followed his advice and threw the ball to Durani. There was also an element of pragmatism in his call, as India were a bowler short with Prasanna off the field due to injury. The left-armer kept his word. He bowled one to Sobers that landed on the rough created by the fast bowlers outside the left-hander's off-stump and sneaked between the bat and pad to dislodge the bails. Seventeen runs later, Durani had Lloyd caught by Wadekar at mid-wicket. Those two strikes opened the floodgates, and the West Indies were all out for 261.

India knocked off the target of 124 with seven wickets in hand. Abid Ali passed on the distinction of striking the winning runs to Gavaskar, who completed his second fifty in his first Test.

India had never beaten the West Indies in a Test before, either at home or overseas. Thousands of miles away, Indian cricket-lovers who had reconciled themselves to viewing draws against the Windies as an achievement, could not believe it.

Gavaskar scored his maiden Test century and followed it with an unbeaten 64 in the second innings of the third Test in Georgetown (Guyana), which was drawn. India's next stop was Bridgetown, Barbados, home to the fastest wicket in the Caribbean. A West Indies victory was predicted when Barbados beat the Indians by nine wickets in a three-day game that preceded the Test.

Put in by Wadekar, the West Indies scored 501-5, with Sobers contributing 178. India were struggling at 70-6 in response, when Sardesai (150) and Solkar (65) came to the rescue again. Bishan Bedi helped Sardesai save the follow-on with a last-wicket stand of 62.

Shortly after Sobers set India 335 to win in five hours, Ashok Mankad had his right wrist broken by Uton Dowe, the paceman, but he refused to come off and carried on till he was dismissed. His resilience rubbed off on his teammates. Gavaskar batted with aplomb to score his second Test hundred in only his third Test and the Indians achieved a draw.

The last Test belonged to Gavaskar, who scored 124 in the first innings and 220 in the second of what was a six-day game.[26] His skills were on display throughout, as were his powers of concentration, which enabled him to forget a painful tooth. The West Indies took a first-innings lead of 166, but they stumbled in their second innings and were 165-8 when the match ended.

A crowd of over 10,000 welcomed the victors at Bombay airport. The spotlight was on Wadekar and Gavaskar, who had

---

[26]In those days, there were instances of boards of the playing teams deciding mutually to end a series with a six-day game, in case the series was undecided till that point.

scored a record 774 runs in his maiden series. India could not have won the series without Solkar, the spinners and Sardesai, who was hailed by Merchant as the man behind the renaissance of Indian cricket.

Mansoor, who after pulling out of the Caribbean tour had contested the general elections and lost, announced his unavailability for the England tour as well. Chandrasekhar was recalled to the squad after three seasons, but he was upset when Merchant called his selection a 'gamble'. Unlike their 1952 counterparts, the selectors displayed pragmatism by picking Engineer despite his being available for only the Tests. He had been representing Lancashire in county cricket since 1968, and it would have been silly not to utilize his experience of English conditions.

Abbas Ali Baig, who had last played a Test in 1966-67, was brought back as well. Jaisimha and Durani, both of whom had struggled in the Caribbean, were left out. Keki Tarapore was succeeded as manager by Col. Hemu Adhikari.

The victory in the West Indies notwithstanding, India went into the first Test against England at Lord's as the underdogs. They were playing a team that had just won the Ashes in Australia.

Wadekar's 85 ensured a first-innings lead of nine for the visitors. The spinners bowled well in both innings and India found themselves needing 183 to win in a little over four hours on the last day. Rain had been predicted in the afternoon, but the conquerors of the Caribbean decided to go for it.

England struck twice early, but they were then rattled by a partnership between Gavaskar and Engineer. John Snow was flustered enough to tackle Gavaskar with his shoulder when the batters ran a quick single. As if that was not enough, he then picked up Gavaskar's bat and tossed it to him.

Engineer's dismissal a little later, was a setback. Gavaskar was sixth out at 114 for a splendid 53. When the rains came, India were 145-8 and both sides claimed a moral victory.

Gavaskar scored another fifty in the second Test in Manchester, a game that Snow missed on disciplinary grounds because of the incident at Lord's. The game was interestingly poised at the end of day four, with India at 65-3 after being set a target of 420. However, the final day was washed out.

England took a first-innings lead of 71 in the final Test at The Oval. John Jameson, the England opener, was run out early in the second innings. Just before he ran in to bowl to John Edrich, Chandrasekhar heard Sardesai shout 'Mill Reef!' It was the name of a horse on which they had placed a winning bet a few days ago. Chandra reacted by producing a 'Mill Reef' that beat Edrich for pace and bowled him all ends up. Keith Fletcher, the next man, fell first ball to a catch by Solkar at short leg. England were 24-3 at lunch.

After the resumption, Venkataraghavan beat Basil D'Oliveira in flight and induced him to hole out to mid-on. Alan Knott, England's wicketkeeper-batter, who had batted well in the series, then got a thick inside-edge off Venkataraghavan, which Solkar snapped up with a dive. Chandrasekhar proceeded to dispatch three batters in quick succession.

With England eight down, Wadekar replaced Chandrasekhar with Bedi, who had Derek Underwood caught in the deep. Chandrasekhar was then brought back from the same end, and he had John Price leg-before, to finish with 6-38. India needed only 173 to win a series in England for the first time.

Wadekar and Sardesai put together a partnership after the openers fell cheaply. The captain was run out in the first over of the final day, but Sardesai carried on. The target was less than fifty runs away when he and Solkar fell in quick succession. Engineer, the next man in, was assertive and Viswanath patient.

The winning hit was made by Abid Ali, who had been at the non-striker's end when the Port of Spain Test was won earlier that year. Wadekar, who had dozed off in the dressing-room, was woken up and informed that his team had created history.

The plane carrying the players to Bombay was diverted to Delhi, where they were received by Indira Gandhi, the prime minister. When they finally reached Bombay on 24 September 1971, they realized that the BCCI secretary Prof. Chandgadkar's promise of giving them a red-carpet welcome if they won in England was in fact an understatement.

The players drove from the Bombay airport to the Brabourne Stadium in a motorcade, with over a million people lining the streets. The route was dotted with posters and rose petals were showered on the heroes from vantage points.

India's back-to-back victories against two of the game's Big Three changed many things, foremost among them being the expectations of the fans. Never again would they celebrate drawn Tests as moral victories, for instance. They would only be content with the real thing.

WHAT MIGHT HAVE BEEN

England's tour of India in 1971–72 was postponed by a year due to political tumult. The genocide unleashed by Pakistan in its eastern wing triggered a war on two fronts. It was fought for a fortnight, and it ended on 16 December 1971 with an Indian victory and the unconditional surrender of 93,000 Pakistani officers and soldiers in Dhaka. Bangladesh, a new country, came into being.

Around the same time, there was turbulence in the sporting world as well. International condemnation of South Africa's policy of apartheid resulted in the ICC imposing an embargo on the country.

The cancellation of South Africa's tour of Australia in 1971–72 prompted many Indians to suggest that the BCCI offer to tour Australia as South Africa's replacement, for what would be a 'world championship' of Test cricket. The logic was simple—India had beaten the West Indies, who had lost to Australia in 1968–69; India had then beaten England, who beat Australia in the 1970–71 Ashes.

However, a 'Rest of the World' squad, handpicked by Sir Don Bradman himself, ended up touring Australia instead. The team was led by Garfield Sobers and it comprised three Indians: Engineer, Bedi and Gavaskar.

While Gavaskar did not recapture the highs of the West Indies and England, he picked up invaluable lessons on batting from stalwarts like Sobers and Rohan Kanhai, who were his teammates. The experience of facing a fiery Dennis Lillee on lively wickets and his conversations with Bradman himself stood him in good stead. Bedi bowled brilliantly to underscore his reputation as the best left-arm spinner in the world. Engineer was as ebullient as ever on either side of the stumps.

What if the BCCI had been more persistent and managed to convince the Australian Cricket Board to accept its offer?

The battle between the Australian batters, most of whom were good players of spin, and the Indian spinners, backed by an extraordinary close-in cordon of catchers comprising Wadekar, Engineer, Abid Ali, Solkar and Venkataraghavan, would have been enthralling. The Indian batters would have handled the Australian quicks. Wadekar, Engineer, Abid Ali and Sardesai were no strangers to the country, having toured as recently as 1967–68. Possibly, the absence of a genuine fast bowler would have made it difficult for India to win the series, but the assignment would have definitely toughened the players up for future battles.

As it turned out, India played no international cricket for 16 months after The Oval Test of 1971.

20
STAGNANCY

There was outrage when England announced its team for a tour of India in 1972–73. Once again, the *big guns* had opted out, citing the usual heat-and-dust excuses. For the Indians, who believed that they could not be taken lightly after 1971, it was a bitter pill to swallow.

In the first Test in Delhi in December 1972, India played ten of the eleven men who had played at The Oval in August 1971. The only change was Ramnath Parkar replacing Ashok Mankad, his Bombay colleague, as opener. Chandrasekhar took 8-79 in the first innings, but the outcome was different this time around. The second-string England XI, captained by debutant Tony Lewis, won by six wickets.

The selectors reacted by sacrificing Sardesai, the hero of 1971, for Durani. Venkataraghavan made way for Prasanna, who had spent most of the England tour wondering why he was not being picked in the XI despite his performances from 1967 to 1971. With attacking spinners like Bedi and Chandra already in the XI, Wadekar had preferred a third spinner who could keep it tight at one end, and he believed that Venkataraghavan was a lot better in that regard than Prasanna. That apart, Venkataraghavan was also a brilliant fielder and the vice-captain. However, India needed Prasanna and his guile after the defeat at Delhi.

Prasanna celebrated his return with three wickets in England's first innings of the second Test in Calcutta. Durani scored a belligerent 53 in the first innings. Needing 192 to win, England were all out for 163. Wadekar was unwell for most of the game and Engineer had deputized for him, but the captain returned to the field in the final stages and took a superb catch at slip to dismiss Derek Underwood. Tony Greig, an all-rounder of South African origin, had a good game with six wickets and an innings of 67.

After covering the first two Tests as a journalist, Mansoor scored a century for South Zone against the visitors and declared himself available for the third Test at Madras. The selectors, eager to bolster the batting, acquiesced. In his first Test innings since January 1970, Mansoor went on the offensive and scored 73, putting India on course to overhaul England's 242. Prasanna chipped in with 37 and India reached 316. The off-spinner then took four wickets to terminate England's second innings for 159.

The Indians nearly messed up the 86-run chase, eventually winning by four wickets. They had Durani to thank for his 38, as well as Mansoor, who kept his cool at the end.

The English and Indian batters came into their own in the last two Tests in Kanpur and Bombay, both of which were drawn. In Bombay, Viswanath became the first Indian to score another Test century after scoring one on his debut, thus breaking a jinx that had afflicted all his predecessors, from Lala Amarnath to Hanumant Singh.

Little did anybody know then that the Brabourne Stadium would not host another Test for 36 years.

For decades, the Bombay Cricket Association, which ran and managed official cricket in the city as a member of the BCCI, would stage Test matches that were allotted to it at the Brabourne, as it did not have a ground of its own. This gave the CCI, who owned the arena, the upper hand when it came to discussions on allotments of tickets. The CCI was never inclined to honour the BCA's requirement, which included quotas for its member-clubs and other stakeholders. Matters came to a head in the late 1960s, when Sheshrao Wankhede, the BCA president who had been Maharashtra's finance minister and was later elected as speaker of the legislative assembly, took the initiative to acquire a plot of land close to the CCI, for a new stadium.

The 2-1 win over England meant that Wadekar had led India in three series wins as captain. However, the margins of victory in Calcutta and Madras—28 runs and four wickets, respectively—against a team that was not at full-strength, had not done the Indians any credit.

Bombay won its fifteenth consecutive Ranji title in the 1972–73 season, beating Tamil Nadu in a final that lasted two days and one ball. The spinners of both sides bowled brilliantly on a turner, but Shivalkar was slightly better than his Tamil Nadu counterparts. The game also marked the end of Sardesai's first-class career. Remarkably, he had debuted in 1958–59, the season in which Bombay had begun their winning streak.

Unlike 1971, when India had toured England in the second half of the English summer and therefore played on drier wickets, the team was to tour in the first half in 1974, when it would be colder and the wickets juicier. A competitive international series in the 1973–74 season would have helped the Indian players prepare themselves technically and mentally for the challenges that lay ahead, but all that the BCCI was able to arrange was a tour of Sri Lanka, then an associate member of the ICC. Wadekar was given a team that was a mix of regulars, as well as players who were in the reckoning.

A month after the Indian team's return from Sri Lanka, Karnataka beat Bombay on first-innings lead in the Ranji semi-final at Bengaluru, thus ending the metropolis' 15-year-long winning streak. Centuries by Viswanath and Brijesh Patel enabled Karnataka to score 385. Prasanna and Chandrasekhar then bowled 107 overs between them and shared nine wickets to dismiss Bombay for 307. Gavaskar was bowled by a magical delivery by Prasanna that drifted inwards and then swerved away to hit the stumps. It was what went on to be christened the 'doosra', decades later. Karnataka went on to beat Rajasthan in the final at Jaipur.

Indian selectors had always bemoaned the paucity of fast bowlers who could fight fire with fire on foreign shores. It therefore came as a shock when a selection committee comprising three former quicks—Dattu Phadkar, Bal Dani and Raj Singh Dungarpur—overlooked Maharashtra's Pandurang Salgaonkar, who had done well in Sri Lanka, for the England tour. Madan Lal, the Delhi all-rounder, was picked, but Wadekar's request for either Umesh Kulkarni or Ramakant Desai, both of whom were still going strong in club cricket in Bombay, was turned down. Mansoor had retired from touring and Durani was not considered. This meant that both the players who had essayed match-winning knocks in the series against England in 1972–73, were not in the team.

The board also shot itself in the foot by accepting a playing condition that not more than five fielders would be allowed on the leg-side. This meant that the spinners, especially Prasanna and Venkataraghavan, who were used to bowling to populated leg-side fields, would have to do things differently. The players were livid when they got to know, but it was too late to do anything.

An Indian family invited the team over for dinner during their opening encounter of the tour against D.H. Robins' XI. There, some seniors, including Prasanna and Bedi, asked Wadekar why the team's wins had not resulted in the augmentation of the players' fees. The captain, who was aware that he was being viewed as a man of the establishment for trying to avoid any sort of confrontation with the board, did not take it well. Tempers rose and angry words were exchanged. Although the players made up the following morning, the damage had been done.

21
FALL AND RISE

The Indians went into the first Test in Manchester with numb fingers, running noses and multiple sweaters. The cold was intense. After England declared at 328-9, Gavaskar batted splendidly to score 101, but apart from Viswanath and Abid Ali, nobody else got going.

Leading by 82, England went for quick runs in the second innings. India had a full day in which to score 296, but the batters failed. England won by 113 runs.

Everything went south from that point. England amassed 629 in the second Test at Lord's, making the most of Chandrasekhar's inability to bowl due to a thumb injury. India managed to put up 302 on the board and were asked to follow on. It then took England only 17 overs to seal the series. Chris Old and Geoff Arnold bowled India out for 42, their lowest-ever score. Three years after the highs of 1971, the Indians seemed to have sunk to the lows of 1952.

There were fiascos off the field as well. One of the players was accused of shoplifting. He was innocent but was advised to plead guilty, just because some people wanted to hush up the matter. That did not happen, and the player underwent intense trauma, prompting Gavaskar to share a room with him to intercept abusive calls and talk him out of the crisis. B.K. Nehru, the Indian High Commissioner to the United Kingdom, told the players to 'get out' when they were late for a party at his residence because of the traffic and a delay at a preceding function. The squad trooped back to their bus and refused to return, despite the entreaties of Col. Adhikari, the manager. Venkataraghavan eventually convinced them to do so, and the High Commissioner even apologized to the players, but they were in no mood to socialize—and it showed.

Not surprisingly, India was outclassed in the third Test as well. The only consolation was a 77-run innings by Test debutant Sudhir Naik, Bombay's Ranji Trophy-winning captain in 1970–71.

> Back home, there was the usual probe by a committee [...] It ascribed our defeats to unfavourable weather conditions and poor play. There was no mention of dissensions among the players. I hold the view that the Colonel (Adhikari) did not help in bringing about unity. If he takes credit for the 1971 victory, then he should also take the blame for the 1974 defeats. He crippled Wadekar and made him his mouthpiece.
>
> —E.A.S. Prasanna, *One More Over*[27]

Extreme reactions were only to be expected. The Victory Bat that had been erected in Indore to commemorate the triumphs of 1971 was defaced. The West Zone selectors then decided that the captain of India did not merit a place in the Duleep Trophy squad. Wadekar reacted by announcing his retirement. It was an unfortunate end to an eventful career.

Wadekar's detractors made it a point to gloat and declare that his luck had finally run out. They were the ones who had branded him a lucky captain, conveniently ignoring the fact that luck alone could not have ensured three consecutive series wins, that too without genuine pace.

The national selectors then pulled a tiger out of the hat. Mansoor was offered the captaincy for the first two Tests of the

---

[27]Prasanna, E.A.S., *One More Over*, Rupa & Co., 1977.

upcoming series against the West Indies, but he insisted on all five and had his way.

Bishan Bedi was left out of the first Test in Bangalore (renamed Bengaluru in 2014), because the board wanted to penalize him for appearing in a TV interview in England without permission. However, the bigwigs did not want to labour the point. Hence, Rajinder Goel, the left-arm spinner from Haryana, who like Bombay's Shivalkar was unlucky to be Bedi's contemporary, was picked in the squad, but left out of the XI. A good performance by him would have put the selectors in a quandary as Bedi was to definitely play the next Test.

There was confusion when Mansoor left the field during the Test to tend to an injured finger without indicating who should take over. Venkataraghavan stepped up, but a couple of overs later, Goel ran onto the field with instructions that Gavaskar was to take charge. That was how the world got to know of Gavaskar's appointment as vice-captain, which he had been told to keep under wraps.

The Indians were handicapped by Mansoor and Engineer's inability to bat in the second innings due to injuries and lost by 267 runs. Clive Lloyd, the debutant captain and Gordon Greenidge, the debutant, scored centuries. Andy Roberts, the new leader of the Windies pace attack, took six wickets.

The ghosts of 1958–59 resurfaced before the second Test in Delhi. With Mansoor ruled out, Gavaskar was named captain, but he had his right index finger broken by Maharashtra's Salgaonkar in a Ranji Trophy game. On the eve of the Test, R.P. Mehra, who headed the cricket association in Delhi, announced that Engineer would lead in the Test. People were therefore surprised when they saw Venkataraghavan accompanying Clive Lloyd for the toss on the morning of the game. The appointment had been made just a few minutes before the toss, with the blessings of the board officials and selectors.

Bedi returned for the game at Chandrasekhar's expense.

A youngster named Vivian Richards scored 192 and Lance Gibbs, the veteran off-spinner, exploited a damp wicket to set up a win for the visitors by an innings and 17 runs. Engineer suppressed his disappointment with a knock of 75 in the second innings.

Mansoor's return for the third Test in Calcutta provided Test cricket with its only instance of a captain becoming the twelfth man in the next game. Venkataraghavan, who had led in Delhi, made way for Chandrasekhar. Karsan Ghavri, a left-arm paceman who had represented Saurashtra and Bombay, was brought in for his debut Test. In him and Madan Lal, an Indian XI found a pair of genuine new-ball bowlers after a long time. Another debutant was Aunshuman Gaekwad, son of India's 1959 captain Dattajirao Gaekwad.

Batting first, India struggled. Gaekwad arrived at the crease after Mansoor was hit on the mouth by Roberts and had to go off for repairs. The debutant saw his captain's blood on the pitch, but he steadied his nerves to score 36. Mansoor resumed his innings a little later and hit Vanburn Holder, the paceman, for 19 runs in an over. India was dismissed for 233, but their bowlers then restricted the West Indies to a lead of only seven runs.

Gundappa Viswanath's brilliant 139 in the second innings helped India set the opposition a target of 310. The West Indies were 146-3 at stumps on the fourth day. That evening, Mansoor took two decisions: he would back Chandrasekhar to strike, and he would resign if India lost. Even as the West Indies batters went for the runs on the fifth morning, Mansoor persisted with his leg-spinner. His patience was rewarded when Chandrasekhar dismissed Lloyd and then Alvin Kallicharran. The twin strikes turned the game, and the West Indies was bowled out at 224. India's losing streak had finally ended.

Viswanath's innings on the first day of the Madras Test was appreciated not only by the spectators, but also his opponents. India were 76-6 when Ghavri, who had assisted Viswanath in Calcutta, did an encore. Bedi and Chandrasekhar also dug in.

The score was 190-9 when the latter was caught in the slips. Roberts finished with 7-64, but he was overshadowed by Viswanath, whose unbeaten 97 would never be forgotten.

The spinners then bowled the Windies out for 192, and Gaekwad scored 80 in India's second innings. Needing 255 to win, the West Indies came up against Prasanna at his best. He took 4-41 in the second innings to add to his 5-70 in the first. Bedi and Chandra chipped in with three and two scalps respectively to seal victory by 100 runs.

The decider, a six-day affair at the new Wankhede Stadium in Bombay, got off to an acrimonious start with Gerry Alexander, captain of the 1958–59 West Indies team and now its manager, labelling the wicket as unfit for Test cricket. Lloyd, his own captain, proved him wrong by scoring 242. Play on the second day ended early due to a riot. The official version was that the spectators were incensed by the police's treatment of a fan who ran onto the arena to congratulate Lloyd on his reaching 200. A section of a stand was set ablaze and miscreants ran onto the field, seemingly to scuff up the wicket, but they were thwarted by spectators, who created a cordon around the pitch till reinforcements arrived. The unofficial version was that some individuals—offended by the construction of the new stadium—were looking for an opportunity to create trouble and got one when the police grabbed the spectator. The Windies declared on day three at 604-6.

Gavaskar, whose finger had healed, was joined by Solkar after Engineer fell for a duck. The Bombay boys put up a 168-run partnership, with Gavaskar scoring 86 in his first Test in two months and Solkar completing his maiden Test century. After India avoided the follow-on, the West Indies went on the offensive and set India a target of 404. Holder then tore through the Indian line-up, taking six wickets.

India thus lost the series 2-3, but Mansoor was hailed for resurrecting Indian cricket after the horrific tour of England. Now in his mid-30s, he decided to move on.

22
GLADIATORS

India needed 334 runs to beat England in the opening game of the inaugural cricket World Cup in June 1975. However, they scored only 132-3 in the allotted sixty overs.

It was not that the Indians had no experience of limited-overs cricket. The Padmakar Talim Shield, the oldest limited-overs tournament in the world, had been played in Bombay since 1951 and the BCCI had instituted an inter-zonal limited-overs tournament, which it named after Prof. D.B. Deodhar, C.K. Nayudu's illustrious contemporary, in 1973–74. India had even scored a healthy 265 in their very first One-Day International (ODI) on their tour of England in 1974.

However, the batters just could not get going in the World Cup game. Gavaskar, who nicked the ball to the keeper in the very first over but did not walk because nobody appealed, batted through the innings, scoring only 36. Engineer and he scored fifties in a ten-wicket win over East Africa in the next game, but India was knocked out of the competition when they lost to New Zealand in their last league game.

Venkataraghavan, who had played limited-overs cricket during his stint for Derbyshire county in England, led India in the World Cup, but there was a new captain for the unofficial Test series against Sri Lanka that followed. Bedi, who had impressed with his leadership of Delhi and North Zone, was assigned the job. While he led India to a 2-0 win, some board officials were offended by his protests against the substandard accommodation arrangements for the players in Nagpur, the location of the third Test.

That did not come in the way of his retention as captain for the twin-tour of New Zealand and the West Indies. Sunil Gavaskar, who had been Venkataraghavan's deputy during the World Cup, retained the vice-captaincy.

An injury forced Bedi to withdraw from the first Test of the New Zealand leg, in Auckland. The Indian XI for the game comprised three debutants. One of them was Syed Kirmani, who had been Engineer's understudy in England in 1971 and 1974. His extensive wicketkeeping experience as part of the Karnataka squad alongside spinning greats Prasanna and Chandrasekhar and his prowess with the bat had prompted the selectors to pick him ahead of other candidates. The second debutant was Surinder Amarnath. Despite not being a natural left-hander, his illustrious father had made him bat the *other way* in an era where left-handers were a rarity in Indian cricket. The third was Dilip Vengsarkar, who had scored a belligerent century for Bombay against Rest of India in the Irani Cup at the start of the season. The XI also comprised Surinder's brother Mohinder, who had returned to the Indian team after playing a solitary Test against Australia in 1969–70.

Surinder emulated his father by scoring a century on his Test debut. Gavaskar, who led in Bedi's absence, also scored a century in his first match as a captain. Prasanna bowled superbly, taking eleven wickets in the game, including eight in the second innings. India won by eight wickets.

The visitors then ran into rough weather, literally and figuratively. Even the players from the north were unsettled by the cold. The second Test in Christchurch was drawn. The visitors were then undone by the greenest wicket they had ever seen, in the final Test in Wellington. A sweep by Lance Cairns broke

Gavaskar's cheek bone, necessitating a surgery. India, down to ten men in the second innings, were skittled out for 81, with Richard Hadlee taking 7-23. Bedi remarked after the game that unlike the curators in New Zealand, those in India used grass-mowers with blades.

The Indians then flew across the Pacific to take on the West Indies, who had won the inaugural World Cup in 1975 but were routed 1-5 by Australia in a Test series soon after.

India did not start well, losing the first Test in Bridgetown by an innings and 97 runs. The next Test in Port of Spain was drawn, but it could have gone their way with a bit of luck. Centuries by Gavaskar and Brijesh Patel ensured a big first-innings lead, and the spinners then tied nearly all the West Indies batters down. However, Vivian Richards came to his team's rescue with his second century of the series and the game was drawn.

Incessant rainfall in Georgetown, where the third Test was to be played, resulted in the game being shifted to Port of Spain, India's favourite city in the Caribbean for obvious reasons. The West Indies imitated their opponents by deploying three spinners—Albert Padmore, Raphick Jumadeen and Imtiaz Ali—on the most spin-friendly wicket in the Caribbean.

The search for an opening partner for Gavaskar had still not ended, with Parthasarathy Sharma and Vengsarkar not clicking in the first two Tests. Aunshuman Gaekwad was then requested to give it a go.

In the third Test, the West Indies scored 359 and then bowled India out for 228, with Michael Holding taking 6-65. The hosts stepped on the gas in the second innings.

> When Lloyd declared at 271-6, it was not in charity. He wanted to wrap up the series as they were already 1-0 up. If we were in that kind of position, we would have been a lot happier because Indian spinners have always enjoyed bowling fourth. But in this Test match, we were

batting fourth against an attack which was not always sure of itself.

—Bishan Bedi, *Great Moments of Indian Cricket*[28]

India were set 403 to win. Not only did they have a new opener in Gaekwad, but they also had a new number three. Mohinder Amarnath—selected as a 'medium pacer who could bat'—had been promoted in the batting order after his brother's loss of form.

India were 134-1 at stumps on day four, with Gavaskar on 86. He completed his fourth Test century in Port of Spain on the fifth morning but was stumped soon after. His sequence of scores in four Tests at the venue read 65, 67*, 124, 220, 156, 26 and 102.

Viswanath and Mohinder then batted well in tandem and India were 197-2 at lunch. Lloyd took the new ball, but it started disappearing quicker into the outfield and a lot more regularly to the fence. At tea, India were 289-2. The batters were set, and the summit was in sight.

Only 67 runs were needed when Viswanath was run out at a splendid 112. The final blows were hammered by Patel. Mohinder was run out after a heroic 85 with 11 needed. Moments later, India became the second team after Bradman's 'Invincibles' of 1948 to successfully chase a 400-plus target in a Test. Polly Umrigar, the manager and a witness to many defeats in his playing days, was overwhelmed at the victory.

For Lloyd, the defeat, coming as it did in the wake of the series loss in Australia, was the last straw that broke the camel's back. Although he had already been named captain for the forthcoming tour of England, he felt that he needed to make a statement. The spinners were discarded and a pace quartet comprising Michael Holding, Bernard Julien, Wayne Daniel and Vanburn Holder assembled, for the final Test at Sabina Park, Kingston.

---

[28]This was a documentary film released by Grindlays Bank ahead of the ICC Men's Cricket World Cup in 1987.

India was inserted on a wicket that looked lethal, but the openers held firm. Shortly after Gavaskar and Gaekwad raised the hundred, they were surprised to see a cluster of fielders behind the bat, including a couple of leg-slips. The fast bowlers switched to bowling around the wicket. In an age of minimal protective equipment, the Indians were subjected to bouncer after bouncer, interspersed with beamers, which the bowlers ridiculously claimed were accidental. With the spectators egging the pacemen on to 'kill', the Indians felt like gladiators in the colosseum.

Gavaskar fell at 136. Gaekwad and Mohinder then took India past 200 before the latter was caught off a brute of a ball by Holding. Viswanath then fell in exactly the same manner but broke his finger, as it got jammed between the ball and the handle of his bat. A little later, Gaekwad, who had taken innumerable blows on his body in a defiant innings of 81, was hit behind his left ear by a Holding thunderbolt. For Umrigar, a witness to Contractor's injury, it was 1961–62 all over again. Gaekwad was helped off the field, bloodied and in acute pain. There was a third casualty when Patel was hit on the mouth.

Bedi declared at 306-6 and the West Indies replied with 391. India were 97-4 in their second innings when Venkataraghavan was bowled by Holding. Kirmani, the non-striker, followed him off the field, leaving many wondering why the Indians had declared when they were only 12 runs ahead. Bedi later clarified that the innings had in fact ended as there was nobody left who was fit enough to bat. Chandrasekhar and he had injured their fingers while bowling. The West Indies knocked off the 13 runs they needed to win the series, but not before Gavaskar asked Madan Lal to bowl a beamer and then crib about the ball slipping through his fingers.

As expected, the Windies defended their tactics and attributed the injuries to a 'ridge' on the pitch, from which the ball had reared awkwardly. It was ironic that Clyde Walcott, who had walked to the boundary to waste time and deny India a victory in Bombay in 1948–49, accused the Indians of not knowing how to play fast bowling.

The Indians soon realized that they had changed the course of cricket history with their victory in Port of Spain. They had unwittingly laid the foundation of an institution called the West Indies pace dynasty, which would dominate the sport for the next two decades.

23

TRANSITION-II

India were struggling against England in Madras in January 1977, when umpire Judah Reuben picked up a gauze strip that had fallen off the forehead of John Lever, England's new-ball bowler. The umpire's suspicion that there was Vaseline on the strip was confirmed in a laboratory. Bedi then accused the English of applying the same to the ball to enhance its swing. The BCCI got involved and refused to accept the visitors' explanation that Lever had worn the strip to prevent sweat from running into his eyes. However, the English denied the charge.

The English did not forgive. Northamptonshire, the county Bedi had represented since 1972, announced the termination of his contract after the 1977 season. The Indian captain was also accused by Ray Illingworth, the former England captain, of being a chucker. Although Bedi was cleared, the message sent out by the English was crystal clear; anybody who questioned the integrity of cricketers from the land that was the *custodian* of the game would be punished.

Nothing emerged from the BCCI's involvement. It was a time when the Indian cricket board was not taken seriously. Things had changed by 2001, when half the Indian team was penalized by the match referee during a Test against South Africa in Port Elizabeth.

India's 2-0 win over New Zealand at the start of the 1976-77 season had been peppered with red flags. Both Gavaskar and Viswanath scored a century each, but their colleagues had been inconsistent.

The New Zealanders were followed by the first-ever full-strength England team to tour India. It was captained by Tony Greig, whose batting and attempts to play to the gallery with extravagant gestures like collapsing if a firecracker went off in the stands, or freezing in his follow-through after hitting a boundary, as if to oblige the photographers, made him popular with the spectators. He also courted the Indian umpires by declaring at the start of the series that he believed that they were among the best in the world. England's comprehensive victories in the first three Tests in Delhi, Calcutta and Madras, respectively, made it easy for their media contingent to paint Bedi as a sore loser when the Vaseline allegations came to the fore.

India registered a consolation win in the fourth Test in Bangalore, with debutant Yajurvindra Singh Bilkha equalling the world record for the highest number of catches (seven) in a Test. The hosts also came close to winning the last Test in Bombay, but England forced a draw and took the series 3-1. Gavaskar, who became the first Indian to score 1,000 runs in a calendar year during the first Test in Delhi, scored India's only century of the series in Bombay. Bob Willis and John Lever bowled well, as did Derek Underwood, whose tally of 29 wickets was the highest on either side.

The 129-run victory by Gavaskar's Bombay over Bedi's Delhi in the 1976–77 Ranji final led many to believe that normal service had been resumed, as it was Bombay's third title in a row after the semi-final loss in 1973–74.

That Ranji final was played a couple of weeks after Indira Gandhi, India's prime minister, announced the end of the Emergency that she had controversially imposed in June 1975. The anger of the masses at the excesses committed during the Emergency was reflected in the general elections of 1977, in which

Gandhi's Congress-R was routed, and the Janata Party came to power.

In the off-season, Bedi found himself being targeted once again, this time by his own board, which announced that players who did not report for a camp in Madras by 16 September 1977 would not be considered for the tour of Australia that was to follow. Bedi could not reach Madras on the stipulated date as he was in the process of wrapping things up in England and looking into the possibility of suing Northamptonshire for unfair dismissal. He returned to India a few days later and led North Zone in the semi-final of the Duleep Trophy, but senior board officials continued to be dogmatic.

It was M. Chinnaswamy, the board president, who decided to be pragmatic. He prevailed upon the board to drop the matter, and Bedi was retained as captain for the Australia tour. The board also adopted a similar stance on Gavaskar, who had labelled the selectors as 'court jesters' in an article in the 1 May 1977 edition of *Sportsweek*, the periodical. He was also let off and retained as vice-captain. Umrigar was reappointed manager.

The team for Australia comprised the Amarnath brothers, whose father had led India on the inaugural tour in 1947–48, as well as Ashok Mankad, the son of India's top performer in the Tests on the same tour. Chetan Chauhan, who had last played a Test in 1972–73, was recalled after an outstanding season for Delhi.

The Test series against an Australian team without its stars, who had signed up with World Series Cricket, turned out to be a cracker. Australia scraped through by 16 runs and two wickets respectively in the first two Tests, and India dominated the next two, winning the third by 222 runs and the fourth by an innings and two runs. Needing 493 to win the last Test, the visitors got within striking distance but lost by 47 runs. Bedi took 31 wickets, the highest by an Indian captain in a series. Gavaskar scored three centuries. Viswanath, Mohinder, Chandrasekhar and Prasanna also did well, but the fact was that the Indians lost most of the key moments and with them, a series they ought to have won easily.

In mid-1978, the Cricket Club of India organized a tour of Kenya by a team that comprised stalwarts like Mansoor, Gavaskar and Solkar, as well as youngsters. One of those who impressed on the tour was Kapil Dev Nikhanj, a paceman from Chandigarh, who had done well for Haryana in domestic cricket. He was picked in the Indian team for its first series against Pakistan since 1960-61.

The political dispensations in both countries—the democratically elected Janata government in India and the military dictatorship in Pakistan—had decided to move on from a period fraught with tension.

The first Test in Faisalabad started with Sadiq Mohammed, Pakistan's opener, calling for a helmet—an accessory that batters were seen wearing in the WSC games in Australia—after receiving a bouncer from Kapil Dev, the debutant. For fans in India, who were watching the live telecast of a Test match being played outside their country for the first time, the sight of an Indian paceman making an opposition batter uncomfortable with pace, was exhilarating. However, their excitement abated when they saw the disdainful treatment of their spinners at the hands of Zaheer Abbas and Javed Miandad. Viswanath scored a century and the game was drawn.

Mushtaq Mohammed, Pakistan's captain, got his team off to a dream start in the second Test in Lahore by winning the toss and electing to bowl on a green-top. Imran Khan and Sarfaraz Nawaz, Pakistan's pacers, took four wickets each to dismiss India for 199. Saleem Altaf, the third pacer, took the key wicket of Gavaskar, who had scored 89 at Faisalabad. Zaheer Abbas scored 235 to add to his 176 and 96 in the first Test. Worryingly for the Indians, the spinners were thrashed again.

India, 340 runs in arrears, were given a solid start in their second innings by Gavaskar and Chauhan, who had batted well together since they joined forces at Perth in 1977-78. They put on

192 before falling to dodgy umpiring decisions. However, Surinder and Viswanath fought on, as did the teenager from Chandigarh, who had not heard of the term night-watchman until Bedi told him to go in as one. Kapil Dev scored 43.

On day five, India was at 406-4, with Viswanath batting on 83, when he tried to cut Mudassar Nazar, the medium pacer, but was bowled. That gave the Pakistanis an opening and they clawed back to dismiss the visitors for 465. The hosts had less than two hours in which to score 126 to win, and they got there comfortably.

The garb of cricket diplomacy was shed for good in the third ODI in Sahiwal. With honours even after the first two ODIs, the Pakistanis could not digest the fact that their opponents were cruising to victory in the decider. India needed only a few runs to win when bouncers started sailing way over the heads of Gaekwad and Viswanath, the men in the middle. The umpires refused to intervene, and India needed 23 off 14 balls when a furious Bedi called his batters in. Pakistan was declared the winner.

The third Test in Karachi was the first in which Kapil Dev shared the new ball with Karsan Ghavri. Batting first, India scored 344, with Gavaskar finally getting the hundred that had eluded him in the series. Kapil Dev scored his first Test fifty. Pakistan then declared at 481-9 in response.

At the start of India's second innings, Gavaskar nicked Imran and was caught behind, but he was reprieved by the umpire. Having been at the receiving end of umpiring howlers earlier on the tour, the Indian vice-captain was not going to walk. Once he had got his eye in, he was impossible to dislodge. The bowlers then targeted the other end, and Gavaskar started running out of partners until Ghavri dropped anchor. Gavaskar completed his second century of the Test shortly after surpassing Umrigar's Test aggregate of 3,631.

He had moved to 137 when Sarfaraz, who was bowling around-the-wicket and angling the ball across the right-hander, induced him to nick one to Wasim Bari, the keeper. The innings folded up quickly after that. Pakistan needed 164 to win in twenty mandatory overs plus an extra thirty minutes. They overhauled the target, thanks to bold batting and running by Asif Iqbal and Miandad, and a late assault by Imran Khan. Their exposure to the limited-overs format while playing county cricket in England enabled them to pace the chase to perfection.

The difference between the two teams was the bowling. The Indians could not bowl their opponents out even once in the entire series. The Indian selectors reacted to the defeat by sacking Bedi and entrusting the reins to their premier batter.

24

FROM GAVASKAR TO GAVASKAR

Unlike the Pakistanis, who picked their WSC signatories for the series against India, the West Indies overlooked their WSC players for their tour of India in 1978–79. Some of the biggest names in the game, like Clive Lloyd, Vivian Richards, Gordon Greenidge, Andy Roberts and Michael Holding were thus not considered. Alvin Kallicharran, the left-handed batter who had not been recruited by Packer, was named captain of the touring side. The bowling was led by Sylvester Clarke, a feared name on the English county circuit. He had for company Vanburn Holder, Norbert Philip and a youngster called Malcolm Marshall.

The arrival of Kapil Dev enabled Sunil Gavaskar, India's new captain, to deploy five specialist bowlers—two pacemen and three spinners—in the first two Tests. Kapil Dev and Ghavri were to be supported by Bedi, Chandrasekhar and Venkataraghavan. Prasanna, who had conceded a lot of runs in Pakistan, was no longer in the picture.

Gavaskar's magnificent 205 in the first Test in Bombay elicited an open letter from Vijay Merchant, which appeared in *The Times of India*. The veteran praised his spiritual successor's technique, patience, timing, strokes and temperament among other things, and declared that 'Indian cricket had produced no greater batsman.'

Kallicharran, Gavaskar's opposite number and friend, scored 187 in response. The West Indies took the first-innings lead in Bombay and in the second Test in Bangalore as well. However, both games were affected by rain and drawn.

In the third Test in Calcutta, Gavaskar scored 107 in the first innings and an unbeaten 182 in the second, thus becoming the first batter in Test history to score two centuries in a Test thrice. He scored 1,014 runs in the period from 16 October 1978 to 2 January 1979.

India's second innings also featured the maiden Test century of Vengsarkar, who added an unfinished 344 with his captain. Gavaskar declared on the fourth evening, setting the opposition 335 to win on the last day. Ghavri and Venkataraghavan took four wickets each, but the West Indies managed to avoid defeat, with their last pair hanging on till the umpires called the game off in the twilight.

After the West Indies were dismissed for 228 in the first innings of the fourth Test in Madras, their pacemen went on the offensive on a wicket that had copious bounce. However, they were unable to make an impression on Viswanath, who contributed 124 to a total of 255.

What happened next was breathtaking for Indian cricket fans. Generations of Indians who had been born and bred on spin and seen their heroes struggle against the opposition's pace, saw Kapil Dev and Ghavri make the West Indies batters hop and duck. Needing 125 to win, India lost three wickets for 17, but Viswanath then essayed his second decisive innings of the game. The Indians were steered to victory by Kapil Dev, who came in at 84-6 and attacked the bouncers that were being hurled at him. The scores were level when he and Kirmani, anticipating yet another bouncer, ran as soon as the ball was delivered and completed a bye.

The last two Tests were drawn, and India thus won the series 1-0. Their bowling heroes were their new-ball bowlers. Kapil Dev, who also scored a century in the fifth Test in Delhi, took 17 wickets in the series and Ghavri topped the table with 27. By taking charge of the bowling attack, the pacers had made a statement not only for themselves, but also on behalf of their predecessors like Subroto Guha, Pandurang Salgaonkar, Devraj Govindraj, Kailash Gattani and others who did not get the opportunities they deserved in the late 1960s and early 1970s, due to the preponderance of spinners.

Chandrasekhar was dropped after the second Test against the West Indies and Bedi axed after the third. Although Chandrasekhar was recalled for the last two Tests against the West Indies and both he and Bedi were picked for the tour of England that followed, the fact was that they had lost their bite.

The win against the West Indies gave Indian fans reason to fancy their team's prospects in England, but a storm was brewing. The BCCI was not happy with the fact that some of the players had been speaking to Kerry Packer's representatives.

Not very long ago, Bedi and Gavaskar had initiated discussions with the board on better financial terms for the players. While the BCCI was not averse to raising the pay, its hackles were raised by the revival of the long-dormant Players' Association, of which Gavaskar, Venkataraghavan and Viswanath were secretary, treasurer and executive member, respectively. The board had never been keen to negotiate with an association.

The players who were approached by WSC had made it clear that representing the nation would always be their top priority. However, the BCCI still advised the selectors to not consider Gavaskar as captain for the England tour. Syed Kirmani, whose name was also on the WSC wish-list, was omitted from the team altogether. Venkataraghavan was appointed captain and Viswanath named his deputy. The wicketkeeper's spot went to Bharat Reddy, who had toured Australia and Pakistan as Kirmani's understudy.

> I still do not know the reasons why I was removed from the leadership, but I presume it had to do with the fact that I openly talked about the approach made to me by

> World Series Cricket. Kiri (Kirmani) was also honest about it, while others who had been approached, preferred to indicate otherwise. The real story—about the approaches, the responses and the reactions—is a juicy one, and will blow many a reputation to smithereens, and so it is best to preserve it for a book.
>
> —Sunil Gavaskar, *Sportstar*, 1 May 1993

Ironically, WSC itself was disbanded a couple of months before India's tour of England, with the Australian Cricket Board giving Packer exclusive TV rights for cricket in the country that they had refused to sell to him and prompted him to create WSC in the first place.

The second World Cup in 1979, which preceded the series against England, was catastrophic for India. Venkataraghavan's team lost to New Zealand, West Indies and even Sri Lanka, who had still not secured full membership of the ICC.

India lost the first Test in Birmingham. Gavaskar and Viswanath scored two fifties each and Kapil Dev took his first 'five-for' in Tests, but it wasn't enough. Another defeat seemed imminent in the second Test at Lord's, when England amassed 419-9 after bowling India out for 96. Gavaskar, who had scored 42 in the first innings, then compiled 59 before being caught at slip off Ian Botham, who became the fastest to complete the all-rounder's double of 1,000 runs and 100 wickets.

Viswanath and Vengsarkar then produced a match-saving partnership and had their names added to the board of centurions in the away dressing-room at cricket's premier venue.

Gavaskar scored 78, his fourth fifty of the series, in the third Test in Leeds, which was affected by rain. On the eve of the final Test at The Oval, he mentioned to Mike Brearley, the England captain, that he hadn't yet achieved what he had set out to do. At The Oval, England took a first-innings lead of 103 and declared their second innings on the fourth afternoon, setting India a target of 438. The visitors were 76-0 at stumps on day four.

In the first session of the final day, Chetan Chauhan was compact and his partner, an epitome of flair and fluency. Gavaskar completed his twentieth Test century in only fifty matches.

After lunch, the openers surpassed Merchant and Mushtaq Ali's 1936 stand of 203 at Manchester. Chauhan finally fell at 213. Gavaskar carried on in the company of Vengsarkar. The former captain was on song, cutting and driving imperiously. The spectators rose to him when he completed his double century.

England then sent down only six overs in thirty minutes. They called it gamesmanship; had an Asian team done that, it would have been called a cheat.

India needed just over a hundred when the twenty mandatory overs commenced. The target was 71 runs away when Vengsarkar fell for 52. Aware of his team's inexperience in limited-overs cricket and not wanting to leave it till very late, Venkataraghavan sent in Kapil Dev to throw his bat around. The all-rounder went for a big hit and fell for a duck.

Gavaskar kept going until he drove Botham on the up and was caught by Brearley for 221. He had been batting for 490 minutes and faced 443 deliveries. India was 389-4.

England then got lucky with the umpiring. Viswanath was given out caught to a catch that did not appear to be clean, and Venkataraghavan was declared run-out, although TV replays suggested that he had made his crease. The runs dried up and with two deliveries left, India needed ten runs and England two wickets. When Reddy took a single off the penultimate ball, the English players ran off the field without completing the over.

India's next Test was only a week away. The plane carrying the team home from England was nearing Bombay when the commander used its PA system to congratulate Gavaskar for being reappointed captain of India.

The BCCI ought to have informed Venkataraghavan before making the announcement, but it did not.

25
ALL IN THE MIND

Gavaskar's priority at the start of his second stint as captain was to restructure the bowling line-up. Bedi and Chandrasekhar were out of contention. Dilip Doshi, a 31-year-old left-armer from Bengal, who had been consistent at the domestic level for over a decade and represented Nottinghamshire in the county championship in England, was picked in the squad. Left-armers Goel and Shivalkar were still playing domestic cricket, but Doshi was much younger.

The Australian team that arrived in India in September 1979 for a six-Test series was led by Kimberly Hughes. Although World Series Cricket was disbanded in April 1979, the Australian Cricket Board had opted not to pick Packer's recruits for the World Cup and tour of India.

The first two Tests in Madras and Bangalore were affected by the north-east monsoon. Doshi took 6-103 on his debut, but the Australians batted well in both Tests. They even took the first-innings lead in the third Test in Kanpur, before collapsing in the second innings to lose by 153 runs. Shivlal Yadav, an off-spinner from Hyderabad, took six wickets in the game.

India dominated the second half of the series. The Australians were asked to follow on in the fourth Test in Delhi, but they recovered and forced a draw. Yashpal Sharma, a batter from the Punjab who had scored his maiden Test hundred in Delhi, led

India's chase of a target of 247 on the last day of the fifth Test in Calcutta. However, the Australians managed to curb the scoring and the hosts were 200-4 when the game was called off due to poor light.

Gavaskar scored his twenty-second Test century and second of the series in Bombay. Another centurion was Syed Kirmani, who had been recalled for the series. India declared at 458-8 and then bowled Australia out for 160 and 198, to win a series against Australia for the first time.

The Australians had not been at full-strength of course, but players like Allan Border, Rodney Hogg and Hughes himself, all of whom had their moments on the tour, excelled for the first-choice Australian team in the years to come.

The only blip for India was the manner in which Mohinder was dismissed in Bombay. He had gained a reputation of being suspect against the bouncer after being hit on the head by Imran Khan at Lahore in 1978–79, and then having his skull fractured by Richard Hadlee in India's game against Nottinghamshire on the 1979 tour of England. In Bombay, Mohinder came in to bat wearing a sola hat (pith helmet), the favourite headgear of cricketers of his father's generation. He had tried a helmet but found it uncomfortable. As was expected, Rodney Hogg dug one in short and Amarnath went for the hook, but while doing so, he slipped and fell on the stumps.

The Indians had no time to recharge their batteries. Earlier in the year, Gavaskar had been asked about Pakistan's tour of India, which was to follow the one by the Australians. He had on his mind the possibility of the intensive schedule taking its toll on the players when he replied that 'Pakistan would smash India to pulp.'

His statement may well have been on the mind of Asif Iqbal's men, when they were accorded a warm reception in India. Their swag spoke for itself. Sarfaraz Nawaz, Pakistan's highest wicket-taker in the previous season's tussle in Pakistan, had withdrawn from the India tour, allegedly because of his differences with the captain, but the visitors were still the favourites.

Gavaskar planned methodically. In Kapil Dev, Doshi and Yadav, who had taken 28, 27 and 24 wickets, respectively, against Australia, he had bowlers who were in form. Ghavri had also done well.

Roger Binny, a seamer from Bengaluru, joined Kapil Dev and Ghavri in the playing XI in the first Test of the series, which was played in his hometown and ended in a high-scoring draw. Three pacers in an Indian XI would have been unimaginable even a year ago.

Sikander Bakht, a wiry paceman from Karachi, bowled India out for 126 after Pakistan was dismissed for 273, in the second Test in Delhi. Kapil Dev led India's fightback with the ball and the hosts needed 390 to win. Gavaskar fell early, but Vengsarkar got going. India's bid for victory was hampered by the fall of a wicket whenever a partnership showed signs of developing. They were 364-6 at the close, with Vengsarkar unbeaten on 146. The Pakistanis were as rattled by India's resurgence in the second innings, as they were when they got to know that Imran Khan, their bowling lynchpin, had sustained a rib injury.

When reports emerged that the wicket for the third Test in Bombay was going to turn, Gavaskar indulged in mind games. He announced, 'Doshi would win the game for India.' The captain's exasperation at Kapil Dev's penchant for getting out after getting set also prompted him to pronounce publicly that the all-rounder would never score a half-century again. While Doshi was eager to prove his captain right, Kapil Dev was itching to prove him wrong.

Gavaskar was the first to applaud when Kapil Dev completed a skillful fifty in the first innings in Bombay. The captain's rebuke had had the desired effect. The lower-order rescued India from 154-6 to 334 and the bowlers then dismissed Pakistan for 173. Forties by Gavaskar and Vengsarkar in the second innings took India to an unassailable position. Needing 322 to win, Pakistan collapsed for

190. Doshi took six wickets in the game.

The move to prepare a green wicket to capitalize on Imran's absence from the fourth Test at Kanpur nearly backfired on the hosts. They were dismissed for 162, with Sikander Bakht and Ehtesham-ud-din taking five wickets each. Pakistan then scored 249. India recovered lost ground in the second innings, but the match ended in a stalemate due to poor weather.

With Imran finally fit, the Pakistanis were optimistic about their chances in the fourth Test in Madras, where the wicket was known to favour pace. After they had scored 272, Imran bowled 38 overs and took five wickets, but he could not get past Gavaskar, who batted for nearly ten hours to score 166. Kapil Dev, who had taken four wickets in Pakistan's first innings, scored 84 and India put up 430 on the scoreboard.

The all-rounder then ran through the Pakistanis in the second innings, finishing with 7-56. Unlike Mankad and Umrigar's all-round heroics at Lord's in 1952 and in Port of Spain in 1962, respectively, Kapil Dev's match figures of 11-146 and innings of 84 won his team the match and with it, the series. Gavaskar and Chauhan knocked off the target of 76. The win sealed the 1979–80 series in India's favour, as they were 2-0 up with one to play.

As had been the case in 1952-53, the euphoria of a series win against Pakistan was short-lived. Gavaskar announced that he was stepping down, shortly after the end of the Madras Test. The reason behind the decision was the board's refusal to consider the postponement of a scheduled West Indies tour by just one week to give the tired Indian players an opportunity to recoup. For Gavaskar, mediocrity was never an option and he believed that he was not mentally and physically fit enough to give his best. He therefore pulled out of the tour.

The task of leading India in the last Test against Pakistan in Calcutta and a one-off Test against England in Bombay that had been organized to commemorate the golden jubilee of the BCCI was then assigned to Viswanath. His captaincy debut in Calcutta featured an incident that was to resurface years later in the light of cricket's biggest controversy.

> I flicked the coin and Asif (Iqbal) called. It landed in the middle of the hard pitch and started to roll away from us before coming to a halt. Asif got to the coin before I did, picked it up, turned to me and said, 'You have won the toss, Vishy.' I hadn't seen the way the coin landed, but what reason did I have to doubt Asif?
>
> — Gundappa Viswanath, *Wrist Assured*[29]

The Indians thwarted Pakistan's attempt to seize a consolation win and the match was drawn. Unlike their opponents, India had worn a settled look throughout the series, with the same XI playing the first four Tests and only one change being made for the last two Tests. Zaheer Abbas, India's nemesis of 1978–79, had such a poor series that he skipped the last Test.

Most of India's living Test cricketers were guests at the Jubilee Test against England at the Wankhede Stadium. The likes of Lala Amarnath and Syed Mushtaq Ali would have approved of Gavaskar's lofted drive off John Lever, which cleared the long-on boundary. However, India were overwhelmed by Ian Botham, who became the first player to score a century and take ten wickets or more in the same Test. The Indian bowlers were on top in the first innings when Bob Taylor, England's keeper, was declared out caught behind off Kapil Dev. However, Viswanath wasn't sure that the batter had got an edge and had the appeal withdrawn. Taylor then added a match-winning 171 for the sixth wicket with Botham. Predictably, while some praised Vishwanath for his sportsman-spirit, others criticized him for not leaving it to the umpires.

The tour of the Caribbean was cancelled after Kapil Dev also pulled out citing knee trouble. The West Indies Cricket Board

---

[29]Vishwanath, Gundappa, *Wrist Assured*, Rupa Publications India, New Delhi, 2022.

was not sure if an Indian team without its top two players would draw crowds.

The 1979–80 edition of the Ranji Trophy was also eventful. Bombay lost to Delhi in the final. It was Delhi's second successive triumph and a testimony to Bishan Bedi's efforts to bolster cricket in northern India. After taking over as Delhi's captain in 1972–73, Bedi had built the side by inviting players like Chetan Chauhan, Madan Lal and the Amarnath brothers from other teams. He had also mentored scores of local players and led North Zone to three Duleep Trophy titles during this phase.

On the other hand, Bombay failed to qualify for the knockout stage of the Ranji Trophy for the first time in 1977–78, and lost to Delhi in the knockouts in both 1978–79 and 1979–80. With Karnataka also doing well, the metropolis could no longer take its hegemony for granted.

26

THE WIN OF THE TORTOISE

Sunil Gavaskar was reinstated as captain for the twin-tour of Australia and New Zealand, with Viswanath being named vice-captain. Unlike 1977–78, the Indians were to play the full-strength Australian team, which comprised at least three cricketers who would be contenders for a place in any all-time World XI: captain and premier batter Greg Chappell, paceman Dennis Lillee and wicketkeeper Rodney Marsh.

Gavaskar's decision to bat first in bowling-friendly conditions in the first Test in Sydney boomeranged on his team, with Lillee, Len Pascoe and Rodney Hogg reducing India to 78-5. Sandeep Patil—a dasher from Bombay who had made his Test debut against Pakistan in Madras—counterattacked and scored 65 before he was hit on the left ear by a Pascoe bouncer.

Greg Chappell then scored 204, which was three runs more than India's first-innings total. The visitors came a cropper in their second innings as well, but not before their captain made a statement. Patil, who was in hospital, was told to bat in the second innings. He did not last long, but waiting for him at the gate after his dismissal was Gavaskar himself. It was then that Patil realized why his captain had wanted him to bat.

He had ample time before the second Test in Adelaide to get used to wearing a helmet. India was at 130-4 in response to Australia's 528 when he arrived at the crease. What ensued was a fabulous display of batting. Patil drove, cut, punched and flicked on his way to 174, an innings that enabled India to reach 419. Chappell declared at 221-7 on the fifth morning, giving his bowlers 75 overs in which to bowl India out. The visitors started disastrously, and wickets fell steadily until the ninth-wicket pair of Ghavri and Yadav batted out the last 56 deliveries to keep the series alive.

The Test matches were interspersed with a triangular ODI series, which had New Zealand as the third team. The third and final Test at the Melbourne Cricket Ground began a week after Greg Chappell courted controversy at the same venue in the third of the best-of-five finals of the tri-series. With New Zealand needing six off the last ball to tie the game, he commanded Trevor Chappell, his teammate and brother, to bowl the last ball underarm. It was a dot ball and Australia won, but the New Zealanders were livid.

Greg Chappell was no fan of the MCG wicket, which he believed was substandard. Before the start of India's first game of the ODI tri-series, he had requested Gavaskar to support him in asking for the wicket to be dug up. However, he was rebuffed, as the Indian captain realized that the wicket's low and unpredictable bounce would suit the Indian bowlers.

Like Lala Amarnath in 1947–48, Gavaskar did well in the matches against the states, but failed in the Tests. The technical alterations he had made to his technique to adapt to English conditions during his county cricket stint in 1980 were as much to blame as the proficiency of the Australian pacemen at capitalizing on the tiniest chink in a batter's armour. The Indian captain had developed a sideways shuffle across the crease and was not moving back-and-across before playing the ball, as he had always done. Consequently, he was unsure of where his off-stump was, and this had induced him to nick balls pitched in the 'corridor of uncertainty' to either the keeper or the slips, in three innings out of four. Viswanath was also struggling, with scores of 26, 24, 3 and 16 in the first two Tests.

Gavaskar failed again on the first day of the Melbourne Test, but Viswanath flowered. At 115-6, he gained an ally in Kirmani, who helped him add 49. Ghavri was run out for zero, but Yadav stayed in despite having his toe crushed by a Pascoe yorker. Viswanath completed a century and was on 114 when he was declared out caught at slip, although the ball had flown off the knee-roll of his leg-guard. Yet another umpiring decision had gone against the visitors.

The Australians replied strongly to India's 237, but not without some luck. Chappell survived a leg-before shout even before he had opened his account. Allan Border, who was bowled after scoring a century, nearly got a reprieve because the umpires were not sure whether the Yadav delivery had dislodged the bails or Kirmani, the keeper, had done so with his gloves. Although Border was eventually declared out, Kirmani was upset as he believed that his integrity had been questioned. He told Gavaskar that had the umpires declared Border not out, he would have left the field.

Yadav, whose toe was found to be broken, kept bowling until he crossed the pain barrier. What he and his teammates did not know was that Doshi was also playing with a broken toe. He had been hit by a yorker while batting against Victoria.

> I had a spiral fracture of the first metatarsal. I was still determined to play the Melbourne Test. I told my captain that I had a badly bruised toe and I would not be able to play anything till the next Test. I had a difficult decision in front of me. Either I conceal the nature of my injury from my team and do my best, or miss the Test. The latter was unthinkable as I had, quite frankly, dreamed of helping India win the final Test.
>
> —Dilip Doshi, *Spin Punch*[30]

---

[30]Doshi, Dilip, *Spin Punch*, Rupa & Co., New Delhi, 1991.

Doshi did whatever he could to keep the swelling at bay. By the time Australia were dismissed for 419, the visitors had another setback in the form of a thigh injury to Kapil Dev.

Up against a first-innings deficit of 182 and an imminent defeat, Gavaskar did what he always did in a crisis. It helped that Chauhan, who had scored 97 at Adelaide, was in good nick. The openers batted out the latter half of the third day and extended their stand on the fourth.

India was at 165-0, of which Gavaskar had scored 70, when Lillee won a shout for leg-before. The Indian captain was furious, as he believed he had got an inside-edge. He was on his way to the pavilion when one of the Australians said something unpleasant. Something snapped.

The Indian captain remembered all the umpiring decisions that had gone against his team right through the series. He stopped walking, turned towards Chauhan and called him over. Both batters then started walking towards the pavilion. No one knew where this was headed. Wing Commander Shahid Durrani, the manager of the Indian team, handled the situation tactfully. He met Gavaskar at the gate, told Chauhan to stay back and sent Vengsarkar in to bat.

> I have to admit that it was an absolutely inexcusable behaviour on my part, for whatever the provocation, I should have kept my cool as I was the captain.
>
> —Sunil Gavaskar, *Sportstar*, 20 February 1999

India was dismissed for 341, and Australia had a bit of the fourth day and the whole of the fifth in which to score only 143. But then, batting on an unpredictable wicket was not going to be easy.

Patil took the new ball with Ghavri, who had John Dyson caught behind. The left-hander then tried to bowl Chappell a bouncer, as was planned, but the ball just did not rise. It skidded past Chappell's bat instead to hit the stumps. At the other end,

Doshi drew Graeme Wood out of the crease and Kirmani affected a stumping. Australia was 24-3 at the close of the fourth day.

Back at the hotel, Gavaskar spoke to his main strike bowler. Could he somehow return to action on the last day? Kapil Dev responded by taking a pain-killing injection and going off to sleep after setting the alarm to ring after two hours. When it rang, he took another shot and went off to sleep again, after setting the alarm to ring after two hours. This sequence was repeated through the night. When the Australians arrived at the MCG the following morning, they were surprised to see the all-rounder warming up.

It was all or nothing. Kapil Dev and Dilip Doshi, both less than half-fit, were to bowl unchanged. Doshi conceded two boundaries to Kim Hughes but got back with an armer that reared off the pitch like a cobra and spread-eagled the stumps before Hughes could get his bat down. From then on, it was Kapil Dev all the way. He did not give the Australians the length and room to essay their favourite cuts and pulls and kept landing the ball on the right spots. The wicket did the rest. Doshi did not give anything away at the other end either. Australia was bowled out for 83, with Kapil Dev, who had been in no condition to walk just 24 hours previously, finishing with 5-28. India had squared a series after being outplayed on eleven-and-a-half out of thirteen days of Test cricket. The tortoise had outpaced the hare in the final lap and emerged a joint winner.

The New Zealand leg of the twin-tour did not go as per expectations, with India losing 0-1. The consolation was an impressive debut by Ravishankar Shastri, an 18-year-old left-arm spinner from Bombay. After being flown out as a replacement for Doshi at Gavaskar's behest, he took six wickets on his Test debut.

27
GENERATION-L

As Somerset county's overseas professional in the English summer of 1980, Sunil Gavaskar scored close to 1,300 runs, inclusive of three centuries. Two of those were scored in first-class games, but it was his third hundred that was talked about the most. Chasing 283 against Middlesex in the quarter-final of the limited-overs Benson and Hedges Cup, Gavaskar scored 123 against an attack that comprised the formidable quicks West Indian Wayne Daniel and South African Vincent van der Bijl. His innings featured twelve boundaries and three sixes.

Gavaskar had always possessed all the strokes in the book but had been forced to exercise caution because of the Indian team's over-reliance on him. However, a change in circumstances elicited a change in approach.

His 123 for Somerset heralded another transition in Indian cricket.

The start of the 1960s had witnessed the advent of a generation of batters who revelled in taking risks and thrilling watchers. History repeated itself exactly two decades later, when the start of the 1980s saw the advent of a generation that took to limited-overs cricket, the game's young avatar, like a fish to water. Indian cricket's Generation-Limited-Overs Cricket—Generation-L—was represented by players like Sandeep Patil, Yashpal Sharma and Kapil Dev, all of whom did not hesitate in getting on with it.

The Indian team made its white-ball debut in 1980–81. The players donned blue-and-yellow jerseys in a triangular ODI series, which was to be an annual feature in Australia's international calendar as per the terms that were thrashed out during the rapprochement between WSC and the establishment. The second edition of this annual series saw Australia taking on India and New Zealand. The three teams played each other five times at the league stage and the top two in the points table then played a best-of-five final.

India beat Australia in their first game by 66 runs. Sandeep Patil top-scored with 64 and then Dilip Doshi bowled a match-winning spell of 3-32. The Indians then beat New Zealand in Perth, but ran out of steam thereafter, losing seven of their remaining eight games and not qualifying for the finals as a result. Their only other victory came against New Zealand in Adelaide, a game that featured an audacious 72 by Sharma. In the previous game against the same team, Kapil Dev hit nine fours and three sixes to score 75, an innings that prompted Jeremy Coney, the New Zealand all-rounder, to wave his handkerchief in a gesture of mock surrender.

Even as Generation-L was ushering in a new age 'down under', an old one was ending back home. Bombay beat Delhi by an innings and 46 runs in the 1980–81 Ranji Trophy final. It was the last Ranji Trophy game played by Eknath Solkar and Bishan Bedi, the rival captains.

The next season got off to a shocking start. Sunil Gavaskar and Kapil Dev lost their respective 'opening' partners in a six-Test series against England. Karsan Ghavri, who had taken ten wickets in the Tests in Australia, was dropped, as was Chetan Chauhan, India's most consistent batter in 1980–81. Chauhan was replaced by Krishnamachari Srikkanth, a belligerent opener from Tamil Nadu, while Madan Lal came in for Ghavri.

Statistically, the omissions did not make sense. In the 36 Tests in which they had opened the batting, Gavaskar and Chauhan had compiled nine century stands and one double-century partnership. The greater the pressure, the better they had batted. On a similar note, the new-ball pair of Kapil Dev and Ghavri had not allowed a single century-plus stand by an opposing opening pair in the 28 Tests in which they had bowled together.

The touring England team's weakest link was its captain. Keith Fletcher, who had not played a Test since 1977, was in charge of a team that comprised stalwarts like Geoffrey Boycott, Bob Willis, Derek Underwood, Bob Taylor, David Gower, Graham Gooch, John Emburey and, of course, Ian Botham, who had excelled with bat and ball in the Ashes earlier that year. Fletcher was assigned the job on account of his success as Essex county's captain. India had subscribed to the English approach of first picking the captain and then the team in the early years, but had later shifted to the more practical approach of picking the best XI first and then choosing a captain from among the lot.

The cricketing links of a couple of the English players with South Africa threatened to jeopardize the series, but the decks were cleared when the individuals in question denounced apartheid publicly.

The first Test in Bombay was a low-scoring affair, which India won by 138 runs. Botham took nine wickets, but he was outshone by his Indian rival. Kapil Dev and Madan Lal took five wickets each in the second innings to dismiss England for 102.

The five subsequent Tests turned out to be as tedious as those of 1963–64. Frustrated by England's low over-rates, which was an outcome of there being no agreement between the two boards on the minimum number of overs to be bowled in a day, Gavaskar instructed his bowlers to take their own time as well. The Indians ended up copping the blame for slowing things down, as they had more spinners, who with their shorter run-ups found it difficult to stretch their overs, unlike the English pacemen whose run-ups were longer.

Gavaskar ended a lean trot with an innings of 172 in the second Test in Bangalore. He batted for 11 hours and 48 minutes, thus breaking his own record for the longest Test innings by an Indian, which he had set against Pakistan in Madras. Viswanath ended a bad patch with 107 in the third Test in Delhi and 222 in the fifth Test in Madras. The series ended in Kanpur, where Botham and Kapil Dev scored entertaining hundreds for their respective teams. It was Gavaskar's sixth full series as captain, of which four had been won, one squared, and one lost (against New Zealand). At that point in history, he was India's most successful Test captain by some distance.

In light of subsequent events, the first-ever ODI series to be played on Indian soil was far more significant than the Test series. England won the first game in Ahmedabad and set India a target in the second encounter in Jalandhar.

> On previous occasions ... a reasonable England total of 161 from 36 overs, might well have had India capitulating. Dilip Vengsarkar, however, proceeded to demonstrate that times were changing. Maybe it was the experience he had gained from India's national competition, the Wills Trophy, which had been going on for six years, or perhaps it is easy for a Bombayite like Vengsarkar to match the pace of western living.
>
> —Scyld Berry, *Cricket Wallah*[31]

Vengsarkar was another Indian player who was at home in the shorter format. He batted magnificently along with Sharma and won the match in the last over. Gavaskar led India's chase of 231 in the decider in Cuttack with an innings of 71. Patil and Sharma also batted with abandon and India won with four overs to spare.

Generation-L was in top form on the tour of England that followed. The first Test at Lord's was like India's inaugural Test at the same venue exactly half a century ago. Two Indians

---

[31]Berry, Scyld, *Cricket Wallah: With England in India, 1981-2*, Hodder and Stoughton, London, 1982.

distinguished themselves but still finished on the losing side. Kapil Dev took eight wickets and scored an electrifying 89 off only 55 balls in the second innings to help Vengsarkar, who scored 157, take India to 369 after the visitors had been asked to follow on.

The best performance in the drawn second Test in Manchester was Patil's 129. Out of form and low on confidence, he was considering retirement when Gavaskar included him in the XI. Patil's sails started catching the wind as his innings progressed and he scored a century, the highlight of his innings being six fours in an over by Bob Willis, who had succeeded Fletcher as England's captain. Kapil Dev continued his duel with Botham, scoring 65 in Manchester and 97 in the third Test at The Oval, which was also drawn. While Botham fared better with the bat, scoring a century in Manchester and a double century at The Oval in addition to a fifty at Lord's, Kapil Dev took more wickets and was declared the Player of the Series. However, his brilliance did not obscure the fact that India had lost a series on English soil for the ninth time in ten visits. 1971 almost seemed like an aberration.

Viswanath had a couple of good outings, but Gavaskar did not have a productive time. His series ended when Botham broke his ankle with a fierce drive on the first day of The Oval Test. The Indian captain had to use crutches for a couple of months, but he was fit by the time the Sri Lankans, the ICC's newest full members, arrived in Madras for a one-off Test at the start of the 1982–83 season.

The belligerence of the visitors, especially Duleep Mendis, who scored a century in each innings, took the Indians by surprise. Gavaskar and Patil scored hundreds in the first innings, but the Sri Lankans did not yield. Ultimately, the hosts found themselves needing 175 to win in twenty mandatory overs plus 53 minutes. They went for it, but had to shut shop when Kapil Dev, Patil and Viswanath fell within a few runs of each other. Gavaskar, who had dropped himself down the order, blocked the last five overs.

The ODIs against the Sri Lankans were dominated by another representative of Generation-L. K. Srikkanth scored a match-winning 57 off 43 balls in the first game at Amritsar. Sri Lanka batted brilliantly in the second game at Delhi to score 277-4 in fifty overs, but India won with nearly ten overs to spare, thanks once again to Srikkanth, who blitzed 95 off 66 balls. He ended the series with 92 in the third ODI in Bangalore.

Kapil Dev captained India in the ODIs against Sri Lanka and then led North Zone to victory over the Gavaskar-led West Zone in the final of the 1982–83 edition of the Duleep Trophy. That sealed his appointment as vice-captain for the tour of Pakistan.

28

'JIMMY, JIMMY'

The selection of the teenaged duo of Maninder Singh, a left-arm spinner from Delhi, and Laxman Sivaramakrishnan, a leggie from Tamil Nadu, for the tour of Pakistan, made no sense, although both had done well in the Duleep Trophy. It seemed unwise to take them to a country where India's iconic spinners had floundered in 1978–79. The team also comprised Mohinder Amarnath, who had climbed his way up the ladder after being dropped from the team in 1979-80. With scores of 207, 80 and 67 in the Duleep Trophy, and 127 and 52 in the Irani Cup, he had left the selectors with no option.

Lala Amarnath had nicknamed his sons Tommy (Surinder), Jimmy (Mohinder) and Johnny (Rajinder). 'The Eye of the Tiger', the signature tune of Sylvester Stallone's *Rocky*, had been Jimmy's companion during his years on the sidelines. At a time when it seemed that Indian cricket had forgotten him, he stayed focused and psyched himself to grab the first opportunity that would present itself. Coincidentally, one of the most popular Hindi film songs of the time when Mohinder returned to the team went 'Jimmy Jimmy Jimmy, aaja aaja aaja...'[32]

Mohinder, who had debuted for India in 1969–70 as a bowler

---

[32]This is the hook of the hit Parvati Khan song from the 1982 film *Disco Dancer*, and translates to 'Jimmy Jimmy, come on!'

who could bat, was picked for the Pakistan tour as a batter, but it was his now-ancillary skill as a medium pacer that resulted in his inclusion in the XI ahead of Yashpal Sharma for the first Test. The wicket at Lahore's Gaddafi Stadium had shades of green. In his first Test in three years, Mohinder batted with a helmet and an unconventional open stance to score 109. The match was drawn.

India were bowled out for 169 in the second Test in Karachi, but Madan Lal then struck thrice to reduce the hosts to 18-3. However, the Indians failed to tighten the screws and Pakistan went on to score 452. For India to have any chance of saving the game, they needed to have a partnership, and Gavaskar and Vengsarkar were doing just that when Imran Khan produced an incredible spell, taking five wickets for only three runs in 25 deliveries. Pakistan won by an innings and 86 runs.

India scored 372 in the first innings of the next Test in Faisalabad, but their bowlers were pulverized again. Zaheer Abbas scored his third consecutive century of the series, and Javed Miandad, Salim Malik and Imran also reached triple figures. When India batted a second time, 280 runs in arrears, Gavaskar held one end up and carried his bat through the innings to score 127. Unfortunately, Mohinder apart, no other batter got going. Pakistan needed only seven to win.

The Indians then sank by an innings and 119 runs in Hyderabad, on a wicket on which Pakistan had scored 581-3. There appeared to be no demons in the pitch when Miandad and Mudassar Nazar compiled a stand of 451, but they sprung to life when Imran bowled.

Imran's bowling in the series was one of the grandest exhibitions of what came to be known as 'reverse swing'. Some credit Farrukh Ahmed, a Pakistani who played nine first-class matches, for pioneering the art, while others attribute the same to Sarfaraz Nawaz, who represented Pakistan with distinction in the 1970s and early 1980s. Whoever the originator was, he essentially discovered that if one side of the ball were to be kept shiny by consistently applying saliva or sweat and the other side were to get rougher, the cherry would swing late and prodigiously, if bowled at a decent pace. In fact, the ball, if *looked after* like this, would swing inwards if it were to be gripped like a conventional outswinger, and vice versa. Sarfaraz passed on the art to Imran.

It has been contended by some that there was more to the art than met the eye.

> I would categorically state without any fear of recrimination that on that tour, we regularly played against 14 players. Eleven official players—who were a handful by themselves, two umpires and the 12th man who brought in crown caps of bottles and other material required to prepare the ball for reverse swing. Led by the redoubtable Imran Khan, who was more powerful than the BCCP[33] president then, the umpires and officials bent over to please him in every way. Umpires turned a blind eye to no-balls and gave dubious decisions. The way the ball swung around after the drinks break as if by magic perplexed us first, but when we came to know of their modus operandi, we accepted our fate—we were on a 'goodwill' tour, remember?
>
> —B.S. Sandhu, *The Devil's Pack*[34]

A decade later, Imran admitted to using a bottle-top to rough up the ball in a county game for Sussex in 1981.

The diplomatic skills of Fatehsinghrao Gaekwad, who had been reappointed manager for another tour of Pakistan, were tested by the partisan umpiring, but Gavaskar was determined to ensure that the players behaved like sporting ambassadors. He even issued a statement that the Tests were being played in great spirit.

---

[33]The Board of Control for Cricket in Pakistan was renamed the Pakistan Cricket Board in 1994.
[34]Sandhu, B.S., *The Devil's Pack*, Rupa Publications India, New Delhi, 2011.

The Indians felt the pinch of the decision to jettison Chauhan in 1981. As many as five players—Srikkanth, Pranab Roy (son of Pankaj Roy), Ghulam Parkar, Ravi Shastri and Arun Lal—had partnered with Gavaskar since the start of the England series of 1981-82, with varying degrees of success. For the last Test in Karachi, which followed a draw in the fifth Test in Lahore, Gavaskar told Shastri, who had missed four Tests due to a hand injury, to have the stitches on his arm taken off. Shastri opened with his captain and scored his maiden Test century.

Imran finished with 40 wickets in the series. India's star of the series was Mohinder with three centuries to his name. His success apart, India's only moment of joy was a victory in the third ODI on faster run-rate. Pakistan won the ODI series 3-1.

When the series ended, Kapil Dev wanted to go home to Chandigarh by road via Lahore, but Bedi advised him to fly to Bombay with the rest of the team. Change was nigh. The captaincy for the subsequent West Indies tour was assigned to the all-rounder.

Tragically, the doors were shut on Gundappa Viswanath, who had served Indian cricket with distinction for 14 years. Both he and Doshi had struggled in Pakistan and were therefore excluded, but Maninder Singh, who had failed to take a single wicket in five Tests in Pakistan, was retained. Back in the team after three years because of his record against the West Indies, was Aunshuman Gaekwad. Venkataraghavan, now 38, was also recalled.

Compared to what befell Australia and England in the Caribbean in later years[35], Kapil Dev's team did rather well to draw three Tests and lose two. The first, played in Kingston, seemed headed for a draw when India were 165 runs ahead with four wickets in hand, at tea on the last day. However, Andy Roberts ran through the lower order after the resumption and the hosts then raced to the target of 172 from 26 overs, with Vivian Richards scoring 61 off 36 balls.

---

[35] Australia lost 0-3 in 1983–84 and England were routed 0-5 in 1985–86.

Centuries by Amarnath and Kapil Dev enabled the visitors to draw the second Test. Gavaskar ended a lean patch with a century in the drawn third Test, which like the first two games, was affected by rain. His innings was not without its share of drama. The former captain was in his 40s when he failed to pick a Malcolm Marshall snorter in time and was hit on the head. Even as the fielders rushed to check if he was all right, Gavaskar stood unruffled. His unbeaten 147 was his seventh Test hundred in the West Indies and his 27th overall.

Mohinder was at his best in the fourth Test at Bridgetown, which India lost by ten wickets. He contributed 91 to India's 209 in the first innings. In the second, he went in at 61-1, his team well behind West Indies' total of 486. He batted with panache until a Marshall bouncer proved to be too quick for him and rammed into his mouth.

Mohinder was escorted off the field. He washed his blood-soaked shirt before going to the hospital to have the wound stitched and wore it when he returned to the ground the next day. He returned to the middle when the fifth wicket fell at 139. Waiting for him was Marshall, who welcomed him with a perfume ball that flew past his nose. The next delivery was dug in as well. Amarnath saw it early and hooked it for four. He was last out for 80 and was declared the player of the match despite finishing on the losing side.

The last Test in Antigua was a high-scoring draw. Shastri, not even 21 at that stage, batted as well as he had done in Karachi earlier in the season, to score 102. Kapil Dev and Vengsarkar were unlucky to fall in their respective 90s. Mohinder scored 116 in the second innings.

From three years in the wilderness to 1,182 runs in eleven Tests against Imran and the tornadoes of the Caribbean, Jimmy's comeback was straight out of an epic.

29

RULING THE WORLD

We here to win...what else we here for?

—Kapil Dev's character in *83*[36]

Kapil Dev, his deputy Mohinder and a couple of the junior players apart, everybody else seemed to believe that India were only making up the numbers in the third edition of the World Cup. People seemed to remember only the poor performances of the team in the first two World Cups, and not those in ODI series against England and Sri Lanka at home in subsequent seasons.

Berbice, a town in Guyana where India had beaten the West Indies by 27 runs in an ODI on their tour of the Caribbean just before the World Cup, featured prominently in the team meeting that the Indians had in the bus on their way from London to Manchester, where they were to play the two-time champions West Indies in their first game of the tournament. Nine of the 14 members of the World Cup squad had played in that game in Berbice. Gavaskar had scored 90 and Kapil Dev had blasted 72 off only 38 balls. The captain made the point on the journey

---

[36] *83* is the 2021 Hindi film by director Kabir Khan, where Ranveer Singh played Kapil Dev. The movie follows the Indian cricket team—with a focus on the captain—on its path to victory in the 1983 ICC Cricket World Cup.

to Manchester that the team could do it again.

There were no surprises in the World Cup squad, which was picked by a panel comprising as many as four former India captains. Ghulam Ahmed (chairman), Chandu Borde, Pankaj Roy, Bishan Bedi and Chandu Sarwate selected a mix of seniors and Generation-L representatives. Patil and Srikkanth returned after missing the West Indies tour. There were many all-rounders: Binny, Madan Lal, Kirti Azad, Shastri, Mohinder and the captain himself. Balwinder Singh Sandhu, a pacer from Bombay who had toured both Pakistan and the West Indies, was no mug with the bat either. Delhi's Sunil Valson was to lend variety to the bowling with his left-arm pace. Sharma, Gavaskar and Vengsarkar were the specialist batters, and Kirmani, the keeper.

The Indian selectors did not know it then, but by packing the team with all-rounders, they had created a template that would inspire other teams in the years to come.

The 1983 World Cup was the first in which a team played the other three in its group twice instead of just once at the league stage. The rationale given for the same was that it would be unfair if a prominent team's campaign was jeopardized due to one bad day at the league stage. The organizers wanted to nullify the effects of upsets, if any.

This was ironic in the light of what was to follow.

At Manchester, the Indians did it again. They beat the defending champions by 34 runs. Sharma and Binny led the way with the bat and ball, respectively, and the others chipped in. They then beat new entrants Zimbabwe, who had beaten Australia in their first game. However, the Indians were then brought down to earth by Australia and then the West Indies, who avenged their loss in the first game. This meant that if India wanted to qualify for the semi-finals, then they needed to win their last two league matches against Zimbabwe and Australia.

Vengsarkar had been ruled out of the second game against Zimbabwe after being hit on the mouth by Marshall in the second match against the West Indies. He was replaced in the XI by Gavaskar, who had missed two games earlier.

The Indians were so caught up with the thought of batting first against Zimbabwe and scoring 300 from the allotted sixty overs to not only win by a big margin but also improve their run-rate that they overlooked the dampness in the wicket at the Neville Ground, Tunbridge Wells, after winning the toss. The Zimbabwean pacers exploited it to perfection and Kapil Dev found himself rushing to the middle with the scoreboard reading 9-4. Sharma's dismissal made it 17-5. The captain steered India through to the lunch interval with the help of Binny and then Madan Lal. The score at that point was 106-7.

Kapil Dev was angry with his batters, but he could not help but laugh when he entered an empty dressing-room. His teammates had vanished, after leaving behind a glass of water for their skipper. By the time they resurfaced, he had cooled down.

The Indian captain decided to heat things up in the middle after the resumption. Madan Lal fell at 140, but Kirmani dropped anchor. The spectators were then dazzled by a display of pyrotechnics, all emanating from the blade of Kapil Dev. He scattered the bowlers all over the ground and occasionally, beyond it. India finished with 266-8, of which Kapil Dev's contribution was an unbeaten 175, at that stage the highest individual score in an ODI. India went on to win by 31 runs. Inspired by the captain, the team outplayed Australia in the last league game to set up a semi-final clash against England—three-time hosts and runners-up in 1979—who had won five of their six league matches.

The English began well, but the Indians did not let up. After Binny dismissed both openers, Kapil Dev decided to get rid of the fifth bowler's quota of 12 overs as quickly as possible, by getting Mohinder and Azad to bowl in tandem. However, so well did both bowl that they sent down 24 overs in all, during which England lost four key wickets, including those of their mainstays—David Gower, Allan Lamb and Ian Botham. England could only make 213.

India started their chase with Gavaskar playing his first substantial innings of the competition. He was on 25 when he fell, and Srikkanth followed him four runs later to make it 50-2. Mohinder and Sharma then added 92 and set the stage for Patil to do what he did best. Sharma joined him in the carnage and India won in a canter. The West Indies made short work of Pakistan in the other semi-final.

The final was played on a Lord's strip that seemed to have been made to order for the defending champions. The West Indies supporters were delighted when Lloyd won the toss and elected to bowl. Gavaskar fell early, but Srikkanth and Mohinder batted well until the pacemen struck. At 111-6, the end was near, but India's last four wickets added 72.

Vivian Richards seemed in a hurry to finish the game after Greenidge fell to Sandhu's banana inswinger. Kapil Dev sensed his opponent's urgency and persisted with Madan Lal, who had been hit for three fours in an over. Seven runs after Madan Lal had Desmond Haynes caught in the covers, he dug one in short to Richards, who pulled, but got a top-edge. Kapil Dev, who was fielding at mid-wicket, ran backwards and judged the descent of the ball perfectly. 57-3.

Richards' dismissal got the Indian players and supporters buzzing. Three more wickets fell in quick succession, including Lloyd's. Jeff Dujon and Marshall then added 43 before Kapil Dev introduced his vice-captain into the attack. Dujon inside-edged Mohinder's first ball onto his stumps. Five runs later, he had Marshall caught at slip. Kapil Dev then trapped Roberts leg-before at the other end. West Indies' last pair pottered around, and the score was 140-9 when Mohinder struck Holding on his pads and appealed. Umpire Dickie Bird's index finger went up instantly and the Indian players bolted, with thousands in hot pursuit.

On 25 June 1983, exactly 51 years after the start of its inaugural Test match at the same ground, the Indian men's cricket team had completed the greatest upset in cricket history.

The newly crowned world champions managed to extract a promise of a handsome reward from N.K.P. Salve, the BCCI president, who was overwhelmed enough to forget his anger at being denied two extra tickets for the final by the MCC. A couple of days later, he met Nur Khan, his Pakistani counterpart, in London. The board presidents got talking and questioned why only England was deemed fit enough to host the World Cup. Why couldn't India and Pakistan come together to host the next edition?

30
TURBULENCE

Kapil Dev refused to duck when the stones smashed the windows of the team bus as it exited the Eden Gardens. His teammates were wearing helmets and lying on the floor. The fall from the high of June 1983 had taken only six months.

To keep the promise that he had made to the world champions, N.K.P. Salve requested Lata Mangeshkar, vocalist extraordinaire, to perform at a fundraising concert in Delhi. The lady, a cricket connoisseur herself, agreed. That enabled the BCCI to gift a princely sum of ₹1 lakh to every team member.

The Test series against Pakistan in September–October 1983, which the visitors played without Imran Khan, Sarfaraz Nawaz and Abdul Qadir, with which the new season commenced, was affected by rain, but the cricket was also dull. The series witnessed the end of the Test careers of Doshi and Venkataraghavan. Aunshuman Gaekwad scored a double century in the second Test in Jalandhar, which was drawn like the first Test in Bangalore. The Indians had a scare in the third Test in Nagpur, when they were eight down and only 130 runs ahead on the last day. However, Madan Lal and Kirmani batted stubbornly to ensure a draw. Although India won the two ODIs as well as an exhibition day-night game in Delhi, the consensus was that the hosts were unprepared for the visit by the West Indies that was to follow.

The men from the Caribbean extracted a heavy price for their defeat in the World Cup final. They won the Test series 3-0 and the ODI series 6-0. India's nemesis was Marshall, who took eight wickets in the first Test in Kanpur and 25 more in the next five.

One of those who took him on was Gavaskar, who had begun the season with a century in Bangalore and two fifties in Nagpur against Pakistan. He fell for a duck in the first innings of the first Test against the West Indies at Kanpur and was on seven in the second when a Marshall delivery reared awkwardly after pitching. Gavaskar expected the ball to hit the handle of his bat and therefore loosened his grip to prevent his fingers from getting jammed between the handle and the ball. However, the ball hit the handle just below his fingers, and the bat flew out of his hands because of his loose grip. It was not the first time this had happened, yet some people chose to rant about it.

The critics were silenced on the first day of the second Test in Delhi, when Gavaskar countered the speedsters with the hook, a stroke he had not essayed for a long time. He also drove and cut gloriously and drew level with Sir Don Bradman's record tally of 29 centuries. He missed another hundred by only ten runs in the next Test at a new stadium in Ahmedabad, and surpassed Geoffrey Boycott's aggregate of 8,114 to become the highest scorer in Tests. Kapil Dev bowled 30.3 overs to take 9-83 in the second innings, but the wicket had deteriorated rapidly by then and the Indians had no chance of scoring the 242 runs that they needed to win. They rued their decision to bowl first after winning the toss on a pitch that had not hosted any match before and was therefore untested, but then, hindsight always arrived late.

Shivlal Yadav made an impressive comeback to international cricket in the fourth Test in Bombay, but the Indians failed to win the key moments and the game was drawn. In the next Test in Calcutta, the Windies were 213-8 in response to India's 241 when Andy Roberts joined Lloyd in the middle. The veteran fast bowler helped his captain add 161. Thoroughly dispirited by the time they began their second innings, the Indians were routed for

90, with Marshall taking 6-37. The enraged spectators blamed the batters, especially Gavaskar, who had scored 0 and 20. Fortunately, the stones that were hurled at the team bus caused only minor injuries to a couple of the players.

Kapil Dev finally acceded to Gavaskar's request to bat lower down the order in the final Test in Madras. The former captain reckoned that he had reached a stage of his career where he needed more time than the ten minutes between innings to prepare himself to bat. However, he found himself in the middle in the very first over, after Marshall dismissed Gaekwad and Vengsarkar to make it 0-2. Gavaskar stayed in long enough to compile 236, the highest individual score by an Indian in Tests. He had scored 1,310 runs in Tests in a year in which some people had wanted him to be axed.

The other Indian batter who did well was Vengsarkar. He was surprisingly omitted from the Test squad against Pakistan, but there was no way he could be overlooked for the series against the West Indies, given his record against them. He began the series with a knock of 65 in Kanpur, followed by centuries in Delhi and Bombay.

The biggest blow to the Indians was the fall of Mohinder. After single-digit scores in the first two Tests against Pakistan, he fell apart against the West Indies, with scores of 0, 0, 1, 0, 0 and 0.

> It was one of those burnout syndromes actually. When you reach the peak in a very short time, you are bound to go down. I had achieved everything I wanted to in twelve months' time ... So in a way, I had it coming. I was also not keeping too well at the time. I was down with a virus, but still kept playing.
>
> —Mohinder Amarnath, *Sportstar*, 1 May 1993

The Indians would have fared better had Mohinder complemented Gavaskar and Vengsarkar. It would have also helped if any of the bowlers had been even half as consistent as their captain, who took 29 wickets.

Kapil Dev underwent an arthroscopy on his right knee and hence missed the inaugural edition of the Asia Cup in April 1984, organized by the newly formed Asian Cricket Council in Sharjah, United Arab Emirates. India beat Sri Lanka and Pakistan to win the tournament under Gavaskar's captaincy. Chetan Sharma and Manoj Prabhakar—the new-ball pair—and the opening pair of Delhi's Surender Khanna and Bombay's Ghulam Parkar emerged as the heroes for the team. Khanna won the individual award in both games.

Gavaskar was retained as captain despite Kapil Dev's return for the 1984–85 season, which began with a 0-3 loss in an ODI series against Australia. The Indians then flew to Pakistan, where dreadful umpiring threatened to make Gavaskar's hundredth Test a forgettable affair. India was at 114-2 after being asked to follow on, 272 runs in arrears, in the first Test in Lahore, when Mohinder arrived at the crease.

Months after the traumatic West Indies series, Mohinder had dropped in at a trial game before the team's departure to Pakistan and was taken by surprise when Gavaskar told him to play. He then borrowed Gaekwad's kit and played well enough to convince the captain that 1983–84 had been an aberration.

In Lahore in October 1984, Mohinder did an encore of December 1982 by scoring a match-saving century. The second Test in Faisalabad, played on the flattest of wickets, witnessed five centuries—two by the Indians and three by the Pakistanis. Two days later, the Indians had just completed their innings in an ODI at Sialkot when the news of the assassination of Indira Gandhi, the prime minister of India, came through. The tour was aborted and the entire Indian contingent—the players and the media—flew to Delhi that night.

An England team led by David Gower had landed in Delhi on the same day, for a full series. With India having shut down, the English took off to Sri Lanka and played a couple of games there before normalcy returned.

The visitors were clearly the underdogs, going into the first Test in Bombay. Ian Botham had taken the winter off and just before the first Test, his compatriots were defeated by an 'under-25' Indian team. Ravi Shastri, who led the side, informed Gavaskar after the win that three members of the team—Mohammad Azharuddin, a batter from Hyderabad, Sadanand Viswanath, a wicketkeeper from Karnataka, and Sivaramakrishnan, the leg-spinner, who had played a Test in the Caribbean in 1982–83—were ready for Test cricket.

Sivaramakrishnan was accordingly picked in the Test XI, and he spun England out in Bombay with 12 wickets. However, India's joy at ending a sequence of 31 Tests without a victory was short-lived. England, powered by the batting of Mike Gatting, Graeme Fowler and Tim Robinson, and the spin duo of Phil Edmonds and Pat Pocock, won the second Test in Delhi.

The defeat had a controversial fallout. Kapil Dev was dropped from the next Test and ODI for allegedly essaying an irresponsible stroke in the second innings. Patil, who had scored a century in Faisalabad just two Tests previously, was also left out on the same grounds.

> ...When Kapil was dropped ... everybody started saying that it was done at the behest of Sunil. He had to take the blame and public sentiment turned against him. Truth be told that call was taken by the selectors. The late Hanumant Singh, who was also part of the selection committee, had said in an interview with *Sportsweek* that Sunil had nothing to do with Kapil's omission. Let me put that on record once again. In no way did Sunil influence our decision.
>
> —Chandu Borde quoted in *Sunny G*[37]

---

[37]Bhatia, Shyam, Debashish Dutta, *Sunny G*, Deep Prakashan, 2024.

The outcry over the axing of an icon forced the board president to intervene, but the selectors stuck to their guns. The third Test in Calcutta was affected by poor light and it witnessed yet another display of petulance by the spectators, this time because India was not declaring their first innings. The redeeming features were Shastri's second hundred of the series after his 142 in Bombay and a century by Azharuddin on his debut. He went on to create history by scoring centuries in the next two Tests as well.

Kapil Dev returned for the fourth Test in Madras, a disaster for the hosts. Gatting and Fowler scored double centuries and the paceman Neil Foster took eleven wickets to give England a 2-1 lead. India's only hope of saving face was to win the last Test in Kanpur and square the series they were expected to have won easily. The old failing of flattering to deceive when considered the favourite had reasserted itself all over again.

The Kanpur Test was preceded by an ODI in Chandigarh, where the BCCI secretary convened a meeting of the selectors to pick the captain and team for the next assignment. With England having sealed the ODI series already, leading 2-1 in the Test series with one to play and Gavaskar out of form, a change at the top seemed imminent.

31
SEQUEL

Gavaskar was flummoxed by the instructions that were passed on to him by his better half, who had in turn been briefed by the joint secretary of the BCCI. But then, there was no time to argue. The selectors were waiting for him in another hotel in Chandigarh after having decided to retain him as captain for the World Championship of Cricket, a tournament that had been organized to mark the sesquicentennial of the Australian state of Victoria. Gavaskar did as he was told and scaled the wall instead of taking the main exit of the hotel, where the media was waiting. As he made his way to the car that was to drive him to the hotel where the selectors had gathered, Gavaskar decided that the forthcoming assignment would be his last as captain. He had had enough.

The news of Gavaskar's retention created a furore, as did Kapil Dev's appointment as vice-captain. Could the two apparently warring players work together? Prasanna, who had played Test cricket with both, was named manager. The mood of Gavaskar's detractors did not improve when the last Test against England was drawn and India thus lost the series 1-2.

The inclusion of Sivaramakrishnan—left out of the ODIs against England despite his success in the Tests—in the squad bound for Australia was also questioned. It was a time when spinners were considered superfluous in limited-overs cricket.

Sivaramakrishnan himself believed that he had been picked only to gain experience of Australian conditions, where India was scheduled to tour in the next season. He was therefore surprised when Gavaskar asked him and Shastri the day before their opening encounter against Pakistan in Melbourne, what field they wanted. Shastri, who had started opening the batting in ODIs that season, was to continue doing so in the tournament.

The Indians dismissed Pakistan for 183 after Gavaskar won the toss and elected to bowl. Binny, who like Sivaramakrishnan had missed the ODIs against England, took four wickets. Imran Khan struck thrice at the start of India's innings but Azharuddin and Gavaskar, who batted at number five, put together a match-winning stand.

Srikkanth got India off to an electrifying start in the next game against England at Sydney. Azharuddin, Vengsarkar and Kapil Dev did not let the initiative slip and Gavaskar scored a quick 30. India finished with 235-9. England then capitulated for 149 against Shastri and Sivaramakrishnan, who took three wickets each. Viswanath, whose consistency for Karnataka and India under-25 had earned him a spot in the team ahead of Kirmani, held three catches and affected two stumpings.

The victories over Pakistan and England prompted the Indian government to make arrangements to telecast the team's remaining matches live on Doordarshan, the state broadcaster and the only TV channel in the country.

The nation was captivated by what it witnessed on the morning of 3 March 1985, in what was India's only daytime game of the tournament, against Australia in Melbourne. Not only did they see their bowlers pack the opposition off for 163, but they also saw cricket being covered from multiple angles, slow-motion replays as well as an animated weeping duck appearing on the screen if a batter failed to open his account. For a country that was used to watching cricket on a channel that took its name very seriously—Doordarshan literally meant 'a view from afar'—

Channel Nine's coverage was a revelation.

Indian viewers also saw a team that looked a far cry from the outfit that had struggled against England at home. Gavaskar's field-placements and bowling changes were spot-on. It helped that the Little Master had at his disposal an entire bowling attack that was in form. Kapil Dev and Binny were consistent with the new ball, as was Madan Lal, another 1983 hero who had been recalled. Mohinder kept it tight in the middle overs and then there were Shastri and Sivaramakrishnan to turn things around, literally and figuratively. India beat Australia quite comfortably. Shastri and Srikkanth put on 124 and the latter stayed on to remain unbeaten on 93.

As had been the case in 1983, the selectors had picked all-rounders. The team had no tail, with Sivaramakrishnan, who was slated to bat at number eleven, having a Ranji Trophy century to his name. Srikkanth was audacity personified at the top of the order. By using not one but two spinners as attacking options in limited-overs cricket, Gavaskar had turned convention on its head. The bowlers were being complemented by their teammates, who were throwing themselves all over the field.

India's tactics of 1985 would be imitated successfully by other teams in the 1990s.

The Indians encountered their first hiccup of the competition in the semi-final at Sydney. Defending 206, the New Zealand bowlers dried up the runs and dismissed Srikkanth and Azharuddin. When Shastri was dismissed for 51 in the thirty-first over, the target was 104 runs away. Enter Kapil Dev. He took a couple of boundaries off Richard Hadlee and was then deceived by a slower ball, which he hit straight to mid-off. However, the catch was dropped. Kapil Dev reacted by smashing the next ball past the same fielder for another boundary. Vengsarkar, who had batted steadily all along, also opened up and India cruised to a win with six-and-half overs to spare.

For the second match in succession, the individual award was presented to Shastri, who was having the season of his life.

He had started 1984–85 with an ODI century against Australia, followed by Test hundreds against Pakistan and England, and another ODI hundred against England. He also scored the fastest double century in first-class cricket in a Ranji game between Bombay and Baroda, during which he slammed six sixes in an over. He led India under-25 to an outright victory over the English tourists and was also bowling well in both formats. The player who batted at number ten on his Test debut had evolved into one of the top all-rounders in the world.

The Indian bowlers did not put a foot wrong in the final against Pakistan in Melbourne, after Javed Miandad won the toss and opted to bat. The Pakistanis were 33-4 before Miandad and Imran Khan affected a recovery and enabled them to reach 176-9. Kapil Dev and Sivaramakrishnan took three wickets each. The former's yorker that bowled Qasim Omar on his first ball was as stunning as the latter's leg-break that drew Miandad out of his crease and left him stranded. Viswanath, who had had an outstanding tournament behind the wickets, completed a stumping.

Shastri and Srikkanth blunted the Pakistani bowlers with an opening stand of 103. Srikkanth fell for 67, but Shastri carried on. It was appropriate that he and Vengsarkar, both of whom had been a part of the 1983 World Cup side but had not played the final, were in the middle when India completed the sequel. Shastri was declared the Champion of Champions and presented the Audi 100, while Gavaskar announced his decision to relinquish the captaincy.

The margins of India's wins in the tournament spoke for themselves: six wickets, 87 runs, eight wickets, seven wickets and eight wickets, respectively.

> Home are our heroes! Fling wide the gates, hang out the flags, blare the trumpets, crash the cymbals ... Home, from their derring-do in Melbourne and Sydney, are our intrepid,

doughty champs of champ [...] Beat a tattoo. Fire a salute. Home are our gallant soldiers, undisputed champions of one-day cricket not once, but twice over.

—Khalid Ansari, *Mid-Day*, 16 March 1985

Kapil Dev, reinstated as captain, then led India in a quadrangular tournament at Sharjah, where the world champions were bowled out for 125 with Imran Khan taking 6-14. Not to be outdone, the Indians struck back to dismiss Pakistan for 87. The spinners continued from where they had left off in Australia, Kapil Dev took three wickets again and Gavaskar pouched four catches. India then beat Australia by three wickets in the final, thus clinching their fourth ODI title in a multi-nation event in two years.

An eventful season ended with the Ranji Trophy final, in which Bombay beat Delhi despite conceding the first-innings lead. Needing 300 to win, Delhi were undone by Shastri, India's player of the season, who took 8-91 with his left-arm spin to dismiss the opposition for 209.

Two months before Ravi Shastri was declared the Champion of Champions in Australia, Rajiv Gandhi was voted to power with the biggest mandate in Indian electoral history. He was only 40. In one of his first post-election speeches, he paraphrased Martin Luther King by stating that he was young and he had a dream. In 1985, Rajiv Gandhi epitomized modernization, computerization and a bright future.

In much the same vein, Indian cricket looked more robust than ever at the end of the 1984–85 season. The seniors were still going strong, and they now had some extraordinary young talent for company. His all-round accomplishments apart, Ravi Shastri's success as captain for junior and under-25 Indian teams had prompted many to predict a successful future for him as captain as well. He had already superseded many of his seniors by being named Kapil Dev's deputy.

32
SECOND-BEST

On the evening of 18 April 1986, Javed Miandad stood between India and victory in the Austral-Asia Cup final in Sharjah. A brilliant stop by Binny in the last over ensured that Miandad got stuck at the non-striker's end. Pakistan needed five to win in three balls, with two wickets in hand. As a capacity crowd and millions of TV viewers watched, Chetan Sharma bowled Zulqarnain off his fourth ball. When Tauseef Ahmed, the number eleven, reached the crease, Miandad implored him to tap and run. Tauseef did exactly that, and luckily for him and Pakistan, Azharuddin missed an easy run-out. Four were now needed from one, and Miandad was back on strike. Sharma attempted a yorker, but ended up bowling a full-toss, which Miandad hoisted over mid-wicket for six. That one stroke changed the dynamics of India-Pakistan cricket.

A lot had happened in the year that preceded this momentous match. India looked promising on their first official tour of Sri Lanka in mid-1985 but the results turned out to be disappointing. The ODI series was drawn 1-1, with the third game being abandoned. Sri Lanka came close to winning the first Test, registered their first-ever Test win in the second and achieved an honourable draw in the third.

For the Indians, the defining moment of the series was a Sri Lankan umpire grabbing a stump as a souvenir at the end of the second Test. Although they were at the receiving end of some questionable umpiring decisions, the visitors should have done better. The bowlers were ineffective, and the batters did not get going as a unit. Azharuddin and Sivaramakrishnan, heroes of the previous season, failed to fire. Having indicated his reluctance to open, Gavaskar batted in the middle order and scored a couple of fifties, but Kapil Dev, who had allowed his predecessor to drop down in Madras in 1983, was not very happy with the relocation. The captain surpassed Bishan Bedi's tally of 266 to become India's highest wicket-taker in Tests during the series, but the fact remained that he did not have a single victory to his credit, even after 17 Tests at the helm.

Gavaskar displayed his professionalism by agreeing to do what his captain and board wanted him to do. He returned to the opening spot in a tri-series that India played against Pakistan and the West Indies at Sharjah in November 1985. Gavaskar scored 63 and 76 in India's two games, but the world champions lost both. Sadanand Viswanath, one of the major contributors to the victory in the World Championship of Cricket earlier in the year, was a surprise omission for the Australia tour. Kirmani, who had played at Sharjah as well, was picked as the senior wicketkeeper, with Baroda's Kiran More being selected as his understudy. It seemed harsh to single Viswanath out for a lacklustre performance in Sri Lanka, considering that his teammates had floundered as well. More, on the other hand, had reaped the rewards for his consistency in domestic cricket.

In what was more or less a rerun of 1977–78, Australia had lost many of its senior players, this time to a 'rebel' tour of South Africa. The embargo on hosts that was imposed by the ICC in 1970 was still in force and it had prompted South African administrators to entice cricketers from across the world to tour for handsome amounts of money. Many cricketers from England, West Indies, Sri Lanka and Australia had accepted the offers and been slapped with bans by their respective boards. Cricketers from England and Australia were banned from playing first-class cricket for three years, while those from the West Indies and Sri Lanka were banned for life.

Like Simpson in 1977–78, Allan Border, the captain, had the task of hand-holding a group of youngsters against a seasoned opponent. The Australians had just lost back-to-back series against England and New Zealand. Nothing hurt them more than losing to those two teams and the Indians knew it.

Kapil Dev took 8-106 in the first innings of the first Test in Adelaide. Back as Test opener after three Tests in the middle order, Gavaskar scored his thirty-first century, becoming the first batter to score 9,000 Test runs in the process. He was unbeaten on 39 at stumps on the second day, but he did not resume the next morning, as he was tending to a hit on his left arm, which he had sustained the previous day. He resumed at the fall of the fifth wicket and then batted right through to score 166.

The visitors should have won the second Test in Melbourne but they were thwarted by the obduracy of Allan Border, umpiring errors and their own rigidity. They ought to have done something different when Dave Gilbert, the number eleven, kept negotiating the spinners comfortably on the last day, after Border was allowed to take easy singles. When Border eventually fell for 163, leaving India with a target of 126, the visitors inexplicably scored only 59 runs for the loss of two wickets in 25 overs before tea, despite a storm having been forecast. The storm duly arrived and not a single ball was bowled after the interval.

Centuries by India's top three—Gavaskar, Srikkanth and Amarnath—in the last Test in Sydney enabled Kapil Dev to declare at 600-4. David Boon and Geoffrey Marsh, Australia's openers, replied in kind with a double century stand. The complexion of the game changed when the Indian captain heeded the advice of senior players to set a more attacking field. With fielders placed around the bat, Shastri and Yadav triggered a collapse, sharing nine wickets between them and bowling Australia out for 396.

India enforced the follow-on, and the spinners struck again, but the Australians held firm. The series thus ended in a 0-0 stalemate. For the second time in a decade, the Indians had failed to do their abilities justice in a series in Australia.

India qualified for the best-of-three finals of the tri-series against Australia and New Zealand, where they lost to the hosts. While all the batters did well, Gavaskar was the most consistent. He even out-scored Srikkanth on a couple of occasions.

Contrary to what his detractors have alleged, Gavaskar had always done well in the shorter version, starting from his unbeaten fifty against East Africa in the very next game after the controversial 36 not out in the 1975 World Cup. It was only during the 1983 World Cup that he had struggled for a prolonged period. In the Austral-Asia Cup at Sharjah in April 1986, he scored 71 in the semi-final against Sri Lanka and 92 in the final against Pakistan. Chetan Sharma was blamed by everybody for the full-toss that Miandad hit for six, but the fault lay with the Indian batters, who scored only 20 runs in the last five overs of their innings despite being a healthy 225-3 at the end of the forty-fifth.

For once, the Indians were not fazed by the first half of an English summer, when they toured the country in 1986. Sharma, who was under fire after conceding the last-ball six, displayed his resilience with six wickets in the first Test at Lord's. Vengsarkar took the batting honours with his third century at cricket's most venerated shrine. An early burst by Kapil Dev led to England's dismissal in the second innings for 180, leaving India with 134 to win. India were 110-5 when Kapil Dev arrived at the crease and sealed his first Test win as captain, with four boundaries and a six. It also happened to be India's first Test win at Lord's.

Kapil Dev's teammates turned in an outstanding performance in the second Test in Leeds. One of those who starred in the victory was Madan Lal, who was not part of the original squad and was playing league cricket in England. He was invited by the captain to play the second Test after Sharma sprained his back.

Kapil Dev reckoned that his old new-ball partner would exploit the conditions a lot more effectively than Manoj Prabhakar, who was part of the team. Unlike the administrators of 1952, those who ran the BCCI in 1986 backed the captain.

Vengsarkar stood tall with knocks of 61 and 102. India won by 279 runs and the visitors would have won the third Test in Birmingham as well, had it not been for an innings of 183 by Mike Gatting, who had replaced David Gower as England's captain after the Lord's Test. Sharma took ten wickets in the game.

The third Test was Gavaskar's 115th, which, at that point, made him the most-capped player in Test history, ahead of England's Colin Cowdrey. The legend also took his hundredth catch during the game, thus becoming the first Indian fielder to reach the milestone. More was excellent on both sides of the stumps in his debut series. He took 16 catches and averaged 52 with the bat, helping Vengsarkar bail the team out of tricky situations in the first two Tests.

A dominant showing in Australia and a 2-0 triumph in England meant that India could claim to be the second-best Test side in the world in 1986, in addition to being world champion in the shorter format.

It was the ideal note on which to begin a season in which three teams were scheduled to visit.

33

A SEASON OF TWO CHASES

> The way I played my cricket, there was no way I would have put the shutters down and said, okay, relax, we are going to draw the game.
>
> —Kapil Dev, *Madras Magic: The Tied Test of '86*[38]

India's stand-in captain told his teammates that they would not be playing for a draw in the November 2014 Adelaide Test. Instead, the goal would be to go for the target of 364. The incumbent captain, who was not playing the game, advised caution. 'You are an exceptional player, but the others are not as competent as you,' he said. The stand-in's response was prompt: 'How will we know how good we are, unless we go for the target?' He led by example, with an innings of 141. Unfortunately, only one other teammate crossed fifty and two others entered double figures. The target was only 60 runs away when the stand-in captain was seventh out. Australia won by 48 runs, but even they knew that they had only just scraped through.

28 years before that Adelaide Test, another Indian captain did something similar on a fifth-day wicket in Madras.

The 1986–87 series between India and the Australian visitors

---

[38] *Madras Magic: The Tied Test of '86* is a 2006 documentary written and directed by Lincoln Tyner.

began with a thriller. Australia batted till the third morning of the first Test and declared at 574-7. Dean Jones battled the bowlers and the Madras heat and humidity to score 210. Shortly after he completed his century, he started throwing up, but that did not prevent him from punishing the bowling. He lost four kilograms and at one point, control over his bodily functions, during the course of his innings.

India was at 270-7 at the end of day three. After chiding his players for falling to aerial strokes the previous day, Kapil Dev presented a tutorial on the art of essaying aerial strokes in an innings of 119, which enabled India to avoid the follow-on. Australia, 170-5 at stumps on day four, declared overnight at the behest of Bob Simpson, their cricket manager. India had the whole of the last day—at least 87 overs—to score 348 for the win.

What followed caught the Australians unawares. Gavaskar, who was playing in his hundredth consecutive Test, did what he had done at Port of Spain (1976), Brisbane (1977) and The Oval (1979). At tea, India were 193-2 and in control, but Greg Matthews and Ray Bright, the Australian spinners, managed to pull things back. Gavaskar fell for 90 and Kapil Dev fell early, but Ravi Shastri essayed an excellent innings in the company of Chandrakant Pandit, the wicketkeeper from Bombay who was playing his second Test as a specialist batter in the absence of the injured Vengsarkar.

As the Indians edged closer, the tension in the cauldron that was the M.A. Chidambaram Stadium got to the players and even the umpires. There were a couple of nasty altercations. Matthews kept going at one end, even as Border shuffled the other bowlers at the other. Chetan Sharma batted well after Pandit's dismissal. Just when it seemed that India had regained the initiative, the Australians dismissed him and More in quick succession. Yadav, the number ten, hit a six and seemed determined to take India home, but with only four runs needed, he mistimed a sweep off Bright and was bowled. Maninder Singh, the number eleven, defended the last two deliveries of the penultimate over.

Matthews was to bowl the final over. Shastri took a two off the second ball and a single off the third. Maninder defended the fourth and appeared to have inside edged the fifth onto his pads. The Australians appealed, and Vikram Raju, the umpire, raised his finger. It was only the second tie in Test history after the one between Australia and the West Indies in Brisbane in 1960–61, and Bob Simpson had witnessed both.

The climax erased memories of the acrimony that had unfolded a few days previously. With India scheduled to play as many as 16 ODIs in the season and the next World Cup a year away, the selectors decided to rotate players. They accordingly excluded Gavaskar from the first two ODIs against Australia, only to reinstate him in the wake of protests.

Another prominent omission from the ODI squad was Patil. Convinced as he was that the selectors had been giving him a raw deal since 1984, he decided to announce his retirement. However, there was a royal twist in his tale, a couple of years later.

India won the ODI series, but the Test series was undecided, with rain affecting the second Test in Delhi and both teams batting solidly in the third Test in Bombay. Gavaskar, Vengsarkar and Shastri scored hundreds at their home-ground.

The Indians hosted Sri Lanka after a forgettable Champions Trophy campaign in Sharjah, where they lost to Pakistan and the West Indies. They posted 676-7, their highest score in Test cricket, in the first Test against Sri Lanka in Kanpur. Gavaskar scored his thirty-fourth Test century and Kapil Dev blasted his way to 163. India's third centurion was Azharuddin, whose 199 was his first century since his treble in his first three Tests. The game was drawn, but India then won the next two encounters in Nagpur and Cuttack. Maninder Singh, who had become the lynchpin of the attack since the tour of England, took 16 wickets in the last two Tests and Vengsarkar continued his golden run with match-winning knocks of 153 and 166. Rumesh Ratnayake's wicket in the second innings in Cuttack was Kapil Dev's three-hundredth in Tests.

Sri Lanka won the first ODI, dismissing India for 78 to win by 117 runs, but they were beaten in the remaining four games.

All eyes then shifted to the most awaited battle of them all. However, the first four Tests between India and Pakistan were anti-climactic. As had been the case in the 1950s and 1960s, the teams kept waiting for the other to throw the first punch. The closest they got to a result was in the second Test in Calcutta, where Pakistan was dismissed for 229 in response to India's 403, on the fourth day. However, the Indians made no attempt to force the pace in the second innings.

The Calcutta Test also made the news for Gavaskar's withdrawal for 'personal reasons'. The abuse he and his wife had copped in India's last two Tests at the Eden Gardens was believed to be the cause. Back for the third Test in Jaipur, Gavaskar was caught behind off the first ball of the game.

Even as the series was being played, political tensions between the two countries had intensified and there was even talk of war, but sanity prevailed. Zia-ul-Haq, the president of Pakistan, even flew to Jaipur to engage in what was termed as 'cricket diplomacy'.

History was created in the fourth match of the series in Ahmedabad when Gavaskar became the first batter to score 10,000 runs in Tests. He achieved the landmark with a late-cut off Ijaz Faqih, the left-arm spinner.

A minefield, on which the game was unlikely to last beyond three days, awaited the teams in Bangalore. Imran won the toss and batted first, but the visitors were shot out for 116 with Maninder taking 7-27. India was at 126-4 in response, when some daft batting and fine bowling by Pakistan's spin duo of Iqbal Qasim and Tauseef Ahmed resulted in the last six wickets falling for only 19.

In an attempt to take the heat off his team, Imran stated that he did not mind losing, if every player gave it everything. The pep-talk worked, with every Pakistani player applying himself in the second innings and setting India an improbable 221 to win.

Improbable was nearly made possible by Gavaskar, who batted resolutely and authoritatively on a strip on which the spinners were making the ball hop, dart and jump. The master concentrated fiercely and accumulated runs, even as his teammates struggled and the Pakistanis built up the pressure on the umpires with persistent and outrageous appeals. The target was 41 runs away and Gavaskar was on 96 when a Qasim delivery flicked the knee-roll of his pad and went to slip. Another appeal went up and Gavaskar was declared out caught. India was bowled out for 204.

Pakistan won the ODI series as well and returned home to a rapturous welcome. Gavaskar revealed years later that when Imran heard that he was considering retirement in 1986, the latter had suggested that they have a final bash against each other. The Pakistani captain had been contemplating retirement himself.

Imran went on to lead Pakistan to a series win in England. That series was followed by the MCC's Bi-Centenary Test between the MCC and the World XI, which featured the best cricketers on the planet. Gavaskar, who opened for the World XI, scored 188—his first century at Lord's—against an attack that comprised Malcolm Marshall, Richard Hadlee, Ravi Shastri, John Emburey and South Africa's Clive Rice. It was during this game that he announced that the 1987 World Cup would be his last assignment for India. With the Pakistani captain also signalling his intent to retire after the tournament, cricket-lovers of the subcontinent prayed for a final between the co-hosts, with a fairytale ending for either Gavaskar or Imran, depending upon which side of the border they lived on.

34

MISTRUST

The conversation between N.K.P. Salve and Nur Khan in London, a couple of days after India's victory in the 1983 World Cup final, had far-reaching consequences.

The delegation that represented the India-Pakistan Joint Management Committee (IPJMC) at the ICC meeting in London on 19 July 1984 to decide the host of the fourth World Cup, comprised N.K.P. Salve, A.W. Kanmadikar and Jagmohan Dalmiya, the BCCI president, secretary and treasurer, respectively. The £99,500 that the IPJMC offered as prize money was nearly twice the amount being offered by the three-time host. The Asians also offered a minimum guarantee of £200,000 to each of the seven full members of the ICC, as well as £175,000 to the associate member that would qualify for the tournament. This was way above England's offer of £53,900 and £30,200 to the full members and associate member, respectively. The IPJMC's offer of £20,000 each to the other associate members was also nearly twice the amount being offered by England.

Although Australia refused to vote against England in an open ballot, their representative liked the IPJMC's suggestion that Australia and New Zealand could co-host the fifth World Cup.

History was created when the IPJMC bagged 16 votes to England's 12. The World Cup was on its way to becoming a truly global event.

Issues regarding the sponsorship and TV broadcast came up, but they were overcome. The 1987 World Cup was the first to feature 50-over matches. India and Pakistan hosted 17 and 10 matches, respectively, across 21 different venues.

After losing to Australia in their opening game, India won their next five league matches, thanks to enterprising batting and bowling by Shastri and Maninder. Navjot Singh Sidhu, a batter from Punjab who had played a couple of Tests against the West Indies in 1983–84, celebrated his comeback with four fifties.

Needing to score 222 in 42.1 overs to beat New Zealand in their last league game and top the group, India completed the chase in only 32.1 overs, with Gavaskar scoring his maiden ODI hundred. Earlier in the game, Chetan Sharma became the first bowler to perform the hat-trick in the World Cup.

However, India were outplayed by England in the semi-final in Bombay. Graham Gooch employed the sweep magnificently in an innings of 115, and the English bowlers then struck at regular intervals to secure a win by 35 runs. Pakistan's loss to Australia in the other semi-final at Lahore meant that both Gavaskar and Imran were denied their fairytale farewell. Australia beat England in the final in Calcutta.

Even as the BCCI won admirers from across the world for its organizational skills, its relationship with its own players deteriorated. The players had initially refused to sign the tournament contracts, which mandated their sporting the logo of Reliance, the title sponsor, on their apparel. The contracts did not permit them to sport the logos of their individual sponsors, and they were also prohibited from writing for newspapers. A compromise was thrashed out as the World Cup was around the corner, but the board asserted its authority after the tournament ended.

Those weren't the best of times. Mohinder, who had not been picked for the World Cup despite his heroics in 1983, was given the impression that he was to be named captain and summoned to Chandigarh. There, he discovered that the job was to be his only if Vengsarkar did not sign the contract. As it turned out, Vengsarkar did and the captaincy was assigned to him. His first priority as captain was not to prepare the team for a Test series against the formidable West Indies, but to convince his teammates to sign the contracts.

Vengsarkar scored a fine hundred in his first Test as captain against the West Indies in Delhi, but the visitors won the match by five wickets, thanks to a brilliant century by Vivian Richards. They also had the better of the next Test in Bombay, which was drawn. Vengsarkar scored his second century of the series in the drawn third Test in Calcutta, but he had his arm broken by Winston Davis. Ravi Shastri was then named captain for the last Test in Madras.

Given the manner in which Shastri had been groomed for the captaincy, there were many who believed that he ought to have succeeded Kapil Dev. But then, Vengsarkar had forced his way into contention with his performances since 1986, and Shastri had not replicated his consistency of the mid-1980s in the same period.

Shastri led India to victory at Madras, with Narendra Hirwani, a leg-spinner from Madhya Pradesh, taking a record 16 wickets in his debut. The other notable contributors were Kapil Dev, who scored a century, Woorkeri Raman, the left-handed debutant from Tamil Nadu who scored 83, and More, who affected a record five stumpings.

The victory, India's first in Tests against the mighty West Indies since 1979, was impactful enough for all of India to forget the loss of the ODI series. Arun Lal, who succeeded Gavaskar at the top of the order, was India's second-highest scorer of the series after Vengsarkar.

> I was served a show cause notice by the BCCI and I told them that they should also ask the West Indies captain Vivian Richards not to write [columns]. He was putting pressure

on the Indian umpires through his columns. I scored two centuries against them, and I started writing only after I was injured in the Calcutta Test.

—Dilip Vengsarkar, *The Hindu*, 29 September 2005

The board was determined to have the last word on the contract controversy. In February 1988, it banned Vengsarkar from representing India and Mumbai for six months for 'violating the terms'. The team rallied behind him, but he persuaded his teammates to carry on playing.

In Vengsarkar's absence, Shastri led India to victory in a tri-series against Sri Lanka and New Zealand in Sharjah. Vengsarkar returned after serving his ban and led India to victories in the Asia Cup in Bangladesh and a 2-1 triumph in a three-Test tussle against New Zealand at the start of the 1988–89 season. The first Test series on Indian soil since 1974–75 in which all the games ended decisively, was overshadowed by Mohinder's reaction to his omission from the Test squad. His description of the selectors as 'a bunch of jokers' was not too different from Gavaskar's 'court jesters' diatribe a decade previously, but the board adopted a sterner stance against him.

History repeated itself twenty-seven years after Subhash Gupte was not considered for a tour of the Caribbean despite excelling there on India's previous visit. After being overlooked for the tour of the West Indies in early 1989 despite his performances on the previous tour in 1982–83, Mohinder accepted a TV commentary assignment for the series and ended up witnessing a disaster. The fast bowlers were unrelenting. Shastri, Sidhu and Sanjay Manjrekar—the son of Vijay—scored a century each, but Vengsarkar, the captain and the team's premier batter, did not get going. Hirwani, who landed in the Caribbean with 36 wickets from only four Tests, was brutalized by the West Indies batters.

Worse was to follow. Vengsarkar lashed out at some members of the team in a post-tour interview, only for his detractors to point out that he had not been prolific himself and therefore had no right to criticize others. The BCCI was apoplectic when some players flew to the United States from the Caribbean to play exhibition matches without permission. A disciplinary committee announced a one-year ban on six players: Vengsarkar, Kapil Dev, Shastri, More, Azharuddin and Arun Lal.

The cricketers did not take things lying down. They were backed by legal luminaries, senior journalists and the public. They challenged the ban in the Supreme Court, which applied the Monopolies and Restrictive Trade Practices Act to rule in favour of the players. The obstinacy of the BCCI, when directed by the Supreme Court to settle the matter out of court, backfired bigtime, as it was flayed for not giving the players a choice when it came to the contracts, trying to force the latter to accept bizarre terms like one that prohibited them from criticizing board officials and thereby violating a citizen's right to freedom of action. The BCCI eventually revoked the bans, but the mediocrity displayed by the team on the field at the start of the 1989–90 season only widened the chasm between the board and players.

Vengsarkar was replaced as captain by Srikkanth, who had missed the Tests against the West Indies due to a broken arm. India flopped in a tournament at Sharjah and then lost in the semi-final of the Nehru Cup, a six-team ODI tournament organized by the board to commemorate the birth centenary of India's first prime minister. Mohinder, now 39, was recalled for the two tournaments and then dropped again.

On 6 November 1989, two days before the players were to gather in Delhi before flying to Pakistan for a full series, the Association of Indian Cricketers (AIC), a successor of the Players' Association that had been active for a couple of seasons in the 1970s, went public with a charter of demands, among which was a 70 per cent hike in the tour fee, a graded system of payments based on seniority, and the signing of a joint contract as opposed to individual ones. The AIC, which had Kapil Dev as its president,

Vengsarkar as vice-president, Arun Lal as secretary and Mohinder as its spokesperson, also asked for changes in the itinerary.

The BCCI, never a fan of bodies representing cricketers, refused to revise its terms and offer of INR 50,000 per player, and announced that an alternate team would be picked if the selected players did not fall in line. Patil, who was going great guns in his second outing as captain-mentor of Madhya Pradesh, was even sounded out for the captaincy of this alternate team.

Ultimately, 13 of the 16 members of the original squad accepted the board's terms, but they decided not to take any money. Srikkanth was quoted by the media as saying that representing the country was paramount.

Six months after the flop show in the Caribbean, the pundits predicted another disaster in Pakistan.

WHAT MIGHT HAVE BEEN

L. Sivaramakrishnan became a national hero in 1984–85. Maninder became one a season later.

Both bowlers took their time to blossom after being rushed into the Indian team in their mid-teens, but by the mid-1980s, it appeared that the wait had been worth it. Connoisseurs and fans alike could not stop gushing about Sivaramakrishnan's leg-spin proficiency, one of the game's most difficult arts, and his feats in the World Championship of Cricket. In fact, videos of his leg-break that befuddled Javed Miandad in the final still resurface on social media every few months.

Like Bishan Bedi, who nurtured him at the start of his first-class career, Maninder Singh had flight, turn, powers of deception and a flowing action. He had his first brush with stardom after taking 12 wickets in the Test series in England in 1986, which India won. One wonders whether he took note of the fact that Sivaramakrishnan, the hero of 1985, was no longer in the team by then.

Maninder bowled well at home against Sri Lanka and Pakistan in the 1986–87 season and was picked in the World XI squad for the MCC Bi-Centenary Test in August 1987. This was when he started struggling with his bowling action. The issue was exacerbated by the fact that long bowling spells in the nets, which could have helped him regain his rhythm, did not enthuse him. Muscle memory got him through the 1987 World Cup and a couple of subsequent series, but he was never the same bowler again.

In Sivaramakrishnan's case, he struggled to get just about everything right after the 1984–85 season. He was told to toss the ball up more, attack the bat and other things, but no one told him that he was not balanced in his delivery stride. He made a brief return to the national side and played a couple of matches in the 1987 World Cup, but the selectors lost their patience thereafter.

Maninder returned to the Indian team in 1992–93 after a three-year gap and took seven wickets in a Test victory against Zimbabwe, but his performance did not impress those who mattered.

The story of the two spinners could well have been different had they been given timely assistance—technical as well as mental. Unfortunately, sports psychology and psychology in general were taboo concepts in the India of the 1980s. Only weaklings needed psychological assistance, it was believed.

A player who was sailing in the same boat as Siva and Maninder was Sadanand Viswanath. He gave the impression of being brash, but his talent was never in doubt. He ought to have been looked after but he wasn't. It also did not help his cause that More, his wicketkeeping contemporary, was more tenacious.

Had Maninder, Sivaramakrishnan and Viswanath fulfilled their potential, they would have teamed up with the boy wonder to prevent Indian cricket from being swallowed by an anaconda in the 1990s after having scaled multiple ladders in the 1970s and 1980s.

35
BOY WONDER

Sachin Tendulkar does not fail.

This is what Naren Tamhane, former wicketkeeper and West Zone's representative on the national selection committee, said on the afternoon of 5 November 1989, as he sealed the 16-year-old's selection in the Indian team.

Sachin Tendulkar became a household name in India when he and Vinod Kambli added 664 for Shardashram Vidyamandir against St. Xavier's High School in the semi-final of the inter-school Harris Shield in Bombay in February 1988. The 14-year-old's success in inter-school cricket in the preceding seasons had won him a place in Bombay's Ranji Trophy squad in the 1987–88 season. Tendulkar scored a century on his Ranji Trophy debut against Gujarat in the subsequent season, and ended 1988–89 as Bombay's highest scorer with 583 runs. He began the 1989–90 season with a century for Rest of India against Delhi in the Irani Cup, shortly after his selection for the tour of Pakistan.

The teenager was delighted when Srikkanth, his captain, assured him that he would play all four Tests in Pakistan. He scored 59 in the second Test in Faisalabad after an indifferent debut in the first match in Karachi. After a third consecutive draw in Lahore, the local authorities dished out a green-top for the final Test in Sialkot to aid their fast bowlers, only to be stunned when India took the first-innings lead. Vivek Razdan, an alumnus of the MRF Pace Foundation in Madras playing in only his second Test, took five wickets. Imran Khan, who had been talked out of retirement after the 1987 World Cup and was now playing primarily as a batter, then wore his bowling boots to show his teammates how it was done. Wasim Akram and he reduced India to 38-4 in the second innings.

Tendulkar made his way to the middle with India only 112 runs ahead and more than a day's play left. He had barely got his eye in when a delivery by Waqar Younis, another teenage prodigy, reared after pitching. The ball hit Tendulkar on his helmet, off which it ricocheted onto his nose. He bled profusely but carried on and scored a match-saving 57. A few days later, he scored 53 off only 18 balls in an exhibition game in Peshawar. His innings featured four sixes in an over by the legendary leggie Abdul Qadir.

Sanjay Manjrekar scored two centuries in the series, including a double hundred, and Azharuddin ended a lean patch with a hundred and two fifties. Manoj Prabhakar, a pacer and competent batter who had been in and out of the squad since the mid-1980s, established himself in the side with 16 wickets in the series.

To draw a series in Pakistan was no mean achievement. It helped that Imran Khan, an advocate of neutral umpires, walked the talk by inviting John Holder and John Hampshire from England to oversee the four Tests. The Indians could have insisted on calling the tour off after Srikkanth was attacked by a spectator during the first Test, but they chose to be sagacious. Srikkanth impressed many with his man-management skills, and, therefore, his omission for the subsequent tour of New Zealand came as a shock.

'If you become captain, what will you discuss—cricket or contracts?' This was the question posed by Raj Singh Dungarpur, the chairman of selectors, to Azharuddin, and summed up the board's line of thinking. Srikkanth, who had been involved in the discussions on contracts and payments, was made to pay for his batting failures in Pakistan. Azharuddin on the other hand was perceived as non-confrontational.

Vengsarkar, who had taken the Pakistan tour off, was not picked for the New Zealand tour—although he was added later to the squad—and neither was Shastri.

The team of the nineties, as christened by Raj Singh, succumbed to the old first Test jinx in Christchurch. The next two were drawn, and the Indians then came last in a tri-series featuring the hosts and Australia. The highlights of the tour were Azharuddin's 192 in the third Test in Auckland and Tendulkar's 88 in the second in Napier. 80 not out overnight, he got going with two imperious drives off Danny Morrison and then went for a third, only to give a catch at mid-off to John Wright, the New Zealand captain. Twelve more runs and Tendulkar would have become the youngest centurion in Test history.

The series against England that followed in mid-1990 was a batter's dream, played as it was on flat pitches and in glorious sunshine. The bowlers had little or no help. Although all the Indian batters were in form, they managed to maintain their first-Test blues and lost the opening game at Lord's, with the next two Tests being drawn. Shastri, who was recalled as player and vice-captain, took over the opening slot and scored two centuries. Azharuddin extended the run that had begun in Pakistan and scored two delightful hundreds, using his wrists to pierce the gaps in the field. Mike Brearley, the former England captain, spoke for many when he called Azharuddin the modern Ranji. For England, Graham Gooch amassed 752 runs, inclusive of 333 in the first Test at Lord's. However, the adults were overshadowed by the teenager.

After failing in the first Test, Tendulkar sought the counsel of Gavaskar, who was commentating for the BBC. 'Wait for the ball to come to you instead of reaching out for it,' the legend advised. Tendulkar, a quick learner, scored 68 and a match-saving 119 in the second Test in Manchester.

The BCCI's attempt to follow the Australian and English model of appointing a cricket manager who would run things off the field, nearly backfired. Bishan Bedi, the appointee for the series against New Zealand and England, made news for all the wrong reasons. In a sense, he was ahead of his time, with his emphasis on physical fitness and penchant for putting the players through the shredder to achieve that end. However, a single statement of his in New Zealand after the team lost one of the matches in the tri-series, where he said he would not stop the players if they wanted to jump into the Pacific Ocean, overshadowed all the work he put in. If Bedi was to be believed, his statement was distorted beyond recognition.

In England, the cricket manager publicly slammed Gavaskar for turning down an MCC membership. The decision was strictly personal and therefore, Bedi's contention in an open letter to his former teammate that the latter had let down the touring Indian team as well as all Indians living in Britain, was bizarre, to say the least. Bedi was also reported to have openly disagreed with Azharuddin's decision to bowl after winning the toss in the first Test at Lord's, although he claimed later that he had been misquoted.

A full tour by Pakistan was to be the highlight of the home season of 1990–91. However, the Pakistanis cancelled the tour citing 'political disturbances' in India, in what was a classic instance of the pot calling the kettle black. That made it the second series on Indian soil to be cancelled in three years, after England refused to tour in 1988-89 when the Indians objected to the South African links of some of their players.

India's only international assignments in 1990–91 were the Asia Cup and a one-off Test against Sri Lanka, both of which they won. The knockout matches of the Ranji Trophy were delayed due to legal wrangles, and the season ended only in May with a thrilling final between Bombay and Haryana.

For the second time in his career, Kapil Dev led a team of underdogs to victory over a band of heavyweights, but not before

Vengsarkar and Tendulkar gave Haryana a scare with an audacious partnership. Bombay, set 355 to win on the last day, were bowled out for 352 with 14 deliveries left.

The dearth of international cricket in 1990–91 ensured that the performances of the Indian batters in England were on top of people's minds on the eve of the five-Test tour of Australia in November 1991. The confidence of the fans was boosted by the consistency of Sanjay Manjrekar in a tri-series at Sharjah, in which India lost to Pakistan in the final. He also batted well in an ODI series against South Africa before the team flew to Australia.

The Test series in Australia was lost 0-4, but the score-line could well have been 2-3 with a little bit of application and luck. The visitors were also unlucky with the umpiring, which at one point was so bad that Gavaskar was moved to write in his column that India was up against 13 opponents.[39]

After being trounced in the first two Tests, India came close to winning the third one in Sydney, with Shastri, who had already scored a double hundred, taking four wickets in Australia's second innings. The hosts were 173-8 and only three runs ahead when the visitors ran out of time. India bowled Australia out for 145 on the first day of the fourth Test in Adelaide but then squandered the advantage by scoring only 225 in response. Australia batted well in the second innings and set a target of 372. Azharuddin then scored a splendid 106 and Prabhakar got 64, but it wasn't enough. Australia won by 39 runs and went on to dominate the last Test on the world's fastest wicket in Perth.

The Indians bungled by not relying on their traditional strength. Nothing could have been dafter than the visitors playing four pacemen at the expense of a specialist spinner at Sydney, the most spin-friendly wicket in Australia. Shastri's spin nearly won them that game, as it turned out. Venkatapathy Raju, the

---

[39] Harsha Bhogle mentioned this column in *Azhar: The Authorized Biography of Mohammad Azharuddin*.

left-armer, played four Tests, but took only nine wickets. Narendra Hirwani, who had taken 23 wickets for India's under-19 squad on a tour of Australia in 1986–87, did not play a single Test.

Apart from his hundred in Adelaide, Azharuddin failed with the bat. Shastri missed the last two Tests after injuring his thigh during the tri-series, in which India lost to Australia in the best-of-three finals.

India's top performer on the tour was Kapil Dev, who made the ball swing and swerve in his thirteenth year of international cricket. He took 25 wickets in the Test series, including his four-hundredth in the traditional format. The other star was Sachin Tendulkar. He scored a scintillating 148 in the Sydney Test and followed it up with an extraordinary 114 in Perth.

Tendulkar ended the season with individual awards in the two games that India won in the 1992 World Cup co-hosted by Australia and New Zealand. He starred in a victory over Pakistan with an unbeaten 54 and bowling figures of 1-37, and then scored a match-winning 81 against Zimbabwe.

In an interview with *Sportstar*, India's leading sports periodical, later that year, Greg Chappell said, 'If things were handled well, you will have Bradman and then you will have Tendulkar.' The publication, however, did not carry this statement in the final version of the interview[40], as they feared that it might go to the teenager's head. The quote was published only three years later.

---

[40]Chappell's quote was published in the 20 May 1995 issue of *Sportstar*.

36

SPIN RETURNS

The Irani Cup encounter at the start of the 1992–93 season between Delhi, the 1991–92 Ranji winners, and Rest of India, was dominated by Anil Kumble. The leg-spinner from Bangalore had done well on the England tour in 1990, but he had not been picked for the Australia tour the following year. His haul of 13 wickets for Rest of India in the Irani Cup game ensured his recall to the national squad for the historic Zimbabwe and South Africa twin-tour.

The Indians struggled in a one-off Test in Harare, which was Zimbabwe's first after securing full membership of the ICC. Their saving grace was Sanjay Manjrekar, who scored 104 and ensured that they reached 307 in response to Zimbabwe's 456. The match ended in a draw.

South Africa accorded a spectacular welcome to its first official cricketing visitors after being readmitted into the ICC. The locals, whose forefathers had migrated from India decades previously, could not contain themselves. The plethora of get-togethers and parties worried Ajit Wadekar, the new cricket manager.

His apprehensions were not unfounded. Statistically, the Indians were more experienced than their opponents, but then, they were distracted. The South Africans, led by Kepler Wessels, the former Australian international, displayed their mental and tactical superiority in the matches that followed. The Indian batters kept failing and giving their bowlers hardly any runs to bowl with. They were soundly beaten 0-1 in the Test series and 2-5 in the ODI series.

There were some individual highlights, of course. Pravin Amre scored a century in his debut in the first Test in Durban and Sachin Tendulkar scored a hundred in the second Test in Centurion. Trailing by 63 in the first innings of the third Test in Port Elizabeth, India were reduced to 31-6 by the South African pacemen, when Kapil Dev counterattacked to score 129. The lower order did what it could to support him but South Africa needed only 153 to win. The series ended with a draw in Cape Town, where Javagal Srinath, a fast bowler from Karnataka who had made an impressive entry into international cricket in the previous season, bowled with fire to take six wickets.

With Azharuddin having only one victory and seven defeats in 17 Tests as captain, it was predicted that Kapil Dev would be reinstated at the helm of the team for the next assignment against England at home. However, the all-rounder clarified that he would take up the job only if Azharuddin were to step down. He was not interested if the selectors were going to sack the incumbent. Eventually, the selectors, who were headed by Gundappa Viswanath, took cognizance of the fact that of Azharuddin's 17 Tests as the leader, only one had been played at home—and that had ended in victory. He was retained as captain, but only for the first two of six ODIs and the first of three Tests. Wadekar also did his bit to convince the selectors to persist with Azharuddin. However, the fact was that the incumbent was on trial.

Changes were made in the squad. The out-of-form Manjrekar was replaced by Vinod Kambli, Tendulkar's schoolmate, who had impressed in a tri-series in Sharjah in 1991–92, but like Kumble, was left out of the squad for Australia. Sidhu was recalled and Prabhakar asked to continue opening the batting apart from the bowling, with Shastri having broken down again in South Africa.

Wadekar reckoned that India's best bet was to do what it had traditionally done. Accordingly, Kumble, who had been India's best bowler in South Africa, was joined by Raju, the left-armer, and Rajesh Chauhan, an off-spinner from Madhya Pradesh, in what was an unabashed attempt to replicate the Bedi-Prasanna-Chandrasekhar triumvirate. Playing all three spinners on wickets that were tailored to turn, meant that Srinath had to be benched just days after he had won the individual award against South Africa at Cape Town.

Azharuddin set the ball rolling with a stupendous 182 in the first Test in Calcutta. The spinners then took over and India registered their first Test win in three years. The hosts won the next two Tests as well, thus sweeping a Test series for the very first time since 1932. The batters also flourished, with Kambli leading the pack. He followed an innings of 59 in the second Test in Madras with 224 in the third Test in Bombay. He then bettered that performance with 227 in a one-off Test against Zimbabwe.

The six-match ODI series against England was squared. Trailing 1-3 with two games to go, both of which were to be played at Gwalior, India first chased down 257, with Sidhu scoring a century. Azharuddin's breathtaking 95 off 63 balls in the last game enabled India to overhaul England's 265-4 with nearly two overs to spare.

Credit for the turnaround was also attributed to the Code of Conduct that Wadekar had drafted, ostensibly to keep distractions at bay. It comprised twelve points, some of which were as follows:

- The players must attend the nets well on time with the team, as desired by the manager.
- Must come to the ground properly dressed in white and not in shorts or casuals. The twelfth man will wear India's blazer while carrying the drinks.
- No player will be allowed to go outside the hotel without the permission of the manager.

- No private dinner/function except official ones will be permitted.
- No woman will be allowed in the hotel room of the player.
- No talking to the press by any of the players unless permitted by the manager.

Some of the players were not amused, as the diktats read as if they had been prescribed for a junior team and not a senior international side. However, the team was winning and that was all that mattered.

The team extended its victorious run into a tour of Sri Lanka in mid-1993, where a Test was won abroad for the first time since 1986. India won the series 1-0 but lost the three-match ODI series that followed. After a victory in the first game, the visitors were in a winning position in the second, only to be undone by a bizarre batting collapse. Sri Lanka won the decider to take the series.

The energies invested by the BCCI in winning the bid to co-host the 1996 World Cup with Pakistan and Sri Lanka and helping the Cricket Association of Bengal organize a limited-overs tournament on the occasion of the latter's diamond jubilee in 1993, may well have been responsible for its indifference to Test cricket in the period that ensued.

India played only thirteen Tests in the period from July 1993 to November 1995, three of which—one in Sri Lanka (1993) and two against New Zealand at home (1995)—were badly affected by rain. This effectively meant that the team played only ten full Tests in 2.5 years, after having played nine in just five months from October 1992 to March 1993.

The spinners reigned supreme in a home series against Sri Lanka in early 1994, in which Kapil Dev surpassed Sir Richard Hadlee's record tally of 431 Test wickets. The series marked the Test debut of Nayan Mongia, a wicketkeeper who had been knocking on the doors of the national team for a while.

There was a seminal moment on the short tour of New

Zealand that followed. When Sidhu was ruled out of the second ODI due to a stiff neck, Tendulkar, the vice-captain, offered to open. He proceeded to score 82 in 49 balls, in a way claiming the opening position in the shorter version for himself. After the ploy worked, many people reckoned that the tactic of getting the best batter in the team to face as many balls as possible would work in the long run, especially in the World Cup that was two years away.

The team stuttered in its first tournament in Sharjah since 1990, going down to Pakistan in the final of the Austral-Asia Cup in April 1994. However, it bounced back to win a Quadrangular series in Sri Lanka and a tri-series against the West Indies and New Zealand at home later that year. A bilateral ODI series against the West Indies tourists started on a traumatic note with Kapil Dev, who was bowling first-change by then, being smashed for 37 runs in five overs. He announced his retirement after the game.

The Test series against the West Indies in 1994–95 was a competitive affair. India were professionalism personified in the first Test in Bombay, which they won by 96 runs. Srinath made the most of the opportunity to finally play a Test at home, taking five wickets and scoring a crucial half-century. Tendulkar's 85 in Bombay and 179 in Nagpur, as well as the consistency of Kumble, helped divert some of the attention from Kambli's slump.

After four centuries in his first 12 Tests, the southpaw from Bombay encountered the first major challenge of his career in the form of the West Indies fast bowlers, who detected his weakness against the short-pitched ball and exploited it ruthlessly. Kambli's loss of form resulted in his swapping batting spots with Manjrekar for the third Test at the new venue in Mohali on the outskirts of Chandigarh, but the shift from number three to number six made no difference. His sequence of scores after a brisk 40 in the first innings in Bombay read 0, 0, 6, 18 and 0. Buoyed by the greenish tinge of the Mohali wicket, the West Indies bowled

India out for 114 in the second innings, winning the Test by 243 runs and squaring the series in the process. It was India's first defeat in a home Test since 1988.

Kambli's fans hoped that he would regain his flair on batting-friendly pitches in the 1996 World Cup. As it turned out, a left-handed batter from the subcontinent did take the World Cup by storm, but it wasn't him.

37
REVOLUTIONS

Jasprit Bumrah made India, a batsman-obsessed country, fall in love with fast bowling in the late 2010s. Kapil Dev had done likewise nearly half a century ago. The turning point of his career was a national camp for junior cricketers in Bombay in the mid-1970s. When he complained about the limited food being served and demanded more of it as he was a fast bowler, an official told him that there were no fast bowlers in India.

Kapil Dev proved the official wrong, but he had to sacrifice a bit of pace for longevity when he realized that he had to combine the roles of stock and shock bowler. Many youngsters followed in his footsteps by running in and bowling quick, but an express bowler remained elusive.

In the mid-1980s, Ravi Mammen, the Managing Director of Madras Rubber Factory (MRF) and a cricket aficionado, decided to do his bit to address this issue in the mid-1980s. He offered Dennis Lillee the role of coach at the Pace Foundation in Madras. Lillee's terms and conditions were accepted, one of which was to appoint an active first-class or international cricketer whom he would train—who would, in turn, train with the trainees. T.A. Sekhar, the Tamil Nadu speedster who had played a couple of Tests and ODIs in the early 1980s, ticked all the boxes.

Of the many who attended the selection trials for the Pace Foundation in 1987 and 1988, only a handful made it. In 1989,

Raj Singh Dungarpur, the chairman of selectors, was so impressed by Vivek Razdan, a trainee at the foundation, that he picked the latter for the tour of Pakistan despite his not having played a single Ranji Trophy match.

Over a dozen alumni of the MRF Pace Foundation represented India in the period from 1989 to 2016. These comprised Srinath, Venkatesh Prasad, Zaheer Khan and Irfan Pathan. The foundation also inspired the BCCI and its member associations to create similar fast-bowling schemes across the country. The process that culminated in the 2020s—an India team that boasts of an assembly line of quicks—commenced in Madras in the mid-1980s.

Around the time the MRF Pace Foundation was conceived, Sumedh Shah, a Bombay-based advertising professional with more than two decades of work experience, teamed up with Sunil Gavaskar to establish Professional Management Group (PMG), India's first sports event management and sponsorship company, in 1985.

By this time, Gavaskar was a best-selling author, a print columnist, an entrepreneur, an ambassador of multiple brands, and an activist who in the 1970s had taken up issues related to the players' remuneration and welfare with the board—all in addition to being a cricketing legend. Mindful of the limited career-span of a sportsperson, he had tapped other legitimate avenues to supplement his earnings.

Among PMG's many accomplishments were Gavaskar's debut as a TV host, the inception of the syndicated newspaper column, and the creation of annual awards and ratings for international and Indian cricket, years before the ICC and the BCCI considered doing so themselves.

Others built on the foundation laid by PMG. Sachin Tendulkar became India's highest-earning sportsperson when Mark Mascarenhas, who headed WorldTel, signed him for ₹31.5 crore for five years in 1995. As Tendulkar's manager, Mascarenhas was so successful that the association between the two was renewed in 2000 for ₹100 crore for another five years. By then, all the leading cricketers were being managed by professionals. A successful collaboration in later years was the one between Virat Kohli and Bunty Sajdeh, founder of Cornerstone.

The advent of colour television in India with the Asian Games in 1982 and the cricket World Cup win of 1983 ushered in the era of cricket sponsorship. The Hyderabad-based Vazir Sultan Tobacco Company Limited—which produced Charminar, a popular cigarette brand that was named after the city's most prominent landmark—signed what was the country's first-ever professional sports sponsorship contract, with the BCCI in 1983. The contract covered all cricket—international and domestic—for a period of three years. The ODI series played in India in those seasons were christened Charminar Challenge, with a replica of the Charminar being presented to the winners. VST paid the BCCI ₹3 lakh per ODI.

> VST had been associated with cricket for a long time. It used to field a team called VST Colts in Hyderabad's annual Moin-ud-Dowla tournament. Youngsters from all over the country would be invited to represent this side, many of whom went on to represent India. The 1982 Asian Games gave a fillip to sports sponsorship in India. As the government was reluctant to provide advertising slots for cigarette and alcohol brands on Doordarshan, the only TV channel at the time, VST created special branding for sports sponsorship and a 'spirit of freedom' concept for the sponsorship of cultural events like musical concerts. Sponsorship in Indian cricket had been sporadic till the early 1980s. VST's role was not restricted to merely giving the BCCI money. We travelled to the venues and worked with the local authorities to ensure that the branding and everything else was in place. I remember handling the first-ever international cricket match to be played at Srinagar,

which was an ODI between India and the West Indies in October 1983. The dressing-rooms were still being painted on the eve of the game, and the magnificent chinar trees were literally rising from between the stands! Working with M.L. Jaisimha, who was a consultant with VST, was a pleasure and honour. He was as popular as he was in his cricketing days and he opened many a door for us. The circumstances in which we extended our contract for three more years in 1986 were entirely different. The BCCI had grasped cricket's potential by then. The senior office-bearers made it clear that there were other contenders in the fray. As per the new agreement, we paid the board an astronomical ₹7.5 lakh per ODI. The costs spiralled even higher after 1989 and there were changes within VST as well. It was never the same again.

—Charu Sharma (Media personality and former VST employee)[41]

The liberalization of the Indian economy in 1991 was the catalyst for several tangible and intangible changes. It was also a time of serendipity for the BCCI.

After Nelson Mandela's release from prison and the beginning of the end of apartheid in South Africa, India proposed the country's readmission into the ICC in July 1991. Jagmohan Dalmiya, who had initiated discussions with the newly constituted United Cricket Board of South Africa (UCBSA)[42] in his capacity as BCCI secretary, lost the board elections in September 1991, but Madhavrao Scindia, the new board president, took things forward. It was decided that South Africa would return to international cricket with a three-match ODI series in India in November 1991.

---

[41] Author's interview with Charu Sharma.
[42] Cricket South Africa, established in 2002, succeeded UCBSA as cricket's sole governing body in South Africa, in 2008.

The BCCI was surprised when the UCBSA expressed its desire to purchase the TV rights of what was to be a historic series. Having paid Doordarshan to telecast its matches for years, the BCCI had no clue about TV rights and it had to first check who owned them. The board discovered that it did. The officials then decided to quote $30,000 for the series. However, the South Africans began the discussion by offering the BCCI $40,000 per match.

This was the point at which the BCCI realized that it was sitting on a goldmine.

1991 was also the year in which the Star TV network, which was headquartered in Singapore, commenced operations and transmission in India. The BCCI sold the TV rights for England's tour of India in 1992–93 to Trans World International (TWI) for $60,000. The series was telecast live on Prime Sports, a channel that was part of the Star network. For Indian viewers, the coverage by multiple cameras was a refreshing departure from the amateurish ways of the state broadcaster. The icing on the cake was a star-studded commentary team that comprised Geoffrey Boycott, Sunil Gavaskar, David Gower, Henry Blofeld and Charles Colville.

Doordarshan was incensed at having had to pay TWI $1 million to telecast the England series. DD hit back when its ₹10 million bid to telecast the Hero Cup, the five-team ODI tournament organized by the Cricket Association of Bengal to commemorate its diamond jubilee in November 1993, was rejected in favour of TWI's bid of ₹17.6 million, plus a 70% share of the international revenue. The Ministry of Information and Broadcasting invoked the Indian Telegraph Act of 1885 and argued that only government agencies could do live telecasts by up-linking signals from Indian soil.

The impasse ended when a division bench of the Supreme Court met on the night of 15 November 1993 and ruled that TWI could generate its own signals. The apex court also ordered the release of TWI's equipment that had been seized by the customs.

This verdict enabled fans to watch the exciting conclusion of the Hero Cup. Needing six runs to win in the last over of their semi-final against India, South Africa's lower order choked against Sachin Tendulkar, who had not bowled earlier in the game. India then beat the West Indies in the final, with Anil Kumble finishing 6-12. The semi-finals and final were played under the newly installed floodlights at Calcutta's Eden Gardens.

The telecast issue was resolved for good in February 1995, when the Supreme Court declared that the airwaves or frequencies were public property and stated that a citizen had a fundamental right to 'use the best means of imparting and receiving information and as such to have access to telecasting for the purpose.'[43]

By then, WorldTel, a US-based company headed by Mark Mascarenhas, had offered an astounding $10 million to the Pakistan-India-Sri Lanka Organising Committee (PILCOM), for the TV rights of the 1996 World Cup. This was a revolution in itself, considering that the television rights for the previous World Cup had been sold for around one-tenth that amount. Mascarenhas recovered his costs by on-selling the rights to broadcasters in different territories. His enterprise ensured that PILCOM earned profits worth $50 million, as per *Wisden*, cricket's most venerated publication.

> The tournament was marketed on a scale never before seen in cricket. There was an official sponsor for every conceivable product, including the official World Cup chewing gum.
>
> —Mihir Bose, *Wisden*, 1 January 1997[44]

Like its 1987 predecessor, the 1996 World Cup did not have the fairytale ending that the Indians had prayed for.

---

[43]Majumdar, Boria, *Eleven Gods and a Billion Indians*, Simon & Schuster India, 2018.
[44]Bose, Mihir, 'A Wind Blows from the East', *Wisden CricInfo*, 1 January 1997, https://tinyurl.com/3a74msuf. Accessed on 18 July 2025.

Azharuddin's team won three of its five league matches and then beat Pakistan, the defending champions, in the quarter-final in Bangalore. However, the semi-final was a disaster. Needing 252 to beat Sri Lanka in Calcutta, the Indians slid from 98-1 to 120-8 on an underprepared wicket, at which point the match was called off due to yet another display of petulance by the Eden Gardens spectators. Sachin Tendulkar became the first batter to score over 500 runs in a single World Cup. His aggregate of 523 runs comprised two centuries and three fifties.

Sri Lanka outplayed Australia by seven wickets in the final in Lahore and thus became the third Asian nation to win the World Cup. Sanath Jayasuriya, a member of the champion team, was elected the Most Valuable Player of the tournament. Jayasuriya and his opening partner Romesh Kaluwitharana deserved all the plaudits that came their way for doing successfully at the top of the order what Srikkanth had pioneered a decade previously.

WHAT MIGHT HAVE BEEN

The Indian team was scheduled to tour England in 1994. However, South Africa ended up touring instead. It was insinuated that England gave India the cold shoulder because it lost the bid to host the 1996 World Cup to the subcontinental combine.

Although India toured England in 1996, it can be argued that the postponement of the 1994 tour had an adverse impact on the sport in the country. A series in England in 1994 would have given the Indians an opportunity to show the cricketing world that they could replicate their success at home on foreign soil as well, following their wins within the subcontinent in 1993. The fact that they had emerged victorious in only one Test series outside the subcontinent (England in 1986) since Sachin Tendulkar's birth in 1973 was embarrassing, to say the least.

Ravi Shastri did not play international cricket after the recurrence of his knee injury in South Africa in 1992–93. He returned to domestic cricket the following season, but was ignored by the national selectors. He announced his retirement in 1994 after leading Mumbai to their first Ranji Trophy title in nine seasons and commenced a new innings as a commentator during a quadrangular tournament in Sri Lanka. He was only 32.

Had India toured England in 1994, there is every reason to believe that Shastri would have been recalled. He was used to English conditions, having represented Glamorgan county for years. Moreover, he had also scored two centuries on India's previous tour in 1990. A productive series in 1994 may well have given him a second wind and he could have re-emerged as a candidate for the captaincy.

Javagal Srinath, who had missed eight Tests on turning tracks in 1993–94, would have relished conditions that suited his brand of bowling, and the questions that the England bowlers would have asked of Vinod Kambli, could well have made him a more rounded batter and given him the confidence to tackle fast bowlers from the West Indies later that year.

In 1994, Kapil Dev was past his best as a bowler, but the fact was that he still had plenty to offer as a batter. His knocks against South Africa, England and Sri Lanka in the early 1990s were a case in point. Did the BCCI miss a trick by not asking him to carry on in ODIs till the 1996 World Cup and do what Ian Botham, his illustrious contemporary, had done for England in the 1992 World Cup? As a pinch-hitter at the top of the order and change bowler, Kapil Dev would have been an asset. Without him, India reached the semi-finals. With him, they could well have gone the distance.

38

BIRTH OF THE MIDDLE ORDER

While the selection of Rahul Dravid, a middle-order batter who had been consistent for Karnataka and India A, in the Indian team for the tour of England, was expected, Sourav Ganguly's was not. The selectors were accused of playing the Bengal card to accommodate the left-hander from Calcutta, who had toured Australia with the Indian team in 1991–92 and then been cast aside. A claim often advanced at the time was that the BCCI wanted the East Zone, the weakest of the five zones in cricketing terms, to have some representation in the national side. What added fuel to the fire was that a couple of cricketers from other zones, who had played for India in the late 1980s and early 1990s, were recalled to the national side after shifting to Bengal, the strongest team in the East Zone. Unlike them, Ganguly was a son of Bengal.

The selectors were also slammed for overlooking Kambli, who had been axed after the World Cup despite scoring a century against Zimbabwe. Wadekar, one of his prime backers, was no longer around, having been succeeded as cricket manager by Sandeep Patil.

There was a controversy in England when Sidhu returned home before the start of the ODI series. The official version of the incident was that he was hurt at a remark made by Azharuddin during the ODI series. His teammates and Patil did their best to placate him, but he refused to back down.

The first Test in Birmingham was lost, but it featured a Tendulkar special; the Indian vice-captain scored a glorious 122, an innings that reinforced Sir Don Bradman's pronouncement that had hit the headlines earlier that year. The legend had essentially said that he reckoned Tendulkar was playing much the same as he used to play.

Two Test caps were handed out in the second Test at Lord's. Ganguly, whose form against the counties and knock of 46 in the third ODI resulted in his inclusion, batted at no. 3 and scored a century. Dravid, who was picked after Manjrekar failed a fitness test, scored 95. Venkatesh Prasad, a Karnataka paceman playing in only his second Test, took five wickets in England's first innings. The third Test in Nottingham also featured some outstanding batting, with Ganguly scoring 136, Dravid 84 and Tendulkar scoring 177 and 74.

After the tour ended, it seemed that Sidhu's self-determined exit and Manjrekar's injury had been a blessing in disguise for Indian cricket, as they created two slots in the batting line-up that were filled by Ganguly and Dravid, respectively. Their success brought into focus India's domestic cricket structure, which for years had been accused of not equipping youngsters with the technique and grit to succeed at the international level. Both had played first-class cricket for half a decade before they played Test cricket for India, and were thus exposed to different conditions, wickets and bowlers. At no point did they look out of place against the English bowlers in unfamiliar conditions.

The last two Tests were drawn, which meant yet another tour of England had ended with a loss. The cynical view was that a 0-1 score-line was in fact a relief, considering all that had happened at the start of the tour.

However, Azharuddin's time as captain was up. Tendulkar, only 23, was handed the reins soon after the England tour.

After a couple of disappointing ODI engagements in Sri Lanka and Canada, where India lost to Pakistan, Tendulkar displayed his nous at home. He became the first recipient of the Border-Gavaskar Trophy, which was launched with a one-off Test between India and Australia in Delhi in October 1996. India won by seven wickets, thanks to Nayan Mongia's 152 and Kumble's match haul of nine wickets.

One of the greatest opening combinations in ODI history came together for the first time in the tri-series against Australia and South Africa that followed. Mindful of Ganguly's clean hitting and penchant for finding the gaps, Tendulkar asked the left-hander to partner him at the top.

The captain walked the talk in the tri-series final against South Africa, who had been unbeaten at the league stage. After declaring on the eve of the final that the opposition was beatable, Tendulkar scored a fine 67. With a target of 221 to defend, he appealed to his bowlers to deny the South African batters scoring opportunities on both sides of the wicket. So well did the bowlers respond that he was able to set attacking fields. The South Africans buckled, and India won by 35 runs.

Tendulkar caught the opposition unawares in the first Test of the subsequent series as well. Needing 170 to win on a dusty Ahmedabad wicket, the visitors expected Kumble, Sunil Joshi and Hirwani, India's three spinners, to do most of the bowling, and had readied themselves accordingly. However, the Indian captain unleashed Srinath, his pace spearhead, after instructing him to bowl a fuller length. So well did the pacer respond that by the time the visitors started regretting not having a plan B in place, the match was over for all practical purposes. Srinath took two wickets in three separate bursts to bowl South Africa out for 105. The game also saw the debut of VVS Laxman, a wristy batter from Hyderabad, who scored a priceless 51 in the second innings of the low-scoring game.

The class of '96—Ganguly, Dravid and Laxman—made Indian fans hopeful that the trio, along with Tendulkar, would reverse

Top: *The India and England teams that played the final Test of the first Test series on Indian soil, in Madras in February 1934. Douglas Jardine and C.K. Nayudu, the rival captains, are seated fifth and sixth from left, respectively. [Photo: Nayudu family and Madhya Pradesh Cricket Association]*

Bottom: *When Amarnath took over the captaincy from an injured Vijay Merchant and led India to a dramatic ten-run win—the Indian and South of England teams that played a three-day game at Hastings in 1946.* **Standing back row, from left to right:** *R.T.D. Perks, W.H.R. Andrews, C.S. Nayudu, Gul Mohammad, A.W.H. Mallet, Chandrasekhar Sarwate, Sadashiv Shinde, T.W.J. Goddard.* **Standing middle row, from left to right:** *Umpire (unknown), A.P. Singleton, S.W. Sohoni, G. Cox, Vinoo Mankad, J.D.B. Robertson, Vijay Hazare, H.T. Bartlett, Dattaram Hindlekar, Pankaj Gupta (manager), Frank Chester (umpire), Shute Banerjee.* **Sitting, from left to right:** *Syed Mushtaq Ali, B.H. Valentine, Vijay Merchant (India captain), Sir Pelham Warner, S.C. Griffith (South of England captain), Pelham Warner, Lala Amarnath (acting India captain), L.E.G. Ames. [Photo: Madhav Apte's collection]*

Top: *Members of the Indian team that toured England in 1952.* **From left to right:** *Madhav Mantri, Polly Umrigar, Dattu Phadkar, Ghulam Ahmed, Vijay Manjrekar (partially obscured), Sadashiv Shinde, Hemu Adhikari, Gulabrai Ramchand, Vijay Hazare (captain), Dattajirao Gaekwad and Pankaj Roy. Hazare apart, six players—Umrigar, Ahmed, Adhikari, Ramchand, Gaekwad and Roy—went on to captain India in the 1950s. [Photo: Madhav Mantri's collection]*

Bottom: *Members of the touring Indian team, along with a West Indies cricketing legend, on the ship* Golfito *in Bridgetown, Barbados, on the tour of the Caribbean in 1952–53.* **Standing, from left to right:** *Subhash Gupte, Deepak Shodhan, Gulabrai Ramchand, Vinoo Mankad, Frank Worrell, Vijay Hazare (captain), Pankaj Roy, P.G. Joshi and C. Ramaswamy (manager).* **Sitting, from left to right:** *Madhav Apte, Chandrashekhar Gadkari, E.S. Maka and P.R. Umrigar [Photo: Madhav Apte's collection]*

Top: *Jawaharlal Nehru, India's first prime minister, with Lala Amarnath, independent India's first Test captain (standing eighth from left), and contemporary cricketers. Anthony De Mello, the first BCCI secretary and board president from 1946 to 1951, who fell out with Amarnath during this time, is standing sixth from left. [Photo: Madhav Mantri's collection]*

Bottom: *Queen Elizabeth II is introduced to Nariman Contractor on India's tour of England in 1959. Contractor would be appointed captain of India a year later. [Photo: Madhav Apte's collection]*

Top: *Holkar reached the Ranji Trophy final ten times in eleven seasons from 1944–45 to 1954–55, and won the title four times. Members of the team paying their respects at Rajghat, the memorial of Mahatma Gandhi. Syed Mushtaq Ali is fourth from left. C.K. Nayudu is seventh from right. [Photo: Nayudu family and Madhya Pradesh Cricket Association]*

Bottom: *K.S. Duleepsinhji, after whom the inter-zonal Duleep Trophy is named, presents a memento to Ramakant Desai, the first bowler to take fifty wickets in a single Ranji Trophy season (1958–59). [Photo: Madhav Apte's collection]*

Top: *Mansoor Ali Khan Pataudi with Ajit Wadekar, whom he preceded and later succeeded as captain of India. [Photo: Gopal Bhat]*
Bottom: *The Indian team that created history in the West Indies in 1971.*
Standing, from left to right: *Kenia Jayantilal, Abid Ali, Ashok Mankad, D. Govindraj, Rusi Jeejeebhoy, P. Krishnamurthy, Eknath Solkar, Sunil Gavaskar and Gundappa Viswanath.* **Sitting, from left to right:** *Salim Durani, EAS Prasanna, M.L. Jaisimha, Ajit Wadekar (captain), S. Venkataraghavan (vice-captain), Dilip Sardesai and Bishan Bedi. [Photo: Gopal Bhat]*

Top: *Heroes at the Bombay airport: Ajit Wadekar (captain) and Col. Hemu Adhikari (manager) in the motorcade after the Indian team's return from England in 1971. [Photo: Gopal Bhat]*

Bottom: *The Indian team in Sunil Gavaskar's first Test as captain on home soil, against the West Indies at Bombay in 1978-79.* **Standing, from left to right:** *Dhiraj Parsana, Chetan Chauhan, Bharat Reddy, Karsan Ghavri, Kapil Dev, Dilip Vengsarkar, Mohinder Amarnath and Yashpal Sharma.* **Sitting, from left to right:** *B.S. Chandrasekhar, Bishan Bedi, S. Venkataraghavan, Abbas Ali Baig (manager), Sunil Gavaskar (captain), Syed Kirmani and Gundappa Viswanath. [Photo: Gopal Bhat]*

Top: *Sunil Gavaskar, who masterminded India's series victory over Pakistan in 1979–80, going for the toss with Asif Iqbal, his Pakistani counterpart. [Photo: Gopal Bhat]*

Bottom: *The BCCI's Golden Jubilee Test, 1980. Rival captains Gundappa Viswanath (India) and Mike Brearley (England) being interviewed by commentator Dr Narottam Puri. [Photo: Srenik Sett]*

Top: *The reunion of a lifetime: India's international cricketers snapped for posterity during the BCCI's Golden Jubilee Test in February 1980.* **Top row, from left to right:** M.V. Narsimha Rao, Roger Binny, Bharat Reddy, Yashpal Sharma, Kapil Dev, Sandeep Patil, Shivlal Yadav, Dilip Doshi and Surender Khanna. **Second row, from left to right:** Surinder Amarnath, Dhiraj Parsana, Karsan Ghavri, Aunshuman Gaekwad, Parthasarathy Sharma, Yajurvindra Singh, Madan Lal, Brijesh Patel, Kenia Jayantilal, Eknath Solkar, Ashok Mankad, Chetan Chauhan, Gundappa Viswanath, P. Krishnamurthy, Mohinder Amarnath, Syed Kirmani, Sunil Gavaskar, Hemant Kanitkar and Dilip Vengsarkar. **Third row, from left to right:** Ajit Wadekar, Bishan Bedi, Subroto Guha, Ambar Roy, Hanumant Singh, Rajinder Pal, Salim Durani, A.G. Milkha Singh, Manmohan Sood, Dilip Sardesai, Vasant Ranjane, Ramnath Kenny, M.L. Jaisimha, Arvind Apte, V.M. Muddiah, Abbas Ali Baig, S. Venkataraghavan, Umesh Kulkarni, Sadanand Mohol, Ramesh Saxena and K.S. Indrajitsinhji. **Fourth row, from left to right:** Chandrakant Patankar, Ramesh Divecha, N. Swamy, Vijay Mehra, E.S. Maka, Chandrashekhar Gadkari, Dattajirao Gaekwad, H.T. Dani, Madhav Apte, C.D. Gopinath, Madhav Mantri, P.G. Joshi, Deepak Shodhan, Pananmal Punjabi, Jasu Patel, Chandrakant Borde, Nariman Contractor, Bapu Nadkarni, G.R. Sunderam and A.G. Kripal Singh. **Sitting in the front row, from left to right:** Pankaj Roy, Ghulam Ahmed, C.R. Rangachari, Chandrashekhar Sarwate, K.K. Tarapore, C.S. Nayudu, Shute Banerjee, Mohammad Hussain, M.J. Gopalan, Naoomal Jeoomal, Phiroze Palia, Lall Singh, Lala Amarnath, K.R. Meherhomji, Kanwar Rai Singh, D.G. Phadkar, G. Kishenchand, Hemachandra Adhikari, P.R. Umrigar and S. Banerjee. [Photo: Gopal Bhat]

Bottom: *The 1983 World Cup winners after their return from England, at the Wankhede Stadium.* **Standing, from left to right:** P.R. Mansingh (manager), Roger Binny, B.S. Sandhu, Sandeep Patil, Ravi Shastri, Sunil Valson, K. Srikkanth and Kirti Azad. **Sitting, from left to right:** Yashpal Sharma, Syed Kirmani, Mohinder Amarnath (vice-captain), Kapil Dev (captain), Sunil Gavaskar, Dilip Vengsarkar and Madan Lal. [Photo: Gopal Bhat]

Top: *Architects of an incredible win in Melbourne. The Indian team that toured Australia and New Zealand in 1980–81.* **Standing, from left to right:** *Roger Binny, Sandeep Patil, Kirti Azad, Dilip Doshi, Yashpal Sharma, T.E. Srinivasan, Shivlal Yadav, Bharat Reddy, Yograj Singh and Kapil Dev.* **Sitting, from left to right:** *Dilip Vengsarkar, Chetan Chauhan, Bapu Nadkarni (assistant manager), Gundappa Viswanath (vice-captain), Sunil Gavaskar (captain), Wing Commander Shahid Durrani (manager), Syed Kirmani and Karsan Ghavri. [Photo: Srenik Sett]*

Middle: *Three members of India's famed spin quartet.* **From left to right:** *Bishan Bedi, S. Venkataraghavan and E.A.S. Prasanna. [Photo: Srenik Sett]*

Bottom: *Three members of India's Generation-L of the 1980s, indulging in aquatic antics.* **From left to right:** *Sandeep Patil, Yashpal Sharma and Dilip Vengsarkar. [Photo: Srenik Sett]*

Top: *Sunil Gavaskar, barrier-breaker and world-beater, who instilled self-belief in Indian cricket. [Photo: Srenik Sett]*

Bottom: *Kapil Dev, all-rounder extraordinaire and a man for a crisis. [Photo: Srenik Sett]*

Top: *Giants from three generations. Mohinder Amarnath at his benefit match—an ODI between India and South Africa at the Wankhede Stadium, Mumbai, in 1996–97—with Sachin Tendulkar and Ajit Wadekar (fourth from right). [Photo: Mumbai Cricket Association]*

Bottom: *The start of the greatest Test series to be played on Indian soil: Sourav Ganguly and Steve Waugh at the toss for the first Test of the 2000-01 series at the Wankhede Stadium, Mumbai. Cammie Smith, the ICC match referee, and commentator Ian Chappell look on. [Photo: Mumbai Cricket Association]*

Top: *Anil Kumble, India's greatest wicket-taker in Tests, bids adieu to international cricket at the end of the Delhi Test against Australia in 2008–09. [Photo: Ashutosh Sharma]*

Middle: *Sourav Ganguly's teammates converge on him at the end of his last Test, against Australia in Nagpur in 2008–09. M.S. Dhoni, the captain, paid his predecessor a unique tribute by requesting him to take over in the closing stages of the game. [Photo: Ashutosh Sharma]*

Bottom: *Sachin Tendulkar, Virender Sehwag and M.S. Dhoni, three of India's greatest match-winners, celebrate the fall of an Australian wicket in Delhi in 2008–09. [Photo: Ashutosh Sharma]*

Top: *India's tour of England, 1990.* **From left to right:** *Anil Kumble, Navjot Sidhu, Sanjay Manjrekar, Atul Wassan, Sachin Tendulkar, W.V. Raman, Kiran More, Bishan Bedi (cricket manager), Madhav Mantri (manager), Sanjeev Sharma, Manoj Prabhakar and Mohammed Azharuddin (captain) [Photo: Madhav Mantri's collection]*

Bottom: *World Champions, 2011.* **From left to right:** *Zaheer Khan, M.S. Dhoni (captain), Munaf Patel, Gautam Gambhir, S. Sreesanth, Sachin Tendulkar, Harbhajan Singh, Suresh Raina, Piyush Chawla, Virender Sehwag, Virat Kohli, Yuvraj Singh, Ashish Nehra, Ravichandran Ashwin, Yusuf Pathan. [Photo:Ashutosh Sharma]*

Top: *When one master met another: Sunil Gavaskar with Vijay Merchant. [Photo: Srenik Sett]*

Middle: *Allies-turned-rivals: Raj Singh Dungarpur (right), BCCI president from 1996 to 1999, with Jagmohan Dalmiya, BCCI president from 2001 to 2004. [Photo: Gopal Bhat]*

Bottom: *Ace administrators.* **From left to right:** *Prof. R.S. Shetty (CAO & GM, BCCI, 2006–2018), Niranjan Shah (BCCI secretary, 2001–02, 2005–08), Sharad Pawar (BCCI president, 2005–08) and N. Srinivasan (BCCI president, 2011–14). [Photo: Prof. R.S. Shetty's collection]*

Top: *Sachin Tendulkar with the Ranji Trophy. He represented Mumbai in six Ranji finals and was on the winning side in five of those: 1994–95, 1999–2000, 2006–07, 2008–09 and 2012–13. He led Mumbai to the title in 1994–95, and scored two centuries in the final. [Photo: Gopal Bhat]*

Middle: *Champions forever: Sunil Gavaskar with VVS Laxman. [Photo: Author's collection]*

Bottom: *Maestros: Rahul Dravid with Virat Kohli. [Photo: Author's collection]*

Top: *Winners of the greatest Test series of all time—the Indian team in the dressing room of The Gabba, Brisbane, after winning the Border-Gavaskar Trophy (2020–21).* **Standing back row, from left to right:** *Rishabh Pant, T. Natarajan, Washington Sundar, Ravichandran Ashwin, Mayank Agrawal, Mohammed Siraj, Wriddhiman Saha, Shubman Gill, Abhijit Salvi (doctor), Nick Webb (S&C coach), Rohit Sharma (obscured).* **Standing front row, from left to right:** *Shaminder Sidhu (security liaison officer), Ravi Shastri (head coach), Harvinder Singh (national selector), Bharat Arun (bowling coach), Howard Beer (local security officer), Nuwan Udeneka (throwdown specialist), Rishikesh Upadhayaya (logistics manager), Cheteshwar Pujara, Kartik Tyagi (net bowler), Shardul Thakur, Prithvi Shaw, Jasprit Bumrah, Vikram Rathour (batting coach), Girish Dongre (administrative manager).* **Sitting back row, from left to right:** *Kuldeep Yadav, Navdeep Saini, Ajinkya Rahane (captain).* **Sitting front row, from left to right:** *Hari Prasad Mohan (video analyst), Ramakrishnan Sridhar (fielding coach), Rajeev Kumar (sports massage therapist), Yogesh Parmar (physiotherapist), Arun Kanade (sports massage therapist), Soham Desai (S&C coach), Nitin Patel (physiotherapist), Raghavindraa Dvgi (training assistant), Dayanand Garani (throwdown specialist). [Photo: Moulin Parikh, BCCI]*

Bottom: *Seven India captains snapped at the Mumbai Cricket Association's golden jubilee celebrations of the Wankhede Stadium, Mumbai, in January 2025.* **From left to right:** *Ajinkya Rahane, Diana Edulji (former India women's captain), Dilip Vengsarkar, Sachin Tendulkar, Sunil Gavaskar, Ravi Shastri and Rohit Sharma. They are flanking the ICC Champions Trophy, which India won under Rohit Sharma's captaincy in March 2025. [Photo: Mumbai Cricket Association]*

the team's luck when it toured next.

India lost the second Test in Calcutta but won the decider in Kanpur to take the series. The players were therefore confident of putting up a good show when they flew to South Africa for a return series.

The transition from slow and low Indian pitches to livelier South African tracks, with no time in between to acclimatize, turned out to be dreadful. India was blown away for 100 and 66 in the first Test in Durban, and another rout loomed large when they were reduced to 58-5 in response to South Africa's 529-7, in the second Test in Cape Town.

A counterattack by Tendulkar and Azharuddin produced 222 runs in only 40 overs. While the captain was all majesty, the former captain biffed and blasted his way to his third hundred in four Tests against South Africa. Tendulkar scored 169 before falling to an extraordinary catch by Adam Bacher.

Nevertheless, South Africa won the Test, but India worked their way into a winning position in the third Test in Johannesburg, only to be thwarted by the weather. It was in this game that Dravid scored his maiden Test century. He also excelled in the final of the tri-series that followed, which India lost narrowly.

Srinath's shoulder gave away before the tour of the West Indies that followed, but Prasad and Mumbai speedster Abey Kuruvilla, who debuted in the series, did well. After two draws, the visitors found themselves needing only 120 to win the third Test in Bridgetown. After losing five of their six previous Tests at the venue, it appeared that history was beckoning them. Unfortunately, it all went awry against the pace triumvirate of Curtly Ambrose, Ian Bishop and Franklyn Rose, who were commanded by debutant captain Brian Lara. Tendulkar, who had been disappointed with the draw in Johannesburg, was a broken man after India was dismissed for 81. The last two Tests were ruined by rain and the Windies thus took the series 1-0.

The BCCI was in the mood to experiment in 1997. In April

that year, Mumbai played Delhi in the 1996–97 Ranji Trophy final at Gwalior, in what was the first instance of a domestic first-class game being played under lights. The pink balls that were created for 'day-night' Tests in the 2010s did not exist back then, and the white balls that were used for one-day games were used. Mumbai won the battle for the first-innings lead.

The Ranji final was followed by the Independence Cup, a quadrangular ODI tournament that had been organized to commemorate the golden jubilee of India's freedom. The BCCI sought to counter the heat and humidity at that time of the year by selecting stadia that had been equipped with floodlights during the World Cup the previous year. The matches were scheduled to begin at either 4:00 p.m. or 5:00 p.m., as opposed to the 2:30 p.m. start that was the norm in day-night matches. With all the matches ending around midnight, the Independence Cup was a precursor of sorts to the IPL.

Unfortunately for the hosts, the only Indian representation in the best-of-three finals was at half-time in the second final at Calcutta, when living India captains from Lala Amarnath to Sachin Tendulkar were felicitated. India beat New Zealand in their opening game with Tendulkar scoring a century, but they lost to Sri Lanka and Pakistan. Arjuna Ranatunga's team, which at that point could do nothing wrong in ODIs, prevailed over Pakistan in the finals.

India drew five consecutive Tests against Sri Lanka—two overseas and three at home—later that year. While the Sri Lankans were dominant in ODIs, they continued to be conservative in Tests. However, the Indians were also not incisive enough with the ball.

There were some bizarre selection calls taken during that period, like the one at the start of the West Indies tour to replace the injured Srinath with Noel David, an off-spinning all-rounder from Hyderabad who hadn't exactly set the domestic circuit on fire. Azharuddin's irresponsible batting in the Caribbean resulted in his exclusion from the team for the Independence Cup, and Kambli was recalled. The left-hander scored an excellent 65 in India's last league game against Pakistan, but he was axed for the next assignment—the Asia Cup in Sri Lanka. Azharuddin was brought back.

> Having spent a lot of time with Sachin in Sri Lanka, I had sensed that he was disturbed. He wasn't enjoying the captaincy and I was by no means the only individual who felt that all wasn't well. There were times when information pertaining to the trajectory of games that we were yet to play, would reach us and leave us wondering [...] The timing of some dismissals, especially in the ODIs, was weird, to say the least.
>
> —Ratnakar Shetty, ON BOARD: My Years in BCCI[45]

The captain and manager met board officials to discuss these issues, only to realize that some individuals did not believe in keeping things confidential.

Tendulkar led India to a 4-1 victory over Pakistan in the second instalment of the annual ODI series in Canada, in September 1997. Ganguly was outstanding with bat and ball, and the pacers Kuruvilla, Debasis Mohanty and Harvinder Singh also impressed. India then lost an ODI series in Pakistan, but not before stealing a win in the second game in Karachi. Robin Singh, a pugnacious all-rounder, and Saba Karim, a wicketkeeper-batter, brought India back into the game with a run-a-ball stand. Both players had been on the sidelines since the 1989 West Indies tour. When their consistency in domestic cricket finally bore fruit in the 1996–97 season, they proceeded to show what Indian cricket had missed in an era wherein the team had made a habit of snatching defeat from the jaws of victory. Robin Singh was batting with

---

[45]Shetty, Ratnakar, ON BOARD: My Years in BCCI, Rupa Publications India, New Delhi, 2022.

Rajesh Chauhan when the latter hit fellow off-spinner Saqlain Mushtaq for a six to seal the outcome of the Karachi game.

This was a time when a claim that Tendulkar's captaincy was adversely affecting his batting gained traction, although it did not make sense statistically. Before a quadrangular series at Sharjah in December 1997, he was told by the selectors to bat in the middle order. He complied and scored 91 against England, but India lost. The subsequent matches against Pakistan and the West Indies were lost as well.

Earlier that year, Tendulkar had spoken about the need to organize camps before tours of South Africa, West Indies and Australia, and the creation of appropriate training infrastructure. However, the individuals who mattered, appeared to be indifferent to his views.

Tendulkar scored a thousand runs for India in both formats in 1997. On the second day of 1998, he got to know from the media that he was no longer captain of India.

39

THE LAST CAPTAINCIES

Sachin Tendulkar reacted to his ouster by preparing intensively for the series against Australia, which had been billed as a battle between him and Shane Warne.

Aware of Warne's propensity to target the rough created by the bowlers' footmarks at the opposite end, Tendulkar scuffed up the practice pitches at the specific spot and instructed local leg-spinners and left-arm spinners, all of whom turned the ball from the right-hander's leg-side to the off, to aim for the same. He then honed his slog-sweep against the volunteers. Veteran L. Sivaramakrishnan and Tendulkar's Mumbai teammates Sairaj Bahutule and Nilesh Kulkarni were among them.

The tussle against Mark Taylor's Australians was preceded by a tri-series in Dhaka, in which India beat Pakistan in the third of best-of-three finals, thanks to a century by Ganguly and the enterprise of newcomer Hrishikesh Kanitkar. Azharuddin's return as captain saw Tendulkar being restored to the opening slot, where he blazed away.

Tendulkar went for the opposition's jugular even before the Test series began. He scored a match-winning 211—his first double hundred in first-class cricket—for Mumbai in a three-day game against the visitors.

Warne had Tendulkar caught at slip for four in the opening innings of the first Test in Chennai. After India conceded a 71-run lead, Tendulkar assured Aunshuman Gaekwad, the coach, that he would set things right. When the leggie landed the ball in the rough in the second innings, Tendulkar was ready. He began a counterattack by slog-sweeping Warne into the stands.

The former captain scored 155, one of his grandest hundreds, and the restored spin triumvirate of Kumble, Raju and Chauhan bowled excellently to secure victory by 179 runs. The Indians maintained the momentum in the next Test in Calcutta to win the series. Australia won the third Test in Bangalore, but Tendulkar stole the show with a stupendous 177.

He continued his form in successive tri-series in India and Sharjah. At the latter venue, India needed 285 to win their last league game against Australia and 254 runs to make it to the final, for which Australia had already qualified. Even as Tendulkar held fort at one end, wickets tumbled at the other, and it seemed at one point that New Zealand, the third team, would go through. Play was then interrupted by a sandstorm and the target was revised to 133 in 15 overs, a tall order in the pre-T20 age.

The resumption saw an assault that was as imperious as it was incredible. Not only did India qualify for the final, but an outright victory looked achievable until Tendulkar fell for 143. Just 48 hours later, Tendulkar proved that lightning could strike the same spot twice by contributing 134 to India's successful chase of a target of 273 in the final.

> Richie Benaud, that modern sage, spoke recently of another rare facet to Tendulkar's life. A lot of exceptional players, he said, had the talent, even the temperament, to be the leaders of their generation. But nobody he thought, brought quite the same passion to their game as Tendulkar did. The passion to be Number One.
>
> —Harsha Bhogle, *Sportstar*, 9 May 1998

Tendulkar scored a record 1,894 runs from 37 ODIs with an

average of 65 in 1998. He could have scored a lot more than 647 Test runs with an average of 81, had his team played more than five Tests that year. Once again, commercial considerations and the proliferation of limited-overs tournaments had resulted in the traditional format not getting its due. The Indian team's failures in a one-off Test in Zimbabwe and a series in New Zealand were the consequences of this indifference.

The Indians followed the triumph in Sharjah in April 1998 with victories in ODI tri-series at home and in Sri Lanka, but they lost momentum when pressure from the government resulted in the top players being divided into two teams. One of these teams participated in the Commonwealth Games in Malaysia, where cricket had been included, while the other took on Pakistan in the third season of the annual series at Toronto. Unfortunately, both assignments were disasters. The reunified team then beat Australia in the quarter-final of the inaugural ICC Knockout in Bangladesh but lost to the West Indies in the semi-final.

India won another tri-series in Sharjah in November 1998 before flying to New Zealand, where they lost the Test series and tied the ODI series. The New Zealand tour was followed by a blockbuster. The Pakistani team arrived in January 1999 for a Test series, the first between the two countries since 1989–90.

The first Test in Chennai was a humdinger. Only 16 runs separated the teams in the first innings, and Pakistan were well-placed at 275-4 in their second innings when Venkatesh Prasad triggered a collapse and five wickets fell for the addition of only 11 runs. Needing 271 to win, India began badly and were brought on track only by the sixth-wicket pair of Tendulkar and Mongia. However, both fell when the summit was in sight. The Chennai spectators enhanced their reputation by according a standing ovation to the Pakistanis, who won by 12 runs.

India squared the series in Delhi, where Anil Kumble took all ten Pakistani wickets in the second innings. It was appropriate that the last year of the decade featured a virtuoso performance by a bowler who had made India invincible at home in the 1990s. He had never allowed himself to get bogged down by the negativity around him. Even as his detractors kept harping about his unorthodoxy—his not being a big turner of the ball and all that—he simply kept doing his job, which was to win matches for India.

Srinath, who had gained a second wind since his return after a shoulder surgery, took thirteen wickets in the first game of the inaugural Asian Test championship in Calcutta, but India still finished on the losing side. The team was in control on day one, with Pakistan reeling at 26-6, but the visitors found a way to get back, as they generally did against India in the 1990s. The hosts were set a target of 279, and the game was in the balance when Tendulkar was controversially run out on the fourth evening. A collision with Shoaib Akhtar after he had completed three runs resulted in his bat being airborne when the stumps were broken. His feet were not in the crease yet, which meant that as per the letter of the law, he was out.

The spectators were livid. They lost their patience again the next morning, after Ganguly, the last recognized batter, was dismissed. The hosts lost the game by 46 runs, shortly after the police evicted the spectators from the arena. India's next game against Sri Lanka at Colombo was drawn and as a result, they lost out on a place in the Asian Test Championship final.

However, Indian fans and sections of the Indian media continued to be optimistic and predicted a memorable run in the seventh edition of the World Cup, which was to be played in the United Kingdom in May–June 1999. No effort was spared to remind one and all that India had won the tournament the last time it had been played in that part of the world.

Contrary to expectations, India just about scraped through to the Super Six stage, where they were eliminated. The redeeming features of the campaign were the 318-run stand between Ganguly and Dravid against Sri Lanka and the victory over Pakistan, with which the Indians extended their unblemished World Cup record against their traditional rivals. Dravid, who for two years had challenged the perception that he was a Test specialist, displayed solidity and flair in bowling-friendly conditions to score 461 runs in the tournament, the highest by any batter.

With Azharuddin certain to lose the captaincy, Ajit Wadekar, the new chairman of selectors, asked Tendulkar if he fancied another shot at the job. The answer was no, but the selectors sprung a surprise by reinstating him anyway. Tendulkar had the option of turning it down, but he then decided to take it up as a challenge.

There was reason to believe that things would be different this time around. The captain's relationship with the new selection panel, for instance, was unlikely to be as frosty as it had been in 1997. Wadekar apart, Madan Lal, another former India coach, was part of the panel. Kapil Dev, Tendulkar's old teammate, had succeeded Aunshuman Gaekwad as coach. The new brains' trust commenced its tenure with a series win over New Zealand at home, in which the captain scored his first double century in Tests. His 186 against the visitors in an ODI in Hyderabad was the highest individual score by an Indian in the shorter format until that point.

The Indians then flew to Australia to play a team that had won the World Cup, followed by four consecutive Tests, including three against a strong Pakistani outfit, earlier that year. What did not help was Jaywant Lele, the BCCI secretary, being quoted by media outlets as predicting that India would lose 0-3 in Australia.

On bouncy wickets and against a team of match-winners in their prime, the visitors stood no chance. Tendulkar scored a century in the second Test in Melbourne and VVS Laxman scored 167 in the third in Sydney, but they had no support. India also crashed out of the ODI tri-series against the hosts and Pakistan.

The defeat prompted Tendulkar to conclude that it just wasn't meant to be. He declared that the two-Test series against South

Africa at home would be his last games as captain. He was determined to bow out on a high note and scored an electrifying 97 in the first Test in Mumbai. Azharuddin, who was recalled to the side after being overlooked for the Australia tour, scored a century in the Bangalore Test. However, the others did nothing of note and South Africa won both Tests to hand India their first series defeat at home since 1987.

The fans still refused to give up on the team. Like their 1959 counterparts, they reckoned that things were so bad that they could only get better. They were mistaken.

WHAT MIGHT HAVE BEEN

As 1998 drew to a close, the Pakistani team was in a shambles. A team that had seen only two captains—Javed Miandad and Imran Khan (with a cameo by Zaheer Abbas)—from 1980 to 1992 saw more than thrice that number between 1993 and 1998. There were allegations of infighting and factionalism.

But then, something remarkable happened at the start of 1999 when Pakistan toured India. Wasim Akram was appointed captain a fourth time and Javed Miandad was named coach. Here, the Pakistanis overachieved, as they usually did whenever they played their traditional rivals in the 1990s. It was as if a disjointed group had found a purpose. They sustained the momentum they had gained in India, all the way till the final of the 1999 World Cup, which they lost to Australia.

There is reason to believe that the same would have happened with Team India, had it beaten Pakistan in the first Test of the series in Chennai. The Indian team of the 1990s was not riddled with factionalism, but it was notorious for underperforming when put under pressure by a quality opponent. India was at 6-2 and the target 265 runs away, when Tendulkar arrived at the crease to face an attack that comprised Wasim Akram, Waqar Younis and Saqlain Mushtaq, each one a match-winner in his own right.

The situation only worsened when Akram dismissed Dravid off a peach of an away-swinger and Ganguly was declared out caught behind, although the replays showed that the ball had bounced before wicketkeeper Moin Khan claimed a catch.

Mongia joined Tendulkar at 82-5 and gave the latter the support he was looking for. A fascinating battle of attrition ensued. As the Indians crept closer, the Pakistanis started doubting themselves. Tendulkar was in the zone. He kept going in the enervating heat and humidity despite excruciating back pain. The target was only 56 runs away when Mongia fell owing to a horrendous shot. Tendulkar, who by then was close to crossing the pain-barrier, decided to finish things off with boundaries. He began his mission with a flourish but then holed out to a delivery that Saqlain held back and was caught by Akram. The target was only 17 runs away at that stage and it was not beyond Sunil Joshi, Anil Kumble and Javagal Srinath, all of whom could bat, to take the team home. However, Tendulkar's dismissal invigorated the Pakistanis. When the final Indian wicket fell at 258, the former captain was inconsolable.

A win against the Pakistanis in that Chennai Test would have infused the Indian team with self-belief and it could well have gone the distance in the 1999 World Cup. Having had the better of Warne just the year before, the Indians would have handled him a lot better in the World Cup final than the Pakistanis, who had no answer to his guile. What happened to Indian cricket after the series win over Australia in 2001, could well have happened two years earlier.

How different the contents of this book would have been, had that happened!

40

SILVER LININGS

Delhi Crime Branch sleuths, who had tapped some phones to investigate an extortion case, stumbled upon chats between bookies and South African captain Hansie Cronje during the bilateral ODI series in March 2000 that followed the Test series. South Africa lost the ODI series 2-3, but as the cops listened on, it became obvious to them that the outcome of the series had benefited some people financially.

Insinuations about fixing in cricket had been circulating since the early 1980s, when some people had pointed fingers at the toss in the Test between India and Pakistan in Calcutta. The speculation intensified in the 1990s, with people claiming that Sharjah was a hub of the activity. In 1997, the BCCI constituted a one-man committee comprising V.V. Chandrachud, a retired chief justice of the Supreme Court, whose brief was to delve into the allegations. He interacted with select members of the cricketing ecosystem, but nothing concrete emerged from the exercise and the BCCI declared that all was well.

Cronje made the first of his confessions on 11 April 2000, four days after denying the charges. That triggered an avalanche. Manoj Prabhakar, who had not played for India since the 1996 World Cup, reiterated his claim that a teammate had offered him money to underperform during an ODI against Pakistan in a quadrangular tournament in Sri Lanka in 1994. A senior administrator then named the player who had allegedly made the offer to Prabhakar. The accusations flew thick and fast, as did the denials. Journalists attached to an Indian fortnightly that had done a story on match-fixing in 1997 then teamed up with Prabhakar to undertake a sting operation, wherein the all-rounder furtively recorded conversations with his former teammates, in which he asked them pointed questions. The footage, when released, stunned the nation.

The fans, who had supported the team through thick and thin, were disappointed and disillusioned. The outcry was deafening enough for the government to direct the Central Bureau of Investigation (CBI) to get involved.

However, there was a silver lining. The icons—Tendulkar, Dravid, Kumble, Srinath and Ganguly, who had succeeded Tendulkar as captain—emerged unscathed. There was not a shred of evidence that suggested that they had anything to do with bookies or fixing. In fact, the CBI's report quoted a bookie as saying that 'the fixing process would start only when Tendulkar got out, as he could single-handedly win the match and upset any calculation.'

The BCCI requested K. Madhavan, the former CBI director, to look into the findings of the central agency and make recommendations. Accordingly, two cricketers were banned for life and two others were banned for five years. A former member of the team's support staff was also implicated. Among those banned was an individual who had tried to project himself as a whistle-blower. The banned cricketers apart, a welcome casualty of the scandal was the seemingly meaningless limited-overs tournaments that had sprouted all over the cricketing world in the 1990s. These were identified as hotspots where bookies targeted players.

The BCCI announced the strictures on 5 December 2000, eight months after Cronje's confession. There was a sense of closure that day, as well as an acknowledgement of the fact that cricket's age of innocence had ended for good.

It helped that the Indian team did not have too many cricketing assignments between April and October 2000. This enabled the players to keep a low profile. Ganguly and Dravid played county cricket in England before the team regrouped for the second edition of the ICC Knockout in Nairobi.

India beat Kenya in their first match and then took on the reigning world champions in the quarter-final. The game began with a sensational assault by Tendulkar on Glenn McGrath, the Australian spearhead. The former captain's cameo and an 84 by Yuvraj Singh, the hero of India's triumphant campaign in the under-19 World Cup in Sri Lanka earlier that year, ensured a score of 265-9. Ganguly then threw the new ball to Zaheer Khan, the left-handed paceman, who like Yuvraj was playing in only his second ODI.

Zaheer had started playing competitive cricket in Mumbai and later shifted to Baroda. He had also undergone a stint at the MRF Foundation, which is where he caught the eye of Srinath, who recommended him to Ganguly. With his pace, accuracy and propensity to unleash the yorker almost at will, Zaheer vindicated his captain's decision to bowl him ahead of Venkatesh Prasad and Ajit Agarkar, his seniors. The Indians bowled and fielded superbly to win by 20 runs.

At a time when the wounds inflicted by the match-fixing controversy were still raw, the victory against Australia was a shot in the arm, not only for the players themselves but also their supporters. Six days later, the nation tuned in to the semi-final against South Africa, which India won by 95 runs. Ganguly led his team's charge with an innings of 141. He scored another hundred in the final against New Zealand, but it turned out to be a day when Chris Cairns could do no wrong. The all-rounder bowled superbly and then scored an unbeaten century to take his team to its first ICC title.

India's performance in Nairobi enabled the players to get away with an inept display in a tri-series in Sharjah that followed.

Needing 300 to win the final against Sri Lanka, the Indians were bowled out for 54.

Aunshuman Gaekwad had been reinstated as coach after the untimely resignation of Kapil Dev, but his was a stopgap appointment. In their discussions with BCCI officials, the senior players had reiterated the need for a foreign coach. They wanted an outsider who would rise above all the talk of parochialism and the other banes of Indian cricket. Among the names that cropped up was that of John Wright, the former New Zealand captain and later the coach of Kent, who Rahul Dravid had worked with while representing the county in 2000.

Wright could not have been blamed for thinking that he was third in the pecking order when the BCCI invited him to Chennai for an interview. Geoffrey Marsh, the former Australian coach who had been with the 1999 World Cup winning team, and Greg Chappell, the former Australia legend, were also in the race. With nothing to lose, the New Zealander gave a fine account of himself in front of a panel that comprised two former cricketers—S. Venkataraghavan and Hanumant Singh—and senior administrators—Raj Singh Dungarpur, former BCCI president, A.C. Muthiah, incumbent president, and Jaywant Lele, secretary. Bob Simpson, who had worked with the Indian team as a consultant in 1999, also had good things to say about him.

The official announcement was made on 2 November 2000. Wright commenced his stint with a series against Zimbabwe, shortly after India had beaten Bangladesh in the latter's inaugural Test.

The Zimbabweans began their tour of India with a three-day game against a team representing the National Cricket Academy (NCA), Indian cricket's finishing school, which was based out of Bangalore's M. Chinnaswamy Stadium.[46] The long-overdue

---

[46]The BCCI inaugurated the Centre of Excellence, a modern version of the NCA, on the outskirts of Bengaluru in September 2024.

NCA was modelled on the Australian Cricket Academy, based in Brisbane. The coaching staff was headed by Roger Binny, who had coached the Indian team to victory in the under-19 World Cup, and Vasu Paranjape, one of the most respected coaches in the country. Hanumant Singh was appointed director.

The NCA had its first brush with controversy less than two months after its inauguration by Sourav Ganguly on 30 May 2000. Three cricketers—left-arm spinner Murali Kartik, off-spinner Harbhajan Singh and opener Nikhil Haldipur—were expelled on grounds of indiscipline and academy rule violation. Some of their batchmates claimed that Kartik and Harbhajan, both of whom had already represented India, had complained about the quality of the food being served. For the off-spinner, his expulsion would have seemed like the end of the world. His father had passed away earlier in the year. On the professional front, the legitimacy of his bowling action had been questioned after his first few games for India in the late 1990s, forcing him to take remedial action.

> I also decided to leave everything and go abroad to work. I had a few friends there. I was ready to work at petrol pumps or wash utensils so that my family here would not face any problems.
>
> —Harbhajan Singh, *Scroll.in*[47]

The captain of India did not quite see it that way.

---

[47]Scroll Staff, 'Watch: Harbhajan Singh on how his father's wish and Tendulkar's advice kept his India dream alive', *Scroll.in*, 12 June 2020, https://tinyurl.com/hpy4p92v. Accessed on 18 July 2025.

41

LARGER THAN LIFE

> I believed in [a] certain style of playing. That's how I picked up players. Jo khelega, wo jitayega (Whoever plays, should win the team matches).
>
> —Sourav Ganguly, *The Ranveer Show*[48]

Twenty-five of India's best cricketers attended a camp in Chennai at the start of 2001, to prepare themselves for the upcoming series against Australia. Anil Kumble also attended, but not as a player. He had undergone shoulder surgery and was therefore out of action. The captain and coach requested him to oversee the spinners. However, the question remained: Who would fill his shoes?

The off-spinner from Jalandhar, who was planning to leave everything and go abroad, had made a mark on Ganguly. When VVS Laxman, who led India A against the Australians in Nagpur, informed Ganguly during the game that of the three spinners in the team, Harbhajan Singh was bowling the best, the latter suggested that he should not be exposed too much.

The selectors reminded the captain that Sarandeep Singh—Harbhajan's Punjab teammate, also an off-spinner—had bowled

---

[48]BeerBiceps, 'Sourav Ganguly - Leadership, Life Lessons, Cricket Stories & The World Cup', *YouTube*, 9 September 2022, https://tinyurl.com/2zr4cfbm. Accessed on 18 July 2025.

well against Zimbabwe and therefore, another offie was not the call of the hour. However, Ganguly persevered and prevailed.

As eager as Harbhajan to make his selection in the Indian team count was his India A captain.

Laxman had been pushed up and down the order since his debut in 1996–97. He had even opened the batting and done fairly well in that role, especially against the Australians, but he never felt comfortable. This led him to make a significant decision. He informed the board at the start of the 2000–01 season that he was available for selection only as a middle-order batter. The selectors could not ignore him after his record aggregate of 1,415 runs for Hyderabad in the Ranji Trophy in 1999–2000, but he was aware that the Australia series would either make or break his career.

The first Test in Mumbai began on 27 February 2001 with a minute's silence in the memory of Sir Don Bradman, who had passed away a couple of days previously. Sachin's innings of 76 on day one would have done Bradman proud, but his teammates wilted. The Indian bowlers hit back after their team's dismissal for 176, only to be pulverized by Adam Gilchrist and Matthew Hayden, who came together at 99-5 and launched a counterattack. The visitors took a lead of 173.

Although Sadagoppan Ramesh, the opener, and Rahul Dravid got runs in the second innings, the best knock was inevitably essayed by Tendulkar. He scored 65 before hitting Justin Langer, who was fielding at short leg, with a pull. The ball ricocheted off Langer's shoulder and Ricky Ponting dived to take a stunner of a catch. Australia needed only 47 to complete their sixteenth consecutive Test win.

Instead of the dressing down that the Indian players expected after the defeat, Wright drew their attention to what they had done right. The coach emphasized that the team may have lost, but that was no reason to doubt themselves. For the players, this was new.

Harbhajan dismissed Hayden, Gilchrist and Warne to perform the hat-trick on the first day of the second Test in Kolkata, but

Steve Waugh stood firm. His century enabled Australia to score 445, and he enforced the follow-on after his bowlers dismissed India for 171. Australia's first Test series win in India since 1969-70 seemed imminent.

India's captain and coach refused to buckle. Dravid had done well as the number three since he took up that slot at Tendulkar's behest in South Africa in 1996-97, but the management felt that he had gone into a shell. Laxman, the number six, who had scored 59 and was the last man out in the first innings, was so delighted to be assigned the number three slot in the second, that he forgot what he had been through on the eve of the game.

When asked by Laxman to sort his painful back out, Andrew Leipus, the physiotherapist, had shown the batter the mirror, literally and figuratively. The upper and lower halves of Laxman's body were not in alignment, and he had a slipped disc. But then, Laxman was determined to play.

Ganguly and Wright trusted Leipus' expertise at keeping Laxman going through the game, as well as Laxman's own resolve to go the distance. When he arrived at the wicket in the second innings at 52-1, Laxman also had on his mind his conversation with Wright before the start of the Test series, wherein the coach had expressed his confidence in him.

At stumps on day three, India was at 254-4. Laxman was batting on 109, and he had for company Rahul Dravid, India's new number six. Earlier, Shiv Sunder Das, the opener, and Ganguly had helped Laxman take the score along. With India only 20 runs behind Australia at the end of the third day, the nation was relieved that there would be no innings defeat.

The following morning, Laxman and Dravid took it ball-by-ball, session-by-session. They were inadvertently helped by their opponents, who continued to attack and thereby left a lot of gaps in the outfield. The landmarks kept coming, starting with the 200-run partnership, after which Laxman completed his double century. Dravid then completed his own century with a boundary off Warne. India were at 589-4 at the close. Not a single wicket fell on 14 March 2001, the fourth day of the Test. Laxman, having passed Gavaskar's 236 against the West Indies in 1983-84, was on 275, and Dravid was undefeated on 155.

The Indians batted for more than an hour on the last day, intent on declaring at a point where the only option for the Australians would be to play for a draw. Defensive cricket wasn't something the visitors were used to playing, and the hosts fancied their chances of capitalizing on the same.

A draw seemed certain when Australia, needing an impossible 384 to win, was at 161-3 at tea. But then, Tendulkar took the ball. Ganguly's gestures indicated that the plan was for his predecessor to bowl one or two overs at the most, but no one could have foreseen what was going to happen. After Harbhajan dismissed Waugh and Ponting in the same over, Tendulkar trapped Gilchrist and then Hayden leg-before in his third and fourth overs. He then accounted for Warne in the same manner with a googly that bamboozled the greatest leggie of all time. Australia had lost five wickets for only six runs.

Jason Gillespie was then superbly caught at short leg. Glenn McGrath, the number eleven, batted for half an hour, before offering no shot to a Harbhajan delivery that rapped him on the pads. The umpire's finger went up, and Eden Gardens went delirious. It was India's greatest Test win ever.

Earlier in the series, Ganguly had forgotten to wear his blazer for the toss and had to rush back to the dressing room to wear it. He could not help but notice that the delay had irritated his Australian counterpart, and he accordingly decided to play on the same and took his own time to emerge from the dressing-room for the toss in the subsequent matches as well. Waugh, who thought of himself as a master of psychological warfare, learnt much later that he had been its victim.

Australia were a healthy 340-3 in the decider in Chennai when Steve Waugh, in a classic brain-fade moment, handled the ball.

His dismissal sparked a collapse, and the innings ended at 391. India's openers then put on 123, after which Tendulkar produced his twenty-fifth Test century. Laxman and Dravid contributed 65 and 81, respectively. Trailing by 110 in the first innings, Australia were not allowed to build partnerships after the openers put on 82. Harbhajan kept pegging away. Colin Miller's wicket was his fifteenth of the match and thirty-second of the series. Ganguly had been proved right, and how!

India was 76-1 in pursuit of 155 when Ramesh was run out in a misunderstanding with Laxman. The Australians then showed just why they were such a great side; given an inch, they grabbed a mile. Even as Laxman carried on at one end, Tendulkar, Ganguly and Dravid were dismissed in quick succession. However, the Indians were not unduly worried at the last tea interval of the series, as the target was only 23 runs away and they had five wickets in hand. Significantly, Laxman was still there.

The stadium went eerily silent moments after the resumption, when Laxman's full-blooded pull off Miller was plucked out of the air by Mark Waugh. Sairaj Bahutule, one of two debutants for India, was caught at slip soon after. Was it going to end like the previous Test at the same ground, against Pakistan in 1998–99?

Sameer Dighe, wicketkeeper and debutant, then tried his hand at gamesmanship. He beseeched Zaheer Khan, the incoming batter, loudly and in English, to be careful against Miller, who he said was bowling very well. People expected McGrath to return for the kill, but Miller was given another over, in which Dighe got two boundaries.

The Indians inched closer. Zaheer fell with four needed, but Harbhajan, the number ten, held his nerve. The target was two runs away when he dug a McGrath yorker out. The ball sped off his bat past gully, and the batters ran a frantic two. They confirmed with the umpires that they had won, before throwing themselves into each other's arms.

India had completed the most extraordinary turnaround in Test history.

42

TEAM-REBUILDING

There was national outrage when Sachin Tendulkar was handed a 'suspended one-Test ban for ball-tampering' by Mike Denness, the referee, during the second Test of the 2001–02 series against South Africa. Footage of Tendulkar cleaning the seam with his thumb and forefinger was presented as evidence. However, he had not been reported by the umpires.

The umpires did report Virender Sehwag, Harbhajan, wicketkeeper Deep Dasgupta and Shiv Sunder Das for 'excessive appealing'. Denness imposed suspended one-match bans on three players and banned Sehwag from the next Test for allegedly claiming a catch on the first bounce and using foul language. He also penalized Ganguly for 'not controlling his players'.

Effigies of Denness were torched in India, even as news channels played footage of South African players getting away with incessant appeals. The issue came up in the Indian parliament and the uproar forced the South African government to instruct its cricket board to toe the Indian line. The BCCI's response was led by Jagmohan Dalmiya, who had been elected BCCI president a month earlier. Both cricket boards demanded that Denness be replaced for the next Test, but the ICC refused to yield. Ultimately, an unofficial Test was played instead, with Denis Lindsay, the former South African stalwart, officiating as referee.

The episode left no one in the cricketing world with any doubt that the BCCI meant business.

Highs alternated with lows in John Wright's first two full years as coach. India's victory over Zimbabwe in Bulawayo in June 2001 was their first outside the subcontinent since 1986. However, they lost the next Test at Harare and honours were thus shared. On the next tour of Sri Lanka, they lost the first Test in Galle but produced an extraordinary performance in Kandy. Despite the absence of Tendulkar and Laxman, both of whom were injured, the Indians chased down 264 on a turner against Muttiah Muralitharan at his best. Dravid scored 75 and Ganguly ended a lean trot with an unbeaten 98. But they went down in the decider in Colombo by an innings and 77 runs, thus losing the series.

The Test series in South Africa a couple of months later also began on a losing note. The team went downhill after finishing the first day at a healthy 372-7, thanks to centuries by Tendulkar and Virender Sehwag, the debutant. The second Test in Port Elizabeth, during which Denness courted controversy, was drawn.

After Test series wins over England and Zimbabwe at home, the Indians toured the West Indies for a five-Test series in April 2002. Their 37-run win in the second Test in Port of Spain was their first in the Caribbean since 1976. However, they lost the very next Test in Bridgetown, Barbados. Kumble had his jaw broken by Mervyn Dillon, the paceman, while batting in the fourth Test in Antigua, but insisted on bowling with a bandaged head after Ganguly declared at 513-9. It wasn't often that he got to bowl in a Test overseas with so many runs on the board. He bowled as many as 14 overs and dismissed Brian Lara, but the wicket was too dead to yield a result.

The West Indies managed to stay ahead in the decider in Georgetown. Needing 408 to win, India were 237-7 at stumps on day four. All they had to do was block for an hour or so on the fifth morning, with a downpour having been forecast. However, they surrendered quite meekly to lose the series 1-2, when it could have easily ended in a stalemate. The skies opened minutes after the game ended and did not let up for days. Wright was livid at the team's inability to apply itself.

The team was underperforming in the shorter version as well. India lost three tri-series finals in 2001, to add to the five consecutive defeats in finals of multination events since 1998–99. The story was no different in bilateral series. England squared an ODI series in early 2002 after being 1-3 down, and the Indians just about managed to beat Zimbabwe 3-2. With the World Cup just a year away, Ganguly and Wright were aware that the ODI team needed a reboot.

To beef up the batting, they decided to change Tendulkar's job description from opening aggressor to mid-innings stabilizer. Ganguly returned to the opening slot to partner Sehwag, who had excelled at the top of the order since the 2001 tri-series in Sri Lanka. Tendulkar, ever the consummate professional, did not protest. It was also decided to create a wicketkeeping all-rounder out of Dravid, who had done the job at the junior levels and occasionally at the international level. This enabled the inclusion of seven specialist batters in the XI.

It all came together at Lord's on the afternoon of 13 July 2002. After beating the West Indies in an ODI series, the Indians flew across the Atlantic for a tri-series against England and Sri Lanka. Having gone through the league stage unbeaten, the Indians started the final as favourites, but England batted splendidly to score 325-5. Ganguly and Sehwag started well, but then the wickets started falling. When Tendulkar was fifth out, India needed 180 from 156 deliveries.

Yuvraj and Mohammed Kaif, the seventh specialist batter in the XI, then added 121 against the run of play. Kaif carried on after Yuvraj's dismissal, aided by a Harbhajan cameo. It went down to the wire and with two needed from four balls, Zaheer and Kaif scampered for a single. Paul Collingwood's throw missed the stumps, even as Kaif dived. The ball went down to fine-leg and the Indians ran an overthrow to end their losing streak. On the balcony, Ganguly took his jersey off and did a jig, in what was a riposte to a similar gesture by Andrew Flintoff after England had squared the ODI series in India earlier that year.

The players carried their confidence into the ICC Champions Trophy, the rechristened version of the Knockout, in October 2002. After beating Zimbabwe, England and South Africa, India played Sri Lanka, the hosts, in the final. However, rain played spoilsport, and the teams shared the trophy.

Despite losing the subsequent ODI series against the West Indies and New Zealand, the team retained its conviction that it would fire in the World Cup, which was to be co-hosted by South Africa, Zimbabwe and Kenya in February–March 2003. The players were also fitter than ever before, thanks to Leipus and Adrian Le Roux, who had joined the team as the trainer.

In South Africa, the team was spoken to by Sandy Gordon, noted sports psychologist. One of his tips was that the players ought to get together on the field whenever they could, 'to keep the vibe going'. That was the genesis of the 'team huddle', which captured the attention of the cricketing world and even found its way into advertisements.

India beat the Netherlands in their first match of the World Cup, but not as comprehensively as expected. They then lost to Australia, the defending champions, by nine wickets. By then, Tendulkar had returned to the opening slot. A conversation with Kumble and Srinath after a loss in a warm-up game had convinced Wright that the batting order could do with a rejig. The duo opined that the team's talisman should do what he liked the most. When asked, Tendulkar reiterated that he would bat wherever the team wanted him to, but admitted when prodded that he would prefer to open.

The defeat against Australia sparked protests in India, with some former cricketers-turned-experts behaving as if they won every match they had played in. The situation demanded a display of leadership, and Tendulkar did just that by publicly assuring the nation that the team would do its best in the games to follow.

He then walked the talk, with knocks of 81 against Zimbabwe, 152 against Namibia and 50 against England. Three victories later, India played Pakistan at Centurion. Waqar Younis' side batted first and scored 273-7.

Tendulkar warmed up with a boundary in Wasim Akram's opening over. In the next over, bowled by Shoaib Akhtar, he uppercut the fourth ball for six, flicked the fifth for four and then defended the sixth. However, his timing was so immaculate that the ball sped to the boundary. The momentum was with India, and Tendulkar did not let it slip, not even when Sehwag and Ganguly fell off consecutive balls. In the company of first Kaif and then Dravid, he batted like the champion he was, to score 98, before being caught at gully. India still needed 97 at that stage, but the team of 2003 was a far cry from the one of 1999. Dravid and Yuvraj finished it off with four overs to spare.

That innings by Tendulkar—particularly his assault in the second over itself—liberated an entire generation of Indians from the aftershocks of Miandad's last-ball six of 1986, for good.

Every member of India's playing XI starred in the Super Sixes, the highlight of which was Sri Lanka's annihilation for 109. Srinath, who had announced his decision to retire after the tournament, was keen to finish with a flourish. Zaheer Khan and Ashish Nehra, his fellow pacers, were no less prolific. The team's temperament came through in the matches against Kenya and New Zealand, in which the Indians were 24-3 and 21-3, respectively, before the middle order rallied and took the team home. Ganguly scored his third century of the tournament in the semi-final against Kenya, a team that few people expected to make it this far.

A couple of damp patches on the surface and the form of his fast bowlers prompted Ganguly to bowl first after winning the toss in the final against Australia. However, India was never in the hunt after Zaheer went for 15 in the very first over. The Australians pounded the bowling to score 359-2. Tendulkar fell in the first over of India's innings, and although Sehwag scored 82, the chase was never on. Tendulkar would have gladly traded his aggregate of 673 runs that won him the Player of the Tournament award, for the biggest prize of them all.

43

TIGERS OVERSEAS

On the morning of 22 August 2002, Ganguly won the toss and elected to bat in a Test that was to be played on a damp wicket and under an overcast sky at Headingley, Leeds. Nobody could believe it.

Down 0-1 in the series, the visitors were playing both Kumble and Harbhajan, their two best bowlers, in the wake of the punishment that their pacemen had been subjected to in the first two Tests. It was therefore critical to bat first and big, so that the spinners would have runs to bowl with when the wicket would deteriorate.

The team had taken another tough call. Wasim Jaffer was replaced as opener by Sanjay Bangar, the Railways all-rounder, despite Shiv Sunder Das, the other contender, having scored 250 against Essex before the Test.

Dravid and Bangar battled the conditions with aplomb to add 170 for the second wicket. When Tendulkar arrived at the crease at 185-2, he discovered that the wicket was still so moist that the ball was creating indentations on it after pitching. Dravid scored a classy 148 and Tendulkar went on to get 193. He and Ganguly, who also reached triple figures, feasted on a tiring attack and India declared at 628-8 on the third morning, by which time the wicket had aged. Kumble and Harbhajan shared six wickets in the first innings and five in the second, after England were asked to follow on, 355 runs behind. Bangar vindicated the team management's faith in him with two wickets, in addition to his 68 as opener earlier in the game. India's victory by an innings and 48 runs was among its greatest on foreign soil.

The team management had taken another bold call at the start of the tour. Virender Sehwag was requested to open in the traditional format as well. When he dithered, Ganguly assured him that he would get a long run. Sehwag responded with a belligerent 84 in the first Test. In the second, he scored 106. The Indian captain had no clue at that stage that by merely asking a player to open, he had ushered in an age.

The most consistent batter of the Test series was Rahul Dravid, who scored three consecutive centuries, including a double in the last Test at The Oval. Buoyed by the 1-1 draw, the Indians outclassed the West Indies at home, but flopped in New Zealand, just before the World Cup. Even the New Zealanders struggled against the Indian quicks, but they managed to win both Tests. While it was all very well to dish out pitches that aided the home team, the authorities in New Zealand took things to the other extreme. Both Tests ended in less than three days, which was not the best thing to happen from a commercial point of view in a country where cricket was not the most popular sport.

The 2003–04 season commenced six months after the World Cup, with a thrilling Irani Cup game in which Ganguly's Rest of India overcame the Tendulkar-led Mumbai. Two drawn Tests against New Zealand were followed by a tri-series, in which Australia beat India in the final. All eyes then shifted to India's tour of Australia, where they had been humiliated 0-3 on their previous visit. Ganguly was quoted as saying that the Indian team would know how good it really was after the series in Australia.

The captain had flown to Australia before the start of the season to hone his batting skills against the rising ball under the tutelage of Greg Chappell. Those sessions yielded him a stirring 144 on a spiteful wicket in the first Test in Brisbane. That innings, along with Laxman's 75, enabled India to draw a rain-affected match comfortably.

Dravid and Laxman took a leaf out of their captain's book for the second Test in Adelaide. They did an encore of Kolkata 2001, adding 303 for the fifth wicket and getting their team to within 33 runs of Australia's 556. A brilliant bowling and fielding display on the fourth day left India with a target of 230. Dravid, who had batted for nearly ten hours to score 233 in the first innings, scored an unbeaten 72 in the second to take India through. This was India's first Test win on Australian soil since 1981.

The turning point of the next Test in Melbourne was Sehwag's dismissal for 195 on the first afternoon. Had he lasted for even a couple of hours more, India would have batted Australia out of the game, but that was not to be. The hosts forced their way back and levelled the series.

In the final Test in Sydney, the Australians found the door shut on them by Sachin Tendulkar. Exasperated after being made to reach out to deliveries pitched just outside the off-stump and losing his wicket to catches on multiple occasions, he eschewed his trademark cover-drive and scored an unbeaten 241, of which only 53 runs were scored on the off-side. His innings and Laxman's second century of the series enabled India to cross 700 for the first time in Tests. Australia attempted to reach the 443-run target, but they were forced to shut shop by Anil Kumble, who took 12 wickets in the match. The series was drawn, and India retained the Border-Gavaskar Trophy. It was quite an achievement, given all the predictions of a repeat of the 1999–2000 season.

The fans were so delighted that they passed over the loss to Australia in the best-of-three finals of the tri-series that followed. What they did take note of was Laxman's form. A shock omission for the 2003 World Cup, he showed what India had missed in South Africa by stroking his way to three centuries in the tri-series.

All the attention then shifted to the Pakistan tour, which materialized after a reconnaissance team flew across the border to discuss security and other issues. The tour commenced with an ODI series, which the visitors won 3-2. Each of the Indian batters clicked in at least one game, the standout performance being Laxman's 104 in the decider in Lahore. As was his wont, he scored at more than a-run-a-ball without feeling the need to slog.

In the first Test at Multan, Sehwag went where no Indian batter from Merchant to Dravid had gone before. However, his 309 was overshadowed by a declaration. Dravid, who was leading India in the absence of the injured Ganguly, waved Tendulkar in at 675-5, when the latter was only six short of a double century. It appeared a strange decision, as a lot of time was left in the game. When Tendulkar expressed his disappointment to the media that evening, Wright and Prof. Ratnakar Shetty, the team manager, knew that they had their task cut out.

Even as the media and former cricketers took sides, Dravid and Tendulkar spoke to each other and moved on. They may have disagreed with the timing of the declaration, but both were clear that winning the match was paramount. Their prudence prevented a vertical split in the team that would have set Indian cricket back by years.

The bowlers then dismissed the hosts twice, to seal victory by an innings and 52 runs. It was India's first Test win across the border.

Pakistan hit back in the second Test at Lahore, winning by nine wickets. Ganguly's return for the decider in Rawalpindi resulted in the omission of Akash Chopra, who, as opener, had helped Sehwag get the team off to starts throughout the season. India completed a hat trick of toss wins in the series and elected to bowl. After Pakistan were knocked over for 224, Parthiv Patel, the teenaged wicketkeeper, opened in Chopra's place and scored 69. Laxman, Ganguly and Yuvraj also got runs, but the cornerstone was Rahul Dravid, whose 270 marked the culmination of a remarkable three-year run, the highlights of which were match-winning hundreds in Kolkata, Leeds and Adelaide. There was also his 75 in Kandy. At Rawalpindi, India totalled 600.

The Indian bowlers, whose predecessors had been mauled on previous tours of Pakistan, then ensured victory by an innings and 131 runs.

In the first decade of the new millennium, Ganguly's team had put Indian cricket back on track, after the gains made in the 1970s and 1980s had been undone to a great extent in the 1990s, despite the individual brilliance of Tendulkar and Kumble.

44

FORWARD AND BACK

History repeated itself in the latter half of 2004. The Indian team slid after scaling the peak. An early elimination in the Champions Trophy was followed by a Test series loss to Australia at home.

The Australians came to India having done their homework. They avoided all-out attack and tried the patience of the strokemakers instead. India lost the first Test in Bangalore. Their resurgence in the second Test in Chennai was led by Sehwag, who scored 155, and Kumble, who took 13 wickets. At stumps on day four, India needed 210 runs and Australia ten wickets, but rain played spoilsport. The visitors then pocketed the series with a comprehensive victory in the third Test in Nagpur on a green strip, which suited them more than it did the Indians. A former Australian cricketer even wrote in a newspaper column that it was like playing at Brisbane in the middle of a series in India. Tendulkar returned after missing the first two Tests due to a tennis elbow, but injuries to Ganguly and Harbhajan did not help India's cause.

Dravid, who had taken over in Nagpur, stayed in charge for the last Test, which was played on a square turner in Mumbai. Needing 107 to win, Australia was dismissed for 93 by the spin triumvirate of Kumble, Harbhajan and the left-armer Murali Kartik.

Series wins over South Africa and Bangladesh could not

obscure the fact that the Indian team had plateaued. An exception was Anil Kumble, who regained his eminence after spending two seasons in Harbhajan's shadow. The selectors had made up their minds to discard the leggie for the tour of Australia in 2003–04, but Ganguly repeated what he had done with Harbhajan in 2001 and fought for the inclusion of a player he believed in.

With Harbhajan sidelined due to a finger injury in Australia, Kumble stepped up a gear and nearly bowled India to a series win in the last Test in Sydney. He followed that with a series-winning 15 scalps in Pakistan. 2004 saw him take 74 wickets from only 12 Tests.

The tour of Bangladesh in December 2004 witnessed the debut of Mahendra Singh Dhoni, a wicketkeeping all-rounder and beneficiary of the BCCI's Talent Resource Development Wing (TRDW). The objective of this scheme, which was designed by Makarand Waingankar, a senior cricket journalist, was to identify talent and fast-track its ascent by bypassing the state cricket associations, whose talent-spotters could conceivably be susceptible to favouritism.

The project was greenlighted by Jagmohan Dalmiya, the BCCI president. Teams of Talent Resource Development Officers and video analysts were deputed to watch every junior game and prepare reports. These were sent to Dilip Vengsarkar, who headed the TRDW and was permitted to attend meetings of the national junior selection committee.

Among the TRDW's prominent discoveries was Irfan Pathan, a left-handed pacer from Baroda. His performance in the under-19 Asia Cup in 2003 earned him a spot in the senior team for the tour of Australia. His all-round proficiency in the subsequent series in Pakistan even elicited comparisons with Kapil Dev.

Irfan was followed by Dhoni. The Ranchi resident scored two centuries for India A in a tri-series in Kenya and was picked for the ODIs in Bangladesh. He did not start well, but Ganguly persevered. In the second game of the ODI series against Pakistan in April 2005, Dhoni slammed 148 off only 123 deliveries, inclusive of 15 fours and four sixes.

After struggling to find genuine bowling and wicketkeeping all-rounders for years, India had hit pay dirt.

Pakistan had the better of its Test and ODI series in India in early 2005. They squared the Test series after being 0-1 down and then won the ODI series 4-2 after losing the first two matches. Dravid scored centuries in each innings of the second Test, but his teammates were inconsistent.

The Pakistan series marked the end of John Wright's stint as coach. His contribution to the revival of Indian cricket would never be forgotten. He was succeeded by Greg Chappell, who was chosen by the BCCI's panel over Tom Moody and Mohinder Amarnath. What also went in Chappell's favour was that Ganguly thought highly of him.

However, things did not go according to plan. On the tour of Zimbabwe—Chappell's second as coach—he let it be known to the captain that the latter did not merit a place in the side owing to his form. The fallout between the two was messy. An email by Chappell to Ranbir Singh Mahendra, who had been elected BCCI president in 2004, found its way into the newspapers and created a furore. While some fans supported Chappell, others backed Ganguly for what he had achieved as captain.

The goings-on within the BCCI were no less tumultuous. Dalmiya's group lost the 2005 elections to one led by Sharad Pawar, a senior union minister and president of the Mumbai Cricket Association. Following this development, Rahul Dravid was named captain and his predecessor omitted from the squad altogether.

India proceeded to outplay Sri Lanka 6-1 in an ODI series. The highlight here was Dhoni's 183 in the third game in Jaipur. The next ODI series against South Africa was also eventful. Chappell was accused of gesturing obscenely at fans after the fourth game in Kolkata, during which spectators booed the home team, apparently because Ganguly, the local hero, was no longer in the team. After India squared the series 2-2 in the final game in Mumbai (the third ODI was washed out), Dravid made a statement by acknowledging the support of the spectators at the Wankhede.

The Indians went on to establish a world record for the highest number of consecutive successful chases (17) in ODIs, in the 2005–06 season. They beat Pakistan and England in ODI series, but struggled in the Tests.

After a Test series win against Sri Lanka at home, in which Tendulkar scored his thirty-fifth century in the format, thus surpassing Gavaskar's record tally, the Indians toured Pakistan for the second time in three seasons.

The electronic media went berserk when Dravid, Chappell and Ganguly, who had been recalled to the squad, were spotted having an animated conversation on the boundary line before the start of the first Test in Lahore. One news channel even requisitioned the services of a lip-reader to decode what was being discussed!

The long and short of it was that Dravid decided to open after having initially told Ganguly to do so. The captain reckoned that his predecessor would be better off in the middle order. Dravid and Sehwag nearly created history, coming within three runs of Mankad and Roy's record stand of 413 in 1955–56.

After two high-scoring draws, India reduced Pakistan to 39-6 on day one in Karachi, with Irfan Pathan performing the hat-trick. However, the team frittered away the advantage and lost by 341 runs. They continued with their inconsistent ways against the English tourists, winning the second Test in Mohali but losing the third in Mumbai after Dravid won the toss and astonishingly gave the England batters first use of a wicket that was expected to deteriorate.

Dravid then shone as batter and captain in India's first Test series win in the Caribbean since 1971, which Tendulkar missed due to shoulder trouble.

All was not well by the time Tendulkar returned to the team. Some members of the team, including a couple of senior players, had fallen out with the coach and his man-management techniques. The distrust between the two parties was all too palpable. The situation did not improve when the team flopped in the Champions Trophy in India and was then routed 0-4 in an ODI series in South Africa.

These setbacks ensured that no one gave India a chance in the Test series against the Proteas, which started in December 2006. But then, the old underdog syndrome came to the fore once again. S. Sreesanth, a paceman from Kerala, and Zaheer Khan, who was making a comeback, bowled India to their first-ever Test win on South African soil in Johannesburg, taking eight and five wickets, respectively. Ganguly, who along with Laxman joined the team for the Test series, scored an unbeaten 51 that enabled India to total 249 in the first innings. South Africa never recovered after being bowled out for 84 in response. Laxman scored 73 in the second innings.

The team should not have looked back after the victory, but for the umpteenth time the Indians flattered to deceive, in the last two Tests. South Africa won the series 2-1.

India won the ODI series against the West Indies and Sri Lanka in the lead-up to the 2007 World Cup that was to be played in the Caribbean. However, the cold war between the coach and senior players persisted.

With the West Indian wickets being much slower than those in the subcontinent and the ball therefore not coming onto the bat, Chappell believed that it was imperative for a player to take the bull by the horns in the middle overs. He insisted that Tendulkar move down the order in the interests of the team. Tendulkar did so and even scored a century against the West Indies in the lead-up series, but he was far from happy. As someone who had always put team before self, Tendulkar felt that there was no need for the coach to invoke team interest while talking to him.

> I didn't communicate my plans well enough to the senior players. I should have let guys like Tendulkar, Laxman and Sehwag know that although I was an agent of change, they were still part of our Test cricket future [...] My impatience to see improvement across the board was my undoing in the end.
>
> —Greg Chappell, *Fierce Focus*[49]

Some senior players even requested board officials to not send Chappell with the team for the World Cup. Their plea was rejected.

---

[49]Chappell, Greg, and Malcolm Knox, *Fierce Focus*, Hardie Grant Books, Richmond, 2012.

45
RESURRECTION

Furious fans burnt effigies of the players, stoned their houses and even conducted mock funerals after the Indian team crashed out of the World Cup with losses to Bangladesh and Sri Lanka. The BCCI reacted by convening an emergency meeting of former captains to discuss remedial measures. Some board officials wanted Chappell to continue despite the catastrophe, but he resigned.

The board had to restart from scratch. Venkatesh Prasad and Robin Singh were brought on board as bowling and fielding coach respectively, and Ravi Shastri was asked to take a break from his media commitments to help the team rediscover itself. Paradoxically, it helped that the Indian team's next assignment was against Bangladesh, who had derailed the World Cup campaign.

> The atmosphere in the dressing-room was a lot more relaxed on the tours of Bangladesh, Ireland and England [...] There was greater communication, trust and transparency, and the camaraderie between the players was a lot more pronounced ...
>
> —Sachin Tendulkar, *The Nice Guy Who Finished First*[50]

---

[50]Prabhudesai, Devendra, *The Nice Guy Who Finished First: A Biography of Rahul Dravid*, Rupa & Co., New Delhi, 2005.

The players regained their mojo with victories in the ODI and Test series in Bangladesh. The BCCI's search for a new coach continued, with a panel comprising Sunil Gavaskar and Ravi Shastri, among others, interviewing applicants for the post. Graham Ford, a South African who had coached teams in his homeland as well as in England, was interviewed and selected, but he then sprung a surprise by expressing his inability to take up the job. In the meantime, Chandu Borde was requested to accompany the team to Ireland and England as 'cricket manager'.

India beat South Africa in an ODI series in Ireland, before taking on England in a Test series. The hosts had the better of the first Test at Lord's, but like Sohoni and Hindlekar in Manchester in 1946, India's last pair of Dhoni and Sreesanth managed to hang on and achieve a draw. The Indian bowlers then capitalized on Dravid's decision to bowl first after winning the toss in the second Test in Nottingham, skittling England out for 198. Fifties by five of India's top six batters ensured a first-innings lead of 282. Michael Vaughan, the England captain, scored a hundred in England's second innings, but the deficit was far too big, and the innings disintegrated after he was bowled off his pads by Zaheer Khan. The normally subdued Dravid's fist-pumping after India chased down a target of 73, underscored what the victory meant to him and his team. Zaheer, who had been on a roll since his return to the team for the tour of South Africa, had match figures of 9-134.

The Indians delivered another authoritative batting performance in the third Test at The Oval. None of the specialist batters scored a century, but Kumble did. The match was drawn, and Dravid was presented the Pataudi Trophy[51]—instituted by the ECB for Test series between India and England—by Mansoor Ali Khan Pataudi himself. For Mansoor and Borde, who had been captain and vice-captain, respectively, of the team that had lost

---

[51]The BCCI and ECB instituted the Anderson-Tendulkar Trophy for Test series between India and England, in 2025.

0-3 in England exactly forty years ago, the 1-0 triumph of 2007 was one to savour. The ODI series that followed was a close affair, with England winning 4-3.

The England tour ended a month after the selectors shortlisted thirty probables for the inaugural World Cup in the game's newest format, Twenty20, which was to be played in South Africa in September 2007.

Although the BCCI had instituted the inter-state Syed Mushtaq Ali Trophy in the Twenty20 format in the 2006–07 season, it had done so most reluctantly. It had voiced its opposition to the new format and its representatives had even argued in ICC meetings that Twenty20 would be detrimental to the sport. However, the other nine full members disagreed and voted in favour of a biennial World Cup in the format.

Simultaneously, the Asian combine of India, Pakistan, Sri Lanka and Bangladesh was vying with Australia-New Zealand to bag the hosting rights of the tenth fifty-overs World Cup in 2011. It so happened that the Asians missed the 1 April 2006 deadline to submit the participating nations agreement (PNA). The ICC agreed to give the combine additional time for the submission, subject to the condition that the BCCI confirm India's participation in the inaugural T20 World Cup. The BCCI did and the Asian combine went on to win the hosting rights for the 2011 World Cup.

Vengsarkar, who had been appointed chairman of selectors in 2006, was requested by Dravid not to consider himself, Tendulkar and Ganguly for the T20 World Cup. The official reason provided was that they felt that this was a game for youngsters. Dhoni was named captain of a team that comprised many players who were senior to him in cricketing terms. Endorsements of his tactical nous by Dravid and Tendulkar went in his favour.

Twenty-four hours before Dhoni's team took on Pakistan in a first-round game in Durban, the senior players who had skipped the T20 World Cup flew to Delhi for the launch of the

Indian Premier League, the brainchild of Lalit Modi, who was vice-president of the BCCI. Modi had conceptualized an inter-city, franchise-based annual league in the 1990s, but his proposal was rejected by the board's higher-ups of the time. A believer in the dictum *if you can't beat them, then join them*, Modi had then worked his way through the cricket administration hierarchy in India and eventually got elected as vice-president as a part of Sharad Pawar's group in 2005.

There was a seminal development in April 2007. The Zee Group, one of India's largest media conglomerates, launched the Indian Cricket League in April 2007, with some of the biggest names in Indian cricket on board as mentors and coaches. It also signed up contemporary cricketers from India and overseas, many of whom had played at the international level, to represent city-based teams. Like the Australian Cricket Board in 1977, the BCCI did not appreciate this encroachment on its domain and banned the ICL signatories from international and domestic cricket. It also gave Modi the go-ahead to launch his inter-city league. He rebooted it as a Twenty20 tournament.

It was during the IPL launch that Rahul Dravid informed Sharad Pawar, the board president, that he wanted to resign as captain to concentrate on his batting. He could have walked away after the World Cup catastrophe earlier in the year, but he did so only after resurrecting the team with victories in Bangladesh and England. That spoke volumes about the man.

With India scheduled to play ODI series against Australia and Pakistan after the T20 World Cup, the selectors first tackled the issue of the ODI captaincy and assigned the job to Dhoni, who by then had led India to one victory and one defeat in the T20 World Cup. The victory against Pakistan was achieved through a bowl-out, after the scores had been tied. Five members of both teams were supposed to bowl at and break a set of stumps, in what was cricket's version of a penalty shootout. The Indians had practised for this eventuality, but their opponents had not. It showed. Sehwag and Harbhajan, both of whom had been recalled after being dropped for the England tour, hit bull's eye, as did Robin Uthappa, and the match was awarded to India after the Pakistanis missed their first three attempts.

The loss to New Zealand in their second game made every game a knockout affair for the Indians. Yuvraj Singh exploded in their next game against England, with six sixes in a Stuart Broad over. India's 218-4 proved to be too tall an order for the opposition. An enterprising 50 by newcomer Rohit Sharma enabled India to score 153-5 in their next game against the hosts. The South Africans were never in the match after being reduced to 31-5. Rudra Pratap Singh, a left-handed paceman from Uttar Pradesh, was brilliant and the fielding exceptional.

Yuvraj Singh then smashed 70 off thirty balls in the semi-final against Australia. Set 189 to win, the Australians started well, but they were neutralized by Dhoni's bowling changes. Joginder Sharma, a medium pacer from Haryana, took two wickets in the last over and India prevailed by 15 runs.

The Asian giants clashed in the final at Johannesburg on 24 September 2007, exactly six months after their elimination from the first round of the fifty-over World Cup.

Gautam Gambhir, a belligerent opener from Delhi who had debuted for India in 2003, contributed 75 to India's 157-5. R.P. Singh then struck early, and his colleagues maintained the pressure. When Shahid Afridi was sixth out at 77, the Indians were rampant, but Misbah-Ul-Haq counterattacked and hit Harbhajan for three sixes in an over. The bowlers then targeted the other end. At the end of the penultimate over, Pakistan needed 13 with one wicket standing.

Of all the bowlers he had used in the innings, Dhoni had Joginder, Harbhajan and Yusuf Pathan, Irfan's brother, to choose from. He chose to go with Joginder, considering that Yusuf and Harbhajan, slow bowlers both, would find the going tough against Misbah.

Joginder began with a wide. He then bowled a dot, but Misbah hit the next delivery out of the ground. Six were now needed from four. The pressure was clearly on the bowler. It turned out that Misbah had decided what he was going to do with the next ball, even before it was bowled. The ball was fuller and straighter, and Misbah shuffled across and scooped it over his shoulder. It was not the ideal stroke to essay against a bowler who did not have the pace that the batter could use. The ball ballooned off Misbah's bat and was caught by Sreesanth at short fine leg.

For the second time since 1983, India became the world champion. For the third time after 1971 and 1983, the victors were accorded a red-carpet welcome in Mumbai, with crowds lining the streets to greet their heroes.

The triumph fuelled a transformation. The BCCI fell head over heels in love with a format it had despised till then.

46

THE LEAGUE AND EXTRAORDINARY GENTLEMEN

Jagmohan Dalmiya and the BCCI had planned elaborately for the ICC's presidential election in 1996. Among the many things they did was to bear the travel and accommodation costs of the representatives of the associate members, to ensure that they attended the election in London. Dalmiya won, but Australia and England exercised their veto power and argued that he had not won a two-thirds majority among the full members. In those days, the full members of the ICC had two votes each. The two oldest members also delayed the announcement of the result, and it was only a year later that Dalmiya formally took over. The veto was subsequently abolished.

Dalmiya, who was one of those who had earned respect and revenue for the BCCI in the 1990s, realized that something similar had to be done for the cash-strapped ICC. He accordingly conceived the Knockout, a biennial ODI tournament involving all full member nations. Its objective was to augment the coffers of the ICC through sponsorships, gate collections and, of course, TV rights. After two blockbuster editions in 1998 and 2000, the Knockout was rechristened the Champions Trophy.

As ICC president and office-bearer of the BCCI, Dalmiya was proactive. One of his first decisions after being elected BCCI president in 2001 was to compile a report comprising replies to the charges levelled by the CBI in its report on the match-fixing controversy. He wanted the board's side of the story to be made public.

He and his group were succeeded by Sharad Pawar and his team in 2005. The new dispensation created a permanent HQ for the board in the complex of the Wankhede Stadium in Mumbai in November 2006. The Cricket Centre, as it was called, was a welcome change from the two dingy rooms at the northern end of the Brabourne Stadium, from which the BCCI had operated for decades.

It was during Pawar's three-year stint as president that the board started hiring professionals. Pawar also took forward the pension scheme for former cricketers that Dalmiya had initiated and ensured that the BCCI took over women's cricket in India, as had been done by its counterparts across the cricketing world. He increased the board's annual subsidy to the member associations from INR 4 crore to INR 50 crore. The associations were encouraged to spend the amount on infrastructure and professionals. It was not a coincidence that many state-of-the-art playing and training facilities came up in the decade after 2005. India's successful run in junior-level tournaments and the robust bench-strength of the senior team in the 2020s can be attributed to the changes initiated by Pawar and his 2005–08 team.

The highlight of Pawar's last year as BCCI president was the launch of the Indian Premier League. A committee of the board, headed by Lalit Modi, selected Mumbai, Kolkata, Chennai, Delhi, Jaipur, Mohali, Bengaluru and Hyderabad as the home bases of the eight teams that would participate in the annual league. The base price of each team was $50 million. Of the nine bids that were submitted before the deadline, the highest bid of $112 million was made for Mumbai and the lowest of $67 million was made for Jaipur. The eight team owners ranged from industrialists and entrepreneurs to film stars. The sides were named Mumbai Indians (MI), Kolkata Knight Riders (KKR), Chennai Super Kings (CSK),

Delhi Daredevils, Rajasthan Royals (RR), Kings XI Punjab (KXIP), Royal Challengers Bangalore (RCB) and Deccan Chargers (DC).

The team-owners then got down to the task of preparing for the first-ever player auction, which was held in Mumbai on 20 February 2008. The franchises had a purse of $5 million each, of which they were expected to spend at least $3.3 million. Mumbai, Delhi, Kolkata, Bangalore and Mohali had an 'icon' player on board, in the form of Sachin Tendulkar, Virender Sehwag, Sourav Ganguly, Rahul Dravid and Yuvraj Singh, respectively. Each icon player was to be paid 15% more than what his franchise's costliest buy at the auction would get. Hyderabad had nominated VVS Laxman as its icon player, but he asked not to be considered as one, in order to increase the franchise's purse. In all, 77 players from India and abroad went under the hammer, 75 of whom were sold. Like the teams, every IPL signatory had a base price. Mahendra Singh Dhoni, whose base price was $400,000, was the costliest buy of the auction. He was snapped up by Chennai Super Kings for $1.5 million, or slightly over ₹6 crore, as per the prevalent exchange rates.

The IPL started on 18 April 2008 in Bangalore, with a game between the host franchise and Kolkata Knight Riders. It was preceded by a spectacular opening ceremony, in which there were dances and fireworks. I was working for the BCCI at the time, as the media relations and corporate affairs manager, and was present at the Chinnaswamy Stadium that evening. What has stayed in my memory is a five-second phase, just after all the dancers, platforms and floats had been cleared from the field and just before the teams walked out to begin the match. Lalit Modi, who was standing on the edge of the boundary line, seemed to be the only person on the arena, beholding the fulfilment of his vision.

Brendon McCullum set the tone with his 158 for KKR in the opening game. Every game was watched by capacity crowds. Cheerleaders flown in from other parts of the world danced to music that blared away on the audio systems, to celebrate boundaries and wickets. The first IPL final was a last-ball humdinger. CSK, led by Dhoni, lost to RR, led by Shane Warne.

Those who have played the IPL and those who have worked on it have seen and been through a lot in the last 18 years. The league started with eight teams. The number of teams increased to ten, then fell back to nine and eight, before returning to ten. Many of the original teams are still going strong. Some were terminated and others renamed or resold. A couple of franchises were even suspended for two seasons.

Lalit Modi's enterprise was not restricted to the IPL. As vice-president and head of the board's marketing committee, he got on board an apparel sponsor and a media rights holder, among other things. He also drove the creation of the board's digital archives. And then there were the TV rights. A year after Modi assumed charge, the board's marketing committee sold the TV rights for Indian cricket to Nimbus for a record $612 million for four years. The IPL broadcast rights from 2008 to 2017 were sold separately to the Sony-World Sport Group for $918 million. The number of zeroes in the figures kept increasing in subsequent years.

A spate of controversies in 2010 resulted in Lalit Modi's suspension and a life ban by the board. However, his brainchild continued to thrive.

The IPL has inspired the creation of leagues dedicated to other sports in India. In that sense, the IPL has given a fillip to India's evolution as a sporting nation. It has transformed the lives of not only cricketers, especially those hailing from humble backgrounds, but also those of the professionals who have worked behind the scenes to make the tournament a success. The league has also boosted India's travel and hospitality sectors. Additionally, it deserves credit for the tremendous improvement in India's fielding and fitness standards. Youngsters who have shared dressing-rooms and partnerships with the biggest names in the game, and have played in front of vociferous capacity crowds, are unlikely to be overawed by anything that they are likely to experience, if and when they represent India. The IPL has also encouraged other countries to start their own cricket leagues, like the Big Bash in Australia and the PSL in Pakistan.

There is, of course, a flipside. With leagues gaining prominence across the world, the BCCI might just find it difficult to strike a balance between international cricket and franchise cricket in the years to follow. What if more and more cricketers start preferring a marquee two-month event to a domestic season that stretches to over five months and does not pay them as much? Would it be fair to fault them for wanting to earn their livelihood the way they want to? What if they opt to become freelancers and play in leagues across the world, instead of signing a contract with their national board? This happened in the West Indies in the early 2010s, when prominent cricketers like Chris Gayle, Dwayne Bravo and Kieron Pollard declined to sign central contracts with their cricket board and opted to play in the leagues in different countries instead. The BCCI and other cricket boards might find themselves in a similar situation sooner or later.

Some leading international cricketers had skipped the 1987 World Cup because it was being played in the subcontinent. Three-and-a-half decades later, the compatriots of those cricketers will do anything to bag an IPL contract. How times have changed!

47
ASCENT

On 14 December 2001, India had 97 overs to score 374 to win a Test against England in Ahmedabad. The hosts decided to play safe, and they were 198-3 when the game ended. Exactly seven years later, England declared their second innings in a Test match in Chennai at 311-9, leaving India with four sessions in which to score 387 to win. Memories of insipid last-day batting performances like the one at Ahmedabad in 2001 made Indian fans expect a dull draw. In fact, some pundits even criticized England for declaring late and not giving themselves more time in which to take ten Indian wickets.

At stumps on day four, India was a sensational 131-1. Sehwag had turned the game on its head with an audacious 83 off 68 balls. Gambhir, Yuvraj and Tendulkar guided India to a six-wicket win on the last day.

Sehwag had played in the 2001 Ahmedabad Test as well, but he had batted at number 7 in the first innings and not got to bat in the second. The Chennai Test of 2008 underscored his impact on India's approach in Test cricket in the 2000s.

With Dravid having resigned and Tendulkar reluctant to take up the captaincy, Anil Kumble was designated the Test captain for the series against Pakistan in 2007–08. India's top batter in a series that they won 1-0 was Sourav Ganguly, who scored two centuries, including a double, and a 91.

Sehwag, who had been discarded after the World Cup on grounds of poor form and missed the series against Bangladesh, England and Pakistan as a result, was left out of the probables for the Australia tour in December 2007. However, Kumble insisted on his inclusion in the final squad.

India were outplayed in the first Test in Melbourne and went down against Australian gamesmanship and umpiring howlers in the second in Sydney. It was naïve on the part of the Australians to expect the opposition to overlook their histrionics, which had pressured the umpires into declaring Dravid out caught behind, although the ball had flicked his pad. Ganguly was given out caught although the ball had been grounded.

The Indians were also upset with the three-Test ban slapped on Harbhajan for allegedly hurling racial abuse at Andrew Symonds. Harbhajan denied the charges and was backed by Tendulkar who was batting with him at the time, but the match referee accepted Symonds' version.

Even as the BCCI appealed against the ban, it was 2001 all over again, with Indian fans calling for the termination of the tour. It helped that the team had a statesman at its helm at a time when tempers were running high. When Kumble pronounced after the Sydney Test that only one team had played in the right spirit, the world listened.

The Indians then played exhilarating cricket in the third Test in Perth, Australia's unconquerable bastion for decades, to win by 72 runs. With Australia chasing 413 and 65-2 at stumps on day four, the key wicket on day five was Ricky Ponting's. He came up against a 19-year-old from Delhi, who would not have played had Zaheer not broken down on the tour.

Ishant Sharma tested and teased the Australian captain for eight overs. Kumble then asked him to take a break. At this point, the bowler's Delhi captain intervened. Sehwag had on his mind the 16 consecutive overs that Ishant had bowled in a Ranji game in the previous season. Kumble gave Ishant one more over at Sehwag's bidding, in which Ponting nicked him to slip. Later, Sehwag himself took two wickets, and R.P. Singh and Irfan mopped up the tail.

Australia took the series 2-1 after the fourth Test at Adelaide was drawn, but the Indians came away smiling, on and off the field. Tendulkar scored his second century of the series and Sehwag, who had missed the first two Tests, batted as only he could to reach triple figures. After the game, Justice Hansen, who presided over the hearing of Harbhajan's appeal, dropped the charge of racial abuse and accepted the latter's claim that he had used an Indian profanity that sounded similar to 'monkey', the term he had allegedly used for Symonds.

Those who condemned the axing of Ganguly and Dravid from the squad for the ODI tri-series against Australia and Sri Lanka that followed, were silenced when India triumphed. At the forefront was their talisman. Tendulkar essayed some classy knocks, including 117 and 91 in the first two of the best-of-three finals.

Sehwag bettered his Multan performance in the first Test of a three-match series against South Africa, with an innings of 319. India squared the Test series 1-1 and lost their next series in Sri Lanka, but not before Sehwag toyed with Muralitharan and the mystery bowler Ajantha Mendis, to score a match-winning double century in the second Test in Galle. Dhoni achieved yet another distinction when he captained India to their first ODI series win on Sri Lankan soil. For India's white-ball captain, the wins in Australia and Sri Lanka marked the successful beginning of India's preparations for the 2011 World Cup, which was to be played on the subcontinent.

By this time, Gary Kirsten, the former South Africa stalwart, had come on board as coach. It helped that he had been a cricketer who made every ounce of his talent count and had retired only a few years earlier. The players, many of whom had played against him, found it easier to relate to him, and vice versa.

India's 2-0 win in a Test series against Australia in the 2008–09 season was in a way overshadowed by Ganguly and Kumble's exits. Having had enough of selectorial whims and fancies, Ganguly announced at the start of the series that it would be his last. Kumble—who missed the second Test, which India won under Dhoni's captaincy—announced his retirement at the end of the third Test at Delhi. Even as the Indians were wrapping up a victory in the fourth and last Test at Nagpur, Dhoni requested Ganguly, who had scored 85 and a duck in his final Test, to 'take over'. It was the perfect tribute to a player who had made India a force in Test cricket at the start of the millennium. At the end of the game, Dhoni insisted that Kumble accompany him to receive the Border-Gavaskar Trophy from the legends themselves.

India then dominated an ODI series against England, which was called off with two matches left when Pakistani terrorists attacked Mumbai on the fateful night of 26 November 2008. There was uncertainty over the Test series that was to follow, but the English decided to come over after being assured that there would be no security concerns. India won the first Test in Chennai, thanks to Sehwag's belligerence and Tendulkar's coup de grace, and drew the second one in Mohali, in which Dravid ended a prolonged bad patch with a century.

The Indians flew to New Zealand after winning an ODI and T20 series in Sri Lanka in early 2009. Tendulkar set up India's first Test win in the country since 1976 with an innings of 160 in Hamilton. The hosts were thwarted in their bid to get back into the series by Gautam Gambhir, who had been on a roll since the ODIs against Australia. He had already scored a double century and two centuries in the Tests against Australia and England, earlier in the season. When the New Zealanders made India follow on in the second Test in Napier, Gambhir batted for over ten hours to score a match-saving 137, and followed it up with a strokeful 167 in the third Test in Wellington.

While there was no doubt that Wasim Jaffer, who had done well as opener in 2006–07, was unlucky to have lost his place after just one ordinary series in Australia, the fact was that Gambhir had made the most of the opportunities he had got.

The Sri Lankans forced a draw in Ahmedabad in the first of their three Tests in 2009-10, but the Indians defeated them by an innings and 144 runs in the second Test at Kanpur. The top three—Sehwag, Gambhir and Dravid—scored centuries, and then Sreesanth, who returned to the team after battling injuries and disciplinary issues for 18 months, bowled superbly on a batting-friendly strip.

The highlight of the last Test in Mumbai, which India won by an innings and 24 runs, was Sehwag's 293, 284 of which he scored in a single day. It was the first Test to be played at the Brabourne Stadium since January 1973. The Wankhede was not available as it was undergoing renovation for the forthcoming World Cup.

That Mumbai Test concluded on 6 December 2009. The 1990s were just a decade old at that stage, but they seemed a millennium away when Dhoni received the ICC Test Championship Mace at a ceremony in Delhi, later that month. The series win over Sri Lanka had taken India to the top of the ICC's Test Rankings for the very first time. The cricketers who had revitalized the traditional form of the game at the start of the new millennium and convinced fans that an Indian team could win Tests overseas, were as much responsible for the ascent as their 2008-09 counterparts.

WHAT MIGHT HAVE BEEN

Rohit Sharma, a belligerent batter from Mumbai, was picked in the Indian team for the tour of Ireland and England in 2007 on the strength of his performances in junior and domestic cricket. His performances in the inaugural T20 World Cup later that year, as well as his two fifties in the tri-series in Australia in early 2008, prompted many to predict a bright future for him. While he also did well for Deccan Chargers in the first two seasons of the IPL, he ended up losing form at the international level and was dropped from the limited-overs side in 2009. A century in each innings for Mumbai in the 2008–09 Ranji Trophy final and a knock of 309 against Gujarat in a Ranji game in 2009–10 brought him back into the reckoning. When the South Africans arrived in India in early 2010, Rohit was earmarked to play the first Test in Nagpur in case VVS Laxman's finger did not heal. I was in Nagpur a couple of days before the Test, to coordinate the pre-series media events of the visiting team. There, I happened to meet Rohit, who told me that he was ready.

Laxman was ruled out on the morning of the game, but Rohit twisted his ankle, forcing the team management to play Wriddhiman Saha, the reserve wicketkeeper, as a batter. As it turned out, Rohit then had to wait three-and-a-half years to make his Test debut. This was the period in which Virat Kohli, who was India's under-19 captain at a time when Rohit was scoring fifties for the senior Indian team in Australia, made his international debut and kept bettering his own standards. Rohit eventually started his Test career in 2013 with centuries in his first two Tests, but he then lost his way again. It was only in 2019–20, when he started opening the batting in Tests, that he found his bearing in the traditional version.

What if Rohit had played at Nagpur in 2010? Although India lost the game on a lively wicket, a stroke-player like him would have relished the ball coming onto the bat. In all probability, he would have retained his place in the Test squad and toured South Africa in the following season. The experience he would have gained there would have helped him on India's tours of England and Australia in 2011–12, both of which turned out to be disasters. He could have first taken on the vice-captaincy and later, the captaincy.

India did well in all the ICC tournaments between 2013 and 2021, only to stumble at the final or penultimate step. How differently would things have panned out for Indian cricket had Rohit Sharma been in charge? After all, he did lead Mumbai Indians to five IPL titles during the same period.

48
ZENITH

The general elections of 2009 forced the BCCI to shift the second season of the IPL to South Africa. Deccan Chargers and Royal Challengers Bangalore, both of whom had finished at the bottom of the league in 2008, contested the final in 2009, with the former emerging triumphant. The IPL was followed by the second T20 World Cup, this time in England, where the 2007 winners were eliminated in the first round.

The inconsistency of the batters resulted in Rahul Dravid's recall to white ball cricket. He starred in an ODI series win in Sri Lanka and then scored 76 in a losing cause against Pakistan in the ICC Champions Trophy, only to be overlooked for an ODI series against Australia at the start of the 2009–10 season. The team needed him in conditions that challenged the batters, but not on batting beauties. It wasn't the best way to treat an icon, but then, he was not one to complain.

The tightest game of the ODI series that Australia won 4-2 was the fifth in Hyderabad, where India came within four runs of a target of 351. Tendulkar's 175 off 141 deliveries kept his side in the hunt. Earlier that year, he had scored 163 against New Zealand in Christchurch and a match-winning 138 in the final of a tri-series in Sri Lanka.

These scores were the prelude to a double century against South Africa at Gwalior on 24 February 2010, the first ever by a male cricketer in ODIs. Tendulkar was no less prolific in Tests during this period, with centuries in series against Sri Lanka, Bangladesh and South Africa. After series wins over Sri Lanka and Bangladesh in the 2009-10 season, India held the South Africans to a 1-1 draw, losing the first Test in Nagpur and then snatching victory in a thrilling finish in Kolkata.

Tendulkar was 'in the zone' in the third season of the IPL as well, in 2010. He was the top scorer and seemed on course to lead Mumbai Indians to the title, but they lost to Chennai Super Kings in the final.

India won the Asia Cup in Sri Lanka in June 2010, but lost the first Test of the series that followed, with Muralitharan ending his career with exactly 800 wickets. Tendulkar's 84 in the second innings helped avoid an innings defeat. He then scored 203 in the second Test, which was a high-scoring draw. Needing 257 to win the last Test, India was 62-4 when Tendulkar and Laxman came together to add 109. The latter scored a hundred and India squared the Test series.

Tendulkar's consistency in the 2009-10 season won him the ICC Cricketer of the Year award. A spate of niggles and injuries, as well as a first-round World Cup exit had tested his resolve in the period from 2004 to 2007, and he even considered quitting, but then, he was made of sterner stuff.

He was far from satiated, as it turned out. His four outings in the Test series against Australia at the start of the 2010-11 season yielded scores of 98, 38, 214 and 53.

In the first Test in Mohali, India was at 124-8, needing 92 more to win, when VVS Laxman forgot debilitating back pain to essay another second-innings masterclass. He goaded Ishant Sharma, the number ten, to fight it out. The paceman dropped anchor and fell only when the target was just 11 runs away. Pragyan Ojha, the number eleven, also held on, and the Indians had a lucky break when he first survived a leg-before appeal and then a run-out, and got four overthrows in the process. The drama ended when

Ojha and Suresh Raina, who was running for Laxman, ran two leg-byes to secure a famous win. India's top performer in the second Test in Bangalore—Tendulkar apart—was the debutant Cheteshwar Pujara, who had come up the ranks from Saurashtra, the land of Ranjitsinhji. He fell for a duck in the first innings, but scored a match-winning 72 in the second after being sent in at number three, ahead of Dravid.

The Indians then beat New Zealand at home, after which they had their most successful tour of South Africa till date. Morne Morkel and Dale Steyn, his new-ball partner who had taken 10-108 at Nagpur earlier that year, ran through the visitors in the first Test in Centurion, but Tendulkar scored an unbeaten 111, his fiftieth Test century.

The next Test in Durban was a seminal encounter for those who had seen the Indian team being steamrolled for 100 and 66 at the same venue in 1996. Zaheer Khan and Harbhajan took six wickets each and Sreesanth four, to set up victory by 87 runs. Laxman produced another second-innings classic in a tight situation, scoring 96. Rahul Dravid became the first fielder to reach the milestone of 200 Test catches when he snapped up Dale Steyn off Harbhajan in the first innings.

Tendulkar's century in Cape Town in India's last Test of the season marked the culmination of an astounding run. From January 2010 to January 2011, he had scored 1,722 runs in 15 Tests with an astounding average of 82, inclusive of eight centuries, of which two were double hundreds. At 37, he had been more prolific than in 1998, his annus mirabilis.

When the hosts were 130-6 in the second innings in Cape Town, the Indians sensed a chance to create history, as South Africa were only 132 ahead. However, the lower order batted resolutely, and the series ended in a 1-1 tie.

The ICC Cricket World Cup 2011 had undergone structural changes, with Pakistan losing co-hosting rights due to security concerns. The tournament started in Dhaka, with India taking on co-hosts Bangladesh. On the eve of the game, Tendulkar delivered a pep-talk to Yuvraj, who was to essay the crucial fifth bowler's role in the tournament. The southpaw had been through a tough time, both professionally and personally. He had been in and out of the ODI squad prior to the tournament. Health-wise, he was not at his best and had been throwing up blood regularly.

Sehwag set the ball rolling, quite literally, with a boundary off the first ball of the tournament. He scored 175 and Kohli, who had led India to victory in the under-19 World Cup in 2008, got 100, to take India to 370-4. Bangladesh never had a chance. India then tied against England, beat Ireland and the Netherlands, lost to South Africa and defeated the West Indies. Tendulkar scored centuries against England and South Africa.

The little master's 50 put India on course to overhaul Australia's 260-6 in the quarter-final at Ahmedabad, but the defending champions struck back in the middle overs. When Dhoni was fifth out at 187, India needed 74 from 75 deliveries. Yuvraj and Raina then joined forces to take their team through. Yuvraj won his fourth individual award in five games for his bowling and batting. Earlier, he had made people curious by declaring that he wanted to win the World Cup for someone special.

The celebrations on the streets of Ahmedabad were replicated in Mohali six days later, when India beat Pakistan by 29 runs in the semi-final. Tendulkar's 85 won him his third individual award in five World Cup wins against Pakistan.

India took on co-hosts Sri Lanka in the summit clash at the rebuilt Wankhede Stadium on 2 April 2011. Confusion at the toss necessitated a re-toss, which was won by Kumar Sangakkara, the Sri Lankan captain. He opted to bat. India started well, with Zaheer Khan delivering an opening spell that read 5-3-6-1. The Indians were in control until Mahela Jayawardene got going. His century helped Sri Lanka reach 274-6.

Sehwag fell leg-before to Lasith Malinga, Sri Lanka's spearhead, off the second ball of India's innings. Tendulkar looked imperious until Malinga induced him to nick one to Sangakkara. One could have heard a pin drop at the Wankhede Stadium when that happened.

Gambhir and Kohli breathed life into the chase. The latter was on 35 when he was spectacularly caught-and-bowled by Tillekaratne Dilshan. The spectators and TV viewers were shocked to see Dhoni stride in at this stage, ahead of Yuvraj. It was Tendulkar who suggested that Dhoni go in if Kohli were to fall, to keep the left-right combination going. The captain also reckoned that he would handle Muralitharan, his CSK teammate, better than Yuvraj. The catch however was that he had not been in the best of form with the bat. By promoting himself, he had set himself up for brickbats. If he was to fail, that is.

Gambhir and he batted splendidly. Only 52 were needed when Gambhir inside-edged Thisara Perera onto his stumps. He had scored 97. Yuvraj's arrival only accelerated the scoring. Four were needed off eleven balls when Dhoni swung Nuwan Kulasekhara hard and straight, beyond the boundary. The capacity crowd then took over.

Shortly after receiving the player of the tournament award for his 362 runs and 15 wickets, Yuvraj revealed the identity of the special individual for whom he wanted to win the World Cup. Kohli added to this in the post-match intereview, saying, 'Sachin Tendulkar has carried the burden of the nation for 21 years. It was time we carried him.'

One of the chief architects of India's second ODI World Cup triumph was someone who had retired two years before the tournament. Seven of the 15 members of the Indian team that won the title—Virender Sehwag, Gautam Gambhir, Yuvraj Singh, Harbhajan Singh, Zaheer Khan, Ashish Nehra and M.S. Dhoni himself—had either debuted or flowered at the start of their careers under the leadership of Sourav Ganguly.

49
SUNSETS

In the 2012 Tri-series in Australia, Dhoni declared that he can't play all three (Gambhir, Sachin and Sehwag) of us together as he was looking ahead at the 2015 World Cup [...] When we were in a desperate need to win a game, I remember in Hobart, Viru and Sachin opened and I batted at three [...] First you decided that you won't play the three of us together, then you decided that you are going to play the three of us together. Either the original decision was wrong, or the second decision was wrong.

—Gautam Gambhir, *India Today*, 8 December 2018

M.S. Dhoni's rotation policy in the tri-series against Australia and Sri Lanka, which was played after the Indian team's second consecutive 0-4 loss in a Test series overseas in less than a year, did nothing to alleviate the anger of the fans.

It was the 1990s all over again, after a dream run from 2007 to 2011. As had been the case in 1991–92, the youngest member of the batting line-up topped the table on a disastrous tour of Australia. Virat Kohli followed scores of 44 and 75 in the third Test in Perth, with his maiden Test hundred in the Adelaide Test.

The selectors wanted to replace Dhoni as captain after the reverses in England and Australia, but they were overruled by the BCCI president. The selection panel comprised Mohinder Amarnath, who had the year before replaced Yashpal Sharma as North Zone's representative on the selection committee. Amarnath had even been tipped to succeed K. Srikkanth as the chairman of selectors in September 2012, but he ended up being removed from the panel altogether.

The tri-series in Australia was a tighter affair. India needed 321 from 40 overs against Sri Lanka at Hobart to stay in contention for a place in the best-of-three finals. They won in 36.4 overs, thanks to an incredible 133 by Kohli. Gambhir, who had captained India in an ODI series against the West Indies just before the Indian team flew to Australia, scored 64. However, Sri Lanka knocked India out by beating Australia in the last league game.

Tendulkar scored his forty-ninth ODI century and hundredth international hundred against Bangladesh in Mirpur in an Asia Cup league game in March 2012, but the hosts won the game by five wickets. India went flat out in their next game against Pakistan. Needing 330 to win, they lost Gambhir off the second ball of the innings. Tendulkar was then joined by Kohli. The duo added 133 at more than a run-a-ball until Tendulkar fell for 52. Kohli maintained the onslaught, scoring 183 before he was out with only a few runs needed. However, the victory could not secure India a place in the final.

No one knew it then, but Tendulkar's innings of 52 against Pakistan on 18 March 2012 was his last outing in ODIs. He announced his retirement from the format nine months later. His was not the only poignant announcement of the year.

Rahul Dravid's decision to retire after his return from Australia seemed ill-timed, given the way he had batted in the last fifteen months. He scored a match-winning century in the first Test of the 2011 series in the West Indies, which was played after the fourth season of the IPL. The second Test was drawn, and India should have won the third Test, but for a cop-out. They needed 86 to win from 15 overs with seven wickets in hand, when they offered to call the game off. It was a bizarre decision by a team that had recently won the World Cup.

What happened in England a few weeks later was a classic case of misfortune befalling the timid. The team was beset with injuries and poor form, with one exception. Dravid scored three centuries in a losing cause. In the last Test at The Oval, he opened in the absence of Gambhir and carried his bat to score 146. India was asked to follow-on, 291 runs in arrears, and Dravid got a standing ovation when he emerged from the dressing-room to open the second innings, ten minutes after entering it undefeated at the end of the first innings.

India surrendered the ICC Test Championship Mace to England, as well as the Pataudi Trophy. Mansoor Ali Khan Pataudi, who presented the trophy to Alastair Cook, the victorious captain, passed away a couple of months later.

Dravid then scored his thirty-sixth Test century in a victorious series against the West Indies at home, but he then had a tough time in Australia.

When Dravid informed N. Srinivasan, the BCCI president, about his decision to move on, the latter advised him against it and reminded him that India were scheduled to play against New Zealand, England and Australia at home in the 2012–13 season. Dravid explained that while he knew that he would do well in the next season, he felt that Indian cricket stood to gain if a youngster were to play instead. Ten Tests would give a newcomer the opportunity to attune himself to Test cricket in familiar conditions, he explained.

Another selfless character felt the same way. Laxman could not add to his tally of six Test centuries in Australia on the 2011–12 tour. He was keen to bow out on a high note and started training at the NCA for what he believed would be his last season. A couple of weeks before the New Zealand series, he read a newspaper article where the writer wondered whether he would be rested for the New Zealand series, or he would play so that he could regain form before the tussles against England and Australia.

The article made Laxman introspect. He concluded that he had nothing left to prove and reasoned that it would be better if a youngster were to be blooded instead. He too announced his retirement with immediate effect.

India beat New Zealand 2-0, but Dravid and Laxman were sorely missed in the home series against England that followed. In what was a repeat of 1984–85, the visitors recovered from a defeat in the first Test to win the series 2-1. Alastair Cook, who had scored a century on his Test debut on England's 2005–06 tour of India, batted exceptionally, as did Kevin Pietersen. The Indian bowlers were outbowled by their English counterparts. It was India's first series defeat at home since 2004. The mood of the fans did not improve with a 1-1 tie and 1-2 loss in the T20 and ODI series against the Pakistani tourists.

The Australians, who arrived in India for a Test series in early 2013, could not be blamed for fancying themselves as the favourites. India were 12-2 in the first Test in Chennai when Tendulkar initiated a recovery with an innings of 81. Kohli got 107 and Dhoni muscled his way to 224. These knocks turned the match and morale of the players.

The most significant feature of India's 4-0 victory in the Test series was the performance of the youngsters. Pujara, who had scored a double century and a century against England, scored another double century, as well as a couple of fifties. Murali Vijay, the opener, had scores of 167 and 153 in consecutive Tests. Shikhar Dhawan, the left-handed opener who replaced the luckless Sehwag for the third Test, scored 187 on his debut. The bowling table was topped by Ravichandran Ashwin, an off-spinner from Chennai, and Ravindra Jadeja, the left-armer from Rajkot, who took 29 and 24 wickets, respectively.

Speculation on Tendulkar's future was inevitable after the exits of Dravid and Laxman. Ten months after he had announced his retirement from ODIs, the master informed the world through a media release that the two-Test series against the West Indies in November 2013 would be his last. He requested the BCCI to schedule the last Test—his two-hundredth—at the Wankhede Stadium, his home ground.

India won the first Test in Kolkata and the second in Mumbai in less than three days each. Rohit Sharma scored centuries in his first two Tests, but he was overshadowed by the colossus. Much to the disappointment of all those who had flocked to the Wankhede Stadium to bid farewell to their hero, Tendulkar fell 26 runs short of a century in his last Test innings.

After delivering an emotional address and before completing a lap of the ground, the maestro made his way to the centre, all by himself, to pay obeisance to the 22 yards that meant everything to him. Hours after the Test ended, the government announced its decision to confer the Bharat Ratna, the country's highest civilian honour, on the pride of India.

50
BOYS IN BLUE, MEN IN BLACK

Adalat kyun jaayegi? Adalat mein to koi football *khelta nahin.*

(Why go to court? Nobody plays football there.)

This is how Arun, the protagonist of *Mr. India*, one of the most popular Hindi films of all time, reacts when his tenant threatens to take to court the football that a group of children are playing with.

Fact, they say, is stranger than fiction. There came a time in the mid-2010s when people joked that cricket was being played more in the courts than on the field.

Ricky Ponting's acquisition by Mumbai Indians in 2013 meant that the protagonists of the Monkeygate affair—Harbhajan, Tendulkar, Kumble (mentor) and Ponting himself—were now teammates. Andrew Symonds would have also been there, had he not retired in 2012.

This was one of many instances of the IPL bringing together erstwhile rivals and bridging communication gaps.

Ponting, who was appointed captain, subsequently dropped himself and handed the reins to Rohit Sharma, who led Mumbai Indians to their first title. However, the 2013 season of the IPL was overshadowed by a spot-fixing scandal.

It all began with the arrest of three members of a franchise. An individual linked to another franchise whose team was led by Dhoni and owned by the BCCI president was also arrested on charges of betting. Dhoni was criticized for being silent on the controversy before the Indian team left for England to play the Champions Trophy.

This was followed by the resignations of the secretary and treasurer of the BCCI, in protest at the manner in which the issue was being handled. Never before had the board encountered a crisis of this magnitude.

India excelled in the seventh edition of the Champions Trophy, winning all five games. Shikhar Dhawan combined well with Rohit Sharma at the top of the order and scored two centuries, while Jadeja bagged 12 wickets.

The team's success pleased board officials and fans, but the spot-fixing controversy raged on. With the BCCI president refusing to step down, a compromise solution was worked out wherein the former stepped aside till a commission appointed to investigate the charges completed its task. Jagmohan Dalmiya was then named interim president. The commission appointed by the board exonerated the accused and Srinivasan re-assumed charge at the board's AGM in September 2013, but not for long, as it turned out.

The unrest was not confined to the corridors of the BCCI. The same phase also witnessed a standoff between the BCCI and Cricket South Africa over India's proposed tour of South Africa in November 2013. In July 2013, CSA announced the schedule, which comprised three Tests, seven ODIs and two T20 Internationals, but the BCCI raised objections and invited the West Indies over to play two Tests and three ODIs, also in November 2013.

> Every other country, during their main season, has got sufficient international teams touring them. We found that this year, most of the time we are out. So Indian cricket fans

need to see Indian players play in front of them, which is why we invited the West Indies.

—N. Srinivasan, *The Times of India*[52]

The deadlock was broken when the CSA president flew to Mumbai to meet his counterpart. The BCCI agreed to play two Tests and three ODIs in South Africa in December 2013.

The opening Test of the series, played in Johannesburg, was also India's first after the end of the Tendulkar era. It turned out to be a thriller, in which South Africa came close to overhauling a target of 438, but were held to a draw. The hosts won the second by ten wickets. Pujara, Kohli and Ajinkya Rahane, the successors of the batting geniuses of the 2000s, batted well in the series.

The next assignment in New Zealand was one that got away. Leading by 301 in the first innings of the first Test in Auckland, the hosts were bowled out for 105 in their second innings by the fast-bowling combine of Zaheer, Ishant and Mohammed Shami. India then reached 366 in pursuit of a target of 407, with Dhawan and Kohli scoring 115 and 67 respectively. Had even one batter supported them, the match would have been won.

Ishant and Shami bowled New Zealand out for 192 in the second Test in Wellington, after Dhoni inserted the opposition in. India replied with 438. The hosts were 78-3 in their second innings when Kohli, standing at an unorthodox silly mid-on, failed to grab an easy chance offered by Brendon McCullum. The New Zealand captain then made the Indians pay by scoring 302 off his own bat. Although Kohli scored a hundred in the second innings, the match was drawn and New Zealand took the series.

The limited-overs contests in South Africa and New Zealand were equally disappointing. India then failed to qualify for the

---

[52]PTI, 'Srini Says Lorgat Not Reason Behind Not Finalizing SA's Tour', *The Times of India*, 10 October 2013, https://tinyurl.com/5yt7xzy4. Accessed on 18 July 2025.

final of the Asia Cup in Bangladesh, in which Kohli led in Dhoni's absence.

Dhoni was back for the fourth edition of the T20 World Cup, which was also played in Bangladesh. The Indians made it to the final, but 130-4 was all they could score against Sri Lanka, who won easily. Yuvraj, who had battled a tumour and chemotherapy to return to international cricket, was pilloried for his 11 off 21 balls.

The BCCI managed to hold two-thirds of the 2014 season of the IPL in India despite the general elections, but the season was preceded by dramatic developments. The Supreme Court directed Srinivasan to step down after its three-member committee, headed by Mukul Mudgal, former Chief Justice of the Punjab and Haryana High Court, investigated the IPL corruption charges and submitted its first report. This committee was constituted by the apex court after Aditya Verma, the representative of the Bihar Cricket Association, filed a writ petition in the High Court on the grounds that the BCCI's two-member committee that had cleared the accused in 2013 had not been formed in accordance with IPL rules. The HC upheld Verma's contention, as did the SC later.

Shivlal Yadav, the senior-most vice-president of the board, then took over as interim president and Sunil Gavaskar was requested to preside over IPL 2014. It turned out to an exciting season, with Kolkata Knight Riders winning their second title after 2012.

India returned from their England tour in mid-2014 with more questions than answers. After drawing the first Test, they won the second at Lord's by 95 runs. Needing 319 to win, England were 173-5 at lunch on the final day. Dhoni then instructed Ishant, who had taken three of the five wickets to fall, to dig the ball in. The field was set accordingly and the batters kept falling for the bait. Ishant finished with 7-76.

But then, the ghosts of the 2000s resurfaced. England won the next three Tests, including two by an innings. Dhoni was accused of letting things drift on the field, but the biggest setback was the failure of Kohli, who scored only 134 runs in ten innings.

By the time the team flew to Australia later that year, there was a new coaching staff on board, with Duncan Fletcher, who had succeeded Kirsten in 2011, making way for Ravi Shastri. He had for support Bharat Arun, Sanjay Bangar and R. Sridhar to handle the bowling, batting and fielding departments, respectively.

Kohli made his captaincy debut in the first Test in Adelaide in the absence of the injured Dhoni. He went in with India at 111-2 in response to Australia's 517-7, and was hit on the helmet by Mitchell Johnson, who had blown the English away in the Ashes the previous year. Had Kohli taken a backward step, the series could well have become a repeat of 2011-12. But he did not, and scored 115. In the second innings, he stuck to his resolve to go for the target of 364, never mind if that meant risking defeat. India lost by just 48 runs.

Kohli's twin hundreds set the tone for the rest of the series. Australia lost six wickets while chasing 128 to win in the second Test in Brisbane. The next two Tests were drawn. Steve Smith scored 769 runs in the series, but Kohli was not very far behind, with 692 runs and four centuries. Unlike 2011-12, he did not wage a lone battle. Rahane, who had scored a match-winning hundred at Lord's earlier that year, scored 147 in Melbourne. Murali Vijay was also consistent, and K.L. Rahul, a batter from Karnataka, made an impressive entry into Test cricket with a century in the fourth Test in Sydney. Australia won the series 2-0, but the Indians were by no means disgraced as they were in 2011-12.

By the time the series ended, Kohli had been formally appointed Test captain, with M.S. Dhoni announcing his retirement from the traditional format at the end of the Melbourne Test.

The core of the side stayed on in Australia for the 2015 World Cup. The defending champions won seven games in a row before having their first bad day in the semi-final. Australia batted first and scored 328-7, and India could muster only 233 in response.

India toured Sri Lanka later that year. After losing the first Test despite being in a winning position, Kohli's team hit back in the next two games. All the batters got going, with Pujara opening the batting in the last Test and carrying his bat through to score 145. Ashwin took 21 wickets, and Amit Mishra, the leggie, bagged 15. Another highlight of the series was Rahane's eight catches in the first Test, the highest by a non-wicketkeeper in a Test match.

India lost a high-scoring ODI series against South Africa at home at the start of the 2015–16 season, but dominated the Test series that followed. The South African batting disintegrated on turners; their highest score in seven innings was 214. Ashwin took 31 wickets. However, the Indian batters were also tested, and it wasn't until the last game at Delhi that an Indian got the measure of the South African bowling. Rahane scored a century in each innings and Kohli got 88 in the second.

51

WALKING THE TALK

Narendra Modi was sworn in as India's fourteenth prime minister after the Bharatiya Janata Party and its allies swept the general elections in 2014. Coincidentally, Virat Kohli, who gave the impression of being as patriotic, passionate and committed to his cause as the new prime minister, captained India for the first time in the country's most popular sport, in the same year.

The rise of Modi and Kohli coincided with the advent of social media platforms in India, be it Facebook, Twitter (rebranded X in 2023), Instagram and WhatsApp. It happened to be a time when jingoism started getting the better of patriotism. The urge to create a splash on social media, coupled with a decline in the attention spans of people, made it easier for some to foment a narrative that India and Indian cricket had achieved nothing before Modi and Kohli took charge in their respective domains. Nothing could be further than the truth, of course, and the battle against the distortion of history has been going on ever since.

India lost an ODI series in Australia in early 2016, despite two centuries and a 91 by Kohli. He was in tremendous form in the T20 World Cup at home, with match-winning innings against Pakistan and Australia. The quarter-final was preceded by a humdinger in Bengaluru against Bangladesh, who bungled by trying to end the game with big hits, when all they needed was two off the last three balls. Two wickets fell to catches in the outfield and Dhoni affected a run-out off the last ball, to steal victory by one run.

Kohli's 89 in the semi-final against the Windies helped India reach 192-2, but the opposition chased down the score. Royal Challengers Bangalore, the team Kohli led in the IPL, reached the 2016 final on the strength of his 973 runs in the season, but they lost to Sun Risers Hyderabad, the city's new franchise after Deccan Chargers was terminated in 2012.

The IPL defeat was Kohli's last setback of the year. He went on to lead India to a series win in the Caribbean, followed by victories over New Zealand and England at home. He scored a double hundred in all three series and his teammates were also prolific with bat and ball. Karun Nair, a batter from Karnataka, scored 303 against England in Chennai. However, he struggled in the subsequent series against Australia and thus failed to cement his spot in the XI. The preponderance of middle-order batters ensured that anybody who was not consistent, could never get a longer run.

The middle order made up for the absence of a stable opening pair, which had been an issue since the dissolution of the Sehwag-Gambhir partnership in 2012–13. Murali Vijay, K.L. Rahul and Shikhar Dhawan had not been as consistent as expected. Sehwag retired in 2015 and Gambhir was recalled for two Tests in 2016, before being dropped for good. On the other hand, Ashwin and Jadeja, the spin twins, were impossible to get away.

A couple of interesting cricketers had been added to the mix. Zaheer Khan's retirement in 2014 coincided with the rise of Jasprit Bumrah, a paceman from Ahmedabad with a short run-up and unconventional whippy action. He did well for Gujarat in the Ranji Trophy and Mumbai Indians in the IPL. Hardik Pandya, a promising fast-bowling all-rounder, also came to the fore. Wriddhiman Saha had done well on both sides of the stumps after replacing Dhoni in the Test side in 2014–15.

Dhoni stepped down as white-ball captain in January 2017. Kohli, the new all-format skipper, led India to ODI and T20 wins over England. His loss of batting form in the Test series against Australia in early 2017 did not hamper his belligerence. After losing the first Test in Pune, India won the second in Bangalore by 75 runs despite scoring only 189 in the first innings.

The testiness between the two teams intensified when Steve Smith, the Australian captain, looked towards the dressing-room to check if he ought to go for the decision-review system (DRS) after being declared out leg-before in the second innings. The umpires stepped in immediately, but the Indians were not amused. The third Test in Ranchi was drawn and Rahane led India to victory in the fourth Test at Dharamshala in the absence of the injured Kohli. The game saw an impressive debut by Kuldeep Yadav, a member of the rare breed of left-arm wrist spinners.

These successes helped Indian cricket tide over a difficult phase. Two years after the Supreme Court set up a committee headed by R.M. Lodha, former Chief Justice, to recommend changes in the BCCI as a follow-up to the report submitted by the Mudgal Committee, it removed Anurag Thakur, the board president, and Ajay Shirke, the secretary, from their respective posts on the grounds that the board had failed to implement the majority of the recommendations made by the Lodha Committee.

The SC appointed a Committee of Administrators (COA) to run the board till fresh elections were held in accordance with the Lodha Committee's recommendations. The COA comprised Vinod Rai, former Comptroller and Auditor General of India, Ramachandra Guha, historian and cricket writer, Diana Edulji, former captain of the Indian women's team, and Vikram Limaye, CEO and managing director of Infrastructure Development Finance Corporation (IDFC). They were to be assisted by Rahul Johri, who had been appointed CEO of the BCCI in 2016.

The COA took some constructive steps, but it was not a smooth ride. Guha and Limaye quit within a few months, and the other two gave the impression of not being on the same wavelength. The COA was eventually dissolved in 2019 without fulfilling its primary objective, which was to ensure that all the recommendations of the Lodha Committee were adopted by the BCCI and its member associations.

The Lodha Committee banned two IPL franchises, which had been in the eye of the 2013 storm, for two years. The players of both teams were offered to two temporary franchises for the 2016 and 2017 seasons. Both sides did well, with Gujarat Lions reaching the playoffs in 2016 and Rising Pune Supergiants losing the final in 2017.

India's ICC Champions Trophy campaign in 2017 ended in heartbreak. After four wins in five games, the 2013 winners were outplayed by Pakistan in the final at The Oval in London. Fakhar Zaman, the Pakistani opener, made the most of the reprieve that he got after being caught behind off a Bumrah no-ball, to score 114. After Pakistan finished with 338-4, Mohammed Amir shut India out of the match with the dismissals of Rohit, Kohli and Dhawan with only 33 on the board.

Anil Kumble, who had been appointed coach after the end of Shastri's stint in 2016, resigned after the final. While the performances of the team under his watch suggested that he had done well, he had fallen out with Kohli, who was quoted by the media as having said to board officials that the players did not like the 'intimidating' style of the coach. Those who knew Kumble as a players' man found the accusation hard to believe. His exit set into motion a chain of events that culminated with the return of Ravi Shastri.

Yuvraj Singh's 39 in the third ODI of a five-match series in the Caribbean turned out to be his last international appearance. The man who had piloted India to three World Cup triumphs from 2000 (under-19) to 2011 (fifty-over) announced his retirement in 2019.

The first of back-to-back series wins against Sri Lanka in 2017 was hugely significant, as it was the first time India had won all Tests in a series on foreign soil. The Indians had their moments in the first two Tests of their next series in South Africa, but they lost both games.

Intent to prove a point before the series ended, Kohli played five pacemen in the third Test in Johannesburg. From the time he elected to bat on an uneven pitch that was described by many as dangerous, the Indians did not let up. South Africa scored 194 to India's 187 in the first innings, but the Indians got themselves in front in the second innings, with fighting knocks by the captain and Rahane, who was hit on the elbow but defied the pain, in his first Test of the series. Needing 247 to win, South Africa were comfortably placed at 136-1, but once Hashim Amla fell to Ishant, there was a procession. So well did he, Shami, Bumrah and Bhuvneshwar Kumar bowl that Hardik Pandya, the fifth pacer, barely got a look-in. India won by 63 runs.

That victory, as well as the 203-run win over England at Nottingham later that year, prompted Shastri to say that the Indian team had the potential to become the best travelling side in the world. However, the critics sniggered in response after the tour of England in 2018 ended with a 1-4 defeat for Kohli and his team.

However, they could not question Kohli's genius. The batter who had scored 134 runs on the previous tour, scored 593 runs in 2018, inclusive of two centuries. James Anderson, who had toyed with him in 2014, took 24 wickets in 2018, but he could not make an impression on the Indian captain this time around.

52

VICTORS DOWN UNDER

> This is not a team of gods or demigods, or seniors or juniors. This is an Indian cricket team that will jump over a cliff to win a game for the country.
>
> —Ravi Shastri at a media conference in Sydney, January 2019

India defeated Bangladesh in last-ball finishes in two Asia Cup finals in 2018, both under the captaincy of Rohit Sharma, Kohli's white-ball deputy. Dinesh Kartik's 29 off eight balls took the team over the line in the T20 final in Colombo in March. Six months later, India overhauled a target of 223 in the final of the fifty-over version in Dubai. Kohli subsequently led India to victory in a one-sided Test series against the West Indies.

Cricket's oldest format could not have found a bigger and better brand ambassador in the T20 age than Virat Kohli. He did not miss out on a single opportunity to assert Test cricket's paramountcy. He had already displayed his faith in pace, which he believed was the key to success overseas. While he was lucky to have at his disposal a slew of speedsters, it must also be noted that he was competent enough to get the best out of them. He smelt an opportunity to create history when the Indian team, with most of its members in their prime, arrived in Australia for a four-Test series in November 2018.

The visitors were 41-4 in the first innings of the first Test in Adelaide before Pujara came to the rescue with his 123. India's 250 turned out to be a winning score. The Indian bowlers hunted in a pack to secure a victory by 31 runs. Australia levelled the series in the second Test in Perth, but they were outplayed in the Boxing Day Test in Melbourne.

Fine batting by Pujara, Rohit and Kohli himself enabled India to declare at 443-7. The Indians then did not enforce the follow-on despite taking a 292-run lead. Australia, ultimately set a target of 399 to win, were dismissed for 261. India's bowling hero was Bumrah, who took nine wickets in the match.

Pujara's 193 apart, the highlight of the last Test in Sydney was an innings of 159 by Rishabh Pant, a wicketkeeping all-rounder who had first excelled in junior cricket and scored his first Test hundred against England in 2018. India declared at 622-7 and would have won had rain not intervened. Kohli thus became the first Indian captain to win a Test series in Australia. Pujara was declared the player of the series for his three centuries, but Bumrah and Shami ran him close with 21 and 16 wickets, respectively.

England apart, India outplayed every opponent at the round-robin stage of the ICC Cricket World Cup 2019, to top the table with 15 points. Their league encounter against New Zealand was washed out. Rohit scored a record five centuries as opener and—with Kohli and K.L. Rahul—ensured that the withdrawal of Dhawan due to a broken finger was not felt.

In the semi-final, India restricted New Zealand to 239-8, but they started their innings disastrously with Rohit, Rahul and Kohli falling with only five on the board. Dhoni and Jadeja added 116, but for once, the former captain's time-and-tested stratagem of stretching the game as much as possible and then imposing himself on the opposition, backfired. He was run out in the penultimate over and India were dismissed for 221 with three deliveries left.

Dhoni did not represent India again. He formally announced his retirement on 15 August 2020.

An all-format triumph in the Caribbean was followed by a serendipitous development in the first of three Tests against South Africa in Visakhapatnam. Rohit Sharma, who had not been as consistent in Tests as he had been in the white-ball formats, was asked to open in the red-ball format as well. He responded with a century in each innings, setting up a victory by 203 runs.

India swept the series against South Africa as well as Bangladesh, before the law of averages caught up with them in New Zealand. They lost both Tests before the world locked itself up.

The rescheduled 2020 season of the IPL got underway in the UAE in September, amidst a slew of COVID protocols. A group of players flew to Australia after the league, to play a Test series that went down in history.

Honours were shared in the ODIs and T20Is that preceded the Tests. Kohli, who was to go on paternity leave after the first Test—a pink-ball affair in Adelaide—won the toss and batted excellently. He was on 74 when he was run out in a mix-up with Rahane, his deputy. India declined to 244 all out, but their bowlers secured a first-innings lead of 53.

Then came the nightmare. India were blown away for 36 in the second innings, their lowest Test score. Even as the Australians completed an eight-wicket win, the pundits predicted a 4-0 rout for the team that apart from being humiliated, had also lost its skipper and premier batter.

The twist that followed was unexpected. Ashwin's early introduction into the attack in the next Test in Melbourne took the Australians by surprise. India owed its first-innings lead of 131 to Rahane, whose 112 was arguably the greatest Test innings by an Indian captain, considering the circumstances in which it was essayed. The Indian bowlers then ensured that the batters had to score only 70 to win.

Tim Paine, the Australian captain, declared his second innings in the third Test in Sydney, 406 ahead. Pant's arrival at the crease at 102-3 on the fifth morning heralded a storm. With Pujara keeping things steady at the other end, the visitors were on course for an incredible win when Pant fell, only three short of a century. The Australians went for the kill after dismissing Pujara just two runs later, but they were thwarted by an injured duo. Hanuma Vihari, who tore his hamstring on the field, and Ashwin, who was dogged by a painful lower back, stood firm for 42.4 overs. In the final Test at Brisbane, India went the distance in dramatic style.

Kohli returned for the Test series against England in which Chennai and Ahmedabad hosted two games each. India won 3-1 after losing the first Test on tracks that offered generous turn. Ashwin and Axar Patel, the left-arm spinner, shared 59 wickets between them.

The spinners handed over the baton to the quicks at Lord's in the second Test of a five-match series in England in mid-2021. Rahul and Rohit batted well, but the hosts took a first-innings lead of 27. The Indian lower order then batted brilliantly in the second innings, with Shami and Bumrah adding 89. England were set a target of 272 in a minimum of 60 overs.

The Indian pacers proceeded to follow to perfection their captain's instructions to 'give the batters hell'. Shami and Bumrah, both of whom did not need to warm up after their heroics with the bat, reduced the hosts to 1-2. Siraj completed what his seniors had started, finishing with four wickets. England were dismissed for 120 in 51.5 overs.

Joe Root, the England captain, led a comeback in the next Test in Leeds with a century, and the hosts won by an innings and 76 runs. They then took a first-innings lead of 99 in the fourth Test at The Oval, but the Indians scored 466 in the second innings, with Rohit getting 127. Chasing 368, the England openers put on 100 before Shardul Thakur broke through, having Rory Burns caught behind. The visitors then stormed the breach and the next nine wickets fell for 110 runs.

India led 2-1 and therefore held the initiative on the eve of the final Test, but COVID played spoilsport. A member of the team's support staff tested positive, and the other members isolated themselves as a result. The two boards decided to play the final Test in the following year.

The 2021 season of the IPL began in India in April but had to be aborted due to the outbreak of the second wave of COVID. It was rescheduled and completed in the UAE in September 2021. It was followed by the T20 World Cup in the same country. India missed out on a semi-final spot after losing their first two games against Pakistan and New Zealand respectively.

The communal overtones that were laced by some former Pakistani cricketers to their team's ten-wicket win over India, underscored the ideological and intellectual differences between the subcontinental neighbours, which had only widened as the years went by. In 2021, Pakistan was a failed state, stricken by religious bigotry, bankruptcy and terrorism. On the other hand, the Indians, who had chosen nation over religion at the time of Independence, were reaping the benefits of patience and perseverance.

53
CHAMPS AGAIN

As a BCCI employee, I was around when an interesting conversation took place between a national selector and a board official, shortly after the Indian team was picked for the third edition of the T20 World Cup, which was to be played in the Caribbean in May 2010. The selector informed the official that Rohit Sharma had been the last player to be chosen. 'We know that he is talented, but we cannot keep picking someone only because he is talented. Please let him know that he needs to start performing,' the selector advised.

Rohit produced an innings of 79 against Australia in the T20 World Cup, but his performances continued to be erratic, and he consequently missed out on a spot in the Indian team for the fifty-over World Cup in 2011. He later said that the setback changed his life.

More than a decade later, Kohli resigned as India's T20 captain after a disappointing 2021 World Cup in the UAE. He was succeeded by Rohit Sharma, who was also assigned the job for the ODIs, as the selectors made it clear that they wanted the same captain in both white-ball formats. A few days later, Kohli resigned as Test captain as well. That signalled the end of a remarkable run, in which he had led in 68 Tests and won 40, 16 of them overseas. Kohli denied the claim made by Sourav Ganguly, who had been elected board president in 2019, that the selectors had requested him to continue as T20 captain. However, Ganguly's version was corroborated by a senior selector who was stung by a TV network. A story did the rounds that Rohit was not keen on the Test captaincy, but he was convinced to take up the job by the board president.

Kohli's last hurrah as Test captain was a series win against New Zealand at home, the second Test of which witnessed a 'perfect ten' by Ajaz Patel, the Mumbai-born left-arm spinner representing the Kiwis. The South Africa tour that followed was a repeat of 2006–07, in that the visitors won the first Test but squandered away the advantage in the next two.

Rohit Sharma won his first Test series as captain against Sri Lanka, but he missed the rescheduled final Test against England that had been pending since 2021 due to injury. For that one-off Test, India had a new captain in Bumrah. A new support staff with Rahul Dravid, Paras Mhambrey and T. Dilip had also taken over as head coach, bowling coach and fielding coach, respectively, after the T20 World Cup in 2021. Vikram Rathour—the batting coach in the previous dispensation—stayed on. India controlled the Test for three days but eventually lost ground. Needing 378 to win, England won by seven wickets.

Remarkably, seven players—Dhawan, K.L. Rahul, Pant, Pandya, Bumrah, Kohli and Rohit—led India in 2022. The investments made by the board and its member associations in developing infrastructure in the 2000s, as well as the advent of the IPL and the decision to give more exposure to the India A side overseas, had yielded an abundance of cricketing talent, which in turn enabled the selectors to rest and rotate players. Indian cricket was also reaping the benefits of a competitive domestic structure. The sport's transformation from an urban phenomenon to a national entity was evident in the compositions of Indian teams of the 2000s and 2010s. It also became apparent from the winners of the Ranji Trophy; from 2016–17 to 2024–25, the title was won by Gujarat, Vidarbha (thrice), Saurashtra (twice) and

Madhya Pradesh, all of whom had been considered lightweights for decades. The exception was Mumbai, who won in 2023–24.

Every effort was made to ensure that the marquee players were fresh and raring to go for big events like the T20 World Cup in 2022, which was held in Australia. India's last-ball win in their opening game against Pakistan was engineered by Kohli, who scored an incredible 82 off 55 balls. However, the Indians were knocked out by England, the eventual winners, in the semi-final.

India beat Australia 2-1 in the next edition of the Border-Gavaskar Trophy, but the cynics continued to question the wisdom of playing on rank turners, on which matches finished in three days. Ashwin once again topped the table with 25 wickets, with Jadeja and Nathan Lyon sharing the second spot with 22 wickets each.

A loss to Australia in the second ICC Test Championship final in June 2023 did not obscure the fact that the Indians had played excellent Test cricket over a period of four years to reach two consecutive Test championship finals. They had lost the first ICC World Test Championship final to New Zealand in 2021. Having reached at least the final four in all ICC limited-overs tournaments since 2013 (with the exception of the T20 World Cup in 2021), the players—and their fans—hoped to go the distance in their own backyard, in 2023.

The ICC Cricket World Cup 2023 was the first to be hosted exclusively by India. The hosts went into the tournament after winning the Asia Cup and an ODI series against Australia. In earlier World Cups, batters had outshone bowlers, 1983 and 2003 excepted. 2023 was unprecedented, in that the bowlers outdid the batters despite the brilliance of the latter, that too in batting-friendly conditions. India's margins of victory in their last four league matches spoke for themselves. They beat England by 100 runs in Lucknow, then bowled Sri Lanka out for 55 to win by 302 runs in Mumbai, dismissed South Africa for 82 to win by 243 runs in Kolkata, and subsequently trounced Netherlands by

160 runs. The pace triumvirate of Bumrah, Shami and Siraj was unstoppable. India beat New Zealand by 70 runs in the semi-final in Mumbai to set up a title clash with Australia in Ahmedabad.

However, the tournament ended in tears. Australia chased down a target of 240 with seven overs to spare. Kohli scored 765 runs, the highest ever by any player in a single World Cup, and became the first batter to complete a half-century of ODI centuries. Mohammed Shami, who missed India's first four matches, topped the bowling table with 24 wickets in the tournament.

Three months later, India lost to England in the first Test of a five-match series despite taking a first-innings lead of 190. With Kohli on paternity leave again, Rahane and Pujara not considered, and Pant recuperating from a dreadful road accident, it was all up to Rohit to mentor a young batting line-up. The turnaround was sensational.

Yashasvi Jaiswal, who had scored a century on his debut against the West Indies in 2022, scored a record 712 runs in the series, inclusive of two double centuries. He and a slew of young talents—Shubman Gill, Dhruv Jurel, Sarfaraz Khan and Devdutt Padikkal—rallied around their captain, who aggregated 400 runs himself, inclusive of two match-winning centuries. The bowling plans were executed to perfection by Ashwin, Jadeja, Kuldeep Yadav and Bumrah.

The players were determined to break the ICC jinx in the 2024 T20 World Cup. India beat Ireland in their opening game, but the batters struggled in the next encounter against Pakistan. With only 120 to defend, Bumrah led his team's fightback and India won by six runs. The Indians then beat the US, Afghanistan and Bangladesh, before meeting their nemeses of 2023 in the semi-final.

As he made his way to bat after being put in by Australia, the Indian captain was mindful of the need to grab the initiative. He did just that with a sensational 92 off 59 balls, and India finished with 205-5. Travis Head, Australia's hero of the ODI World Cup final, threatened to play spoilsport again, but he fell to Bumrah at a crucial stage. Arshdeep Singh, the left-arm paceman, applied the brakes in the final stages to restrict Australia to 181-7.

For the better part of the final, which was played at Bridgetown, Barbados, on 29 June 2024, it seemed that the original chokers of limited-overs cricket would prevail over a side that had choked way too often in the previous decade. India batted first and scored 176-7, thanks to Kohli's 76 and Axar Patel's 47. However, the South Africans chased well. With four overs left, they needed only 26, with five wickets in hand.

At this stage, Rishabh Pant, who had returned to the side by then, complained of a niggle in his knee and called the physio. The break gave the Indians a timeout of sorts. The first ball of the seventeenth over, bowled by Hardik Pandya, was slightly wide, which Heinrich Klaasen chased, probably a consequence of his having lost focus after the unforeseen break. The ball kissed his bat and Pant snapped it up. The over produced only four runs.

The situation demanded a Bumrah special. India's premier bowler delivered in the eighteenth over, conceding only two and, most critically, breaching the defences of Marco Jansen. South Africa now needed 20 from 12 balls.

David Miller and Keshav Maharaj could score only four in the nineteenth over, bowled by Arshdeep. On strike for the first ball of the final over, with his side needing 16, Miller biffed a Pandya full toss high and straight. Just when it looked like it would hurdle over the long-off boundary, Suryakumar Yadav came in the way. He caught the ball and then flicked it back into the playing arena, just before his feet crossed the rope. He then stepped back into the arena and caught it again. A boundary by Kagiso Rabada and three extras, including a wide, brought the equation down to nine from two balls.

Rabada swung hard at the next ball but could not clear Yadav. A token final delivery later, Rohit Sharma sank to the ground. The last player to be selected in the Indian team for a T20 World

Cup in the Caribbean in 2010 had led India to victory in the next T20 World Cup that was held there—14 years later.

His teammates, many of whom had been in the XI that had lost the ODI World Cup final just seven months ago, could not hold back tears. At the presentation ceremony, even the stoic Rahul Dravid gave vent to his emotions.

Lakhs turned up for a victory parade on Mumbai's Marine Drive, which culminated with a felicitation of the team at the Wankhede Stadium.

EPILOGUE

Indian cricket was being run and financed by the royalty when the inaugural Test was played in 1932. As the decades passed, the royalty made way for industrialists, lawyers and politicians.

An intense battle for one-upmanship among the royals took place in 1934 during the final of the Moin-ud-Dowlah Gold Cup in Hyderabad, played between the Patiala Retrievers—backed by Bhupinder Singh—and Vizzy's Freebooters. The Retrievers comprised players like C.K. Nayudu, Wazir and Nazir Ali, Mohammed Nissar and Lala Amarnath. On the other hand, the Freebooters had Vijay Merchant and L.P. Jai in the XI. Amarnath scored a match-winning 104.

Decades later, there have been similar contests between IPL teams owned by the *new royalty*, which comprises entrepreneurs and film stars.

The players of 2025 are content to do their bit on the field and leave the rest to the administrators and in the case of the IPL, team-owners, both of whom are taking good care of them. Many of Nayudu's contemporaries, who were on the payrolls of the princes, felt the same way.

In that sense, 1932 is not very different from 2025; except that in this age, cricketers and the game's new patrons have together ensured that India—treated as a cricketing outpost for decades—has become the hub of the sport in terms of popularity, commerce and, most significantly, success.

India's first marquee series after the victory in the T20 World Cup in 2024 was the Australia tour, which took place five months later. It was preceded by visits by Bangladesh and New Zealand. India outplayed its neighbour, first in Chennai and then in a dramatic game in Kanpur. What looked like a certain draw after two whole days were lost to rain and poor drainage facilities, was turned on its head with audacious batting, a timely declaration and then a splendid bowling performance that left the home team with only 95 to get on the last afternoon.

Bengaluru, the venue of the first Test against the touring New Zealanders who had last won a Test in India in 1988, was overcast, and the wicket appeared to have something in it for the quicks. However, the Indians still elected to bat. It turned out to be a monumental blunder.

The New Zealand pacers bowled the hosts out for 46 and their batters then closed the game out with a lead of 356. Although India batted well in the second innings, with Sarfaraz Khan scoring his maiden Test hundred, it was never going to be enough. New Zealand won by eight wickets.

The Indian spinners were then outdone by their New Zealand counterparts on turning tracks in the next two Tests. Left-armers Mitchell Santner and Ajaz Patel as well as offie Glenn Phillips bowled their team to victory in the second Test in Pune by 113 runs and in the third in Mumbai by 25 runs.

India's 0-3 defeat was embarrassing. However, it was by no means the first instance of the Indian team coming a cropper against slow bowling on its own soil. Richie Benaud in 1956–57, Lance Gibbs in 1974–75, Derek Underwood in 1976–77, Phil Edmonds and Pat Pocock in 1984–85, Iqbal Qasim and Tauseef Ahmed in 1986–87 and Monty Panesar and Graeme Swann in 2012–13 had won series for their respective teams in India, years before the New Zealanders caused one of the greatest upsets in cricket history.

Stats suggest that the Indian batters of the 2000s handled spin on turning wickets a lot better than their predecessors and successors. Shane Warne and Muttiah Muralitharan, both of whom are considered the greatest spinners of all time, struggled in India in the late 1990s and 2000s.

The defeat against New Zealand prompted many to predict a 0-5 rout in Australia. However, the underdogs delivered a stunning performance in the first Test in Perth. India's 295-run win changed equations and projections, only for things to fall apart. The batters let the bowlers down badly in the games that followed. Old habits indeed died hard.

Since 2008, it has become customary to blame the IPL whenever Indian batting has flopped. However, the fact that tends to be missed when this happens is that India had been bundled out for double-digit scores and failed to extend matches beyond the third day many times even before the IPL came into being.

The 20th century witnessed some outstanding batting performances by Indians overseas, but it was only in the new millennium that the batters started delivering consistently as a unit—as opposed to individually—on foreign soil. This was the natural consequence of an increase in the number of tours undertaken by the team, which could be attributed to its rising box-office appeal, courtesy the Indian diaspora and the BCCI's own ascent. The batters got more opportunities to play and get attuned to alien conditions. For instance, India toured Australia six times from 1947 to 1992, but eight times between 1999 and 2025.

It could be contended that the wheel came full circle in Australia in 2025. The batters in India's first Test squad of 1932 were overshadowed by the new-ball pair of Mohammed Nissar and Amar Singh. History repeated itself 93 years later, when Bumrah bowled his heart out to take more wickets than some of the greatest fast bowlers of all time in a series on Australian soil until his back acted up in the last Test. It was a heartbreaking end to a series, in which he also led India in the first and last Tests. Ravichandran Ashwin, off-spinner par excellence and one of the greatest match-winners of all time, ended a career in which he did his country and himself proud.

Natwarsinghji Bhavsinhji, the captain of the 1932 team, who was mindful of his modest cricketing abilities, stepped aside on the eve of India's inaugural Test, as he was keen that India be represented by its best outfit. Decades later, he was emulated by Rohit Sharma, a far superior cricketer and India's thirty-fifth Test captain, who opted out of the country's 589th Test against Australia in Sydney because he was out of form.

The saga of men's cricket in India has been replete with emotion, drama, tragedy and triumph. It has featured dramatic leaps and plunges, unforeseen twists and turns, as well as traditions that endure. Indian cricket has witnessed some debilitating lows, but every crisis has only made it more resilient. The debutant of 1932 has enjoyed spells at the summit in all three formats of the sport. India first won the World Cup in 1983, triumphed in the inaugural T20 World Cup in 2007 and topped the ICC Test Rankings for the first time in 2009. However, staying on the summit after scaling it has been a challenge.

Indian teams were never as successful as the top Australian and West Indian sides, simply because they struggled to take twenty wickets in Tests overseas. From 1932 to 1999, India won only 13 of 155 away Tests. The paucity of fast-bowling firepower was to blame. A lot of outstanding spinners did play, and they even did the nation proud abroad in 1967–68 and 1971, but there was a limit to their effectiveness in foreign conditions. The wait for a paceman ended with the emergence of Kapil Dev, but his rise coincided with a plateau on the spin front. The slow men who succeeded the illustrious spin quartet and bowled alongside Kapil Dev failed to live up to their potential.

By the time Kumble arrived in the early 1990s, Kapil Dev was past his prime. Srinath had appeared on the scene as well, but he was sidelined on turning wickets at home after playing his first ten Tests overseas. Bizarre scheduling ensured that the Indian team did not undertake a single tour outside the subcontinent from January 1993 to June 1996 but for a one-off Test in New Zealand. Srinath did form a potent new-ball partnership with Venkatesh Prasad in 1996 but the combination ran out of steam because it lacked support in the form of back-up pacemen. The workload took its toll on Srinath's shoulder.

The inability of Kumble to click overseas in the 1990s also did not help. It was not a coincidence that India's overseas record improved when its premier spinner struck form abroad in the early 2000s. The pacemen and spinners combined with splendid effect in the years that followed, especially in the late 2010s. From 2000 to 2025, India has registered 50 wins in 143[53] away Tests.

After the reverses against New Zealand and Australia in the 2024–25 season came the revival. India went into the ninth edition of the ICC Champions Trophy in February 2025 on the back of wins in white-ball series against England. In Dubai, where they played all their matches of the Champions Trophy, the Indians proved just why they were the envy of the cricketing world. Shubman Gill, the new ODI vice-captain, and veterans Kohli and Rohit were outstanding with the bat, as was Shreyas Iyer, who had also done well in the 2023 World Cup. If the pacers had excelled in the recent past, the Indian team returned to its roots in the Champions Trophy, with Rohit Sharma deploying an unprecedented four spinners in the playing XI. Axar Patel, Ravindra Jadeja, Kuldeep Yadav and Varun Chakravarthy were outstanding.

India beat New Zealand in the final on 9 March 2025, exactly forty years after India beat Pakistan in the final of the World Championship of Cricket (10 March 1985). The highlight of that tournament was Sunil Gavaskar's unprecedented use of two specialist spinners in an age wherein it was believed that spinners had no role to play in limited-overs cricket.

---

[53] At the end of the Oval Test against England in August 2025.

Epilogue

Gill became India's thirty-seventh men's Test captain in June 2025, a couple of months before he turned 26. Coincidentally, Vijay Merchant was the same age when he was handed the reins for the unofficial series against Lord Tennyson's team in 1937–38. Both captains happened to be steering sides in a state of transition during their respective tours of England.

However, the players proved that they were quick learners. The quality of their batting against a competitive bowling attack in pressure situations convinced even the cynics that the so-called *IPL generation* not only values the traditional form of the game but also wants to excel at it. Mohammed Siraj, who overcame the loss of his father to play a critical role in a famous series win in Australia in 2020–21, bowled like a champion in England, playing all five Tests and taking 23 wickets to enable his team to square the series.

The performance of the Indian team in England in 2025 suggests that the future of Test cricket is in good hands. It would be safe to conclude that the two limited-over formats will take care of themselves.

The abundance of batting, fast bowling, spin bowling and fielding talent at the domestic and junior levels, coupled with the infrastructure and opportunities provided by the BCCI and its member units for the talent to express itself, will ensure that India will remain a force in all three formats of the sport for times to come.

India has changed beyond recognition from 1932 to 2025, but there has been one constant. Then and now, cricket has transcended barriers of generation, geography, language, religion and economic status to unite a nation.

ACKNOWLEDGEMENTS

I extend my sincere thanks to Kapish Mehra and Rudra Sharma of Rupa Publications for giving me the opportunity to write this book.

I am grateful to the following individuals, groups and associations for their wishes, encouragement and support:

Prof. R.S. Shetty, Clayton Murzello, Charu Sharma, Medha Prabhudesai, Anuradha Satyanarayana, P.V. Satyanarayana, Chinmay Prabhudesai, Sonal Prabhudesai, Chaitanya Satyanarayana, Abhimanyu Prabhudesai, Ira Prabhudesai, Sara Prabhudesai, Rohini Ramnathan, Shailaja Mudhale, Nachiket Joshi, Savitha Vishwanathan, Rajendra Bhat, Prasoon Kanmadikar, Rohit Pandit, Vaman Apte, Arati Mantri, Abhishek Mukherjee, Bhavesh Singh Sabharwal, Timeless Melodies Group, Radio Nasha, Professional Management Group, Mumbai Cricket Association, Madhya Pradesh Cricket Association, and the BCCI.

BIBLIOGRAPHY

Adhikari, Somak, 'When This HUGE Mistake by Virat Kohli Cost MS Dhoni's Team India 293 Runs!', *MensXP*, 24 June 2024, https://tinyurl.com/mvk69mpz. Accessed on 21 July 2025.

Ali, Mushtaq, *Cricket Delightful: Mushtaq Ali's Own Story*, Rupa & Co., New Delhi, 1967.

Alter, Jamie, 'World Cup Countdown: A History of the 1987 Reliance World Cup', *CricketCountry*, 15 May 2019, https://tinyurl.com/yehfcx4m. Accessed on 21 July 2025.

Amarnath, Mohinder, and Rajinder Amarnath, *Fearless: A Memoir*, HarperCollins Publishers, New Delhi, 2024.

Amarnath, Rajinder, *Lala Amarnath—Life & Times: The Making of a Legend*, Rupa & Co., New Delhi, 2004.

Anthony, A. Joseph, and Jayanthi Jaisimha, *My Way: The Biography of M.L. Jaisimha*, Card Box Company, Hyderabad.

Bajaj, Sachin (ed.), *The Sardar of Spin: A Celebration of the Life and Art of Bishan Singh Bedi*, Roli Books, New Delhi, 2021.

Bala, Rajan, *All the Beautiful Boys*, Rupa & Co., New Delhi, 1990.

Berry, Scyld, *Cricket Wallah: with England in India, 1981-2*, Hodder & Stoughton, London, 1982.

Bharatan, Raju, *Indian Cricket: The Vital Phase*, Vikas Publishing House, New Delhi, 1977.

Bhatia, Rahul, 'Before the Flood', *The Caravan*, 1 February 2012, https://tinyurl.com/9a5uwhxr. Accessed on 21 July 2025.

Bhatia, Shyam, and Debasish Datta, *Sunny G*, Deep Prakashan, New Delhi, 2024.

Bhattacharya, Gautam, and Boria Majumdar, *1971: The Beginning of*

India's Cricketing Greatness, Harper Sport India, New Delhi, 2021.

Bhogle, Harsha, *Azhar: The Authorised Biography of Mohammed Azharuddin*, Viking, New Delhi, 1994.

Bhushan, Aditya, *A Colonel Destined to Lead*, Story Mirror Infotech Pvt Ltd, Mumbai, 2017.

Binoy, George, 'The Empire Strikes Back', *ESPNcricinfo*, 25 February 2013, https://tinyurl.com/yf2euvma. Accessed on 21 July 2025.

Biswas, Shom, and Titash Banerjea, *Of Spins, Sixes and Surprises: 50 Defining Moments in Indian Cricket*, Rupa Publications India, New Delhi, 2023.

'Blast From the Past: Top 10 Highest Buys of Inaugural 2008 IPL Auction', *The Times of India*, 14 February 2023, https://tinyurl.com/3tfm4abk. Accessed on 21 July 2025.

Board of Control for Cricket in India, *75 Years of the Ranji Trophy*, BCCI, Mumbai, 2009.

Board of Control for Cricket in India, *From Learners to Leaders*, BCCI, Mumbai, 2008.

Bombay (Mumbai) Cricket Association, *Golden Jubilee Volume*, Bombay Cricket Association, Mumbai, 1981.

Borde, Chandu, *Panther's Paces*, Anubandh Prakashan, Pune, 2018.

Bose, Mihir, *A History of Indian Cricket*, Andre Deutsch Ltd, London, 2002.

Bradman, Don, *Farewell to Cricket*, Rupa & Co., New Delhi, 1980.

Brar, Hemant, 'Maninder Singh: "I Had Nowhere to Go, So I Went to the Bottle"', *The Cricket Monthly*, 7 August 2019, https://tinyurl.com/wu3vv6zx. Accessed on 21 July 2025.

Brearley, Mike, *The Art of Captaincy*, Channel 4 Books, London, 2001.

Cantrell, John, *Farokh Engineer: From the Far Pavilion*, Tempus, Stroud, 2005.

Chappell, Greg, *Fierce Focus*, Hardie Grant Books, Melbourne, 2011.

Chuzzlewit, S.S., 'Bishan Bedi's Comments Predictably Sensational and Devoid of Substance', *CricketCountry*, 22 February 2016, https://tinyurl.com/yrrbee65. Accessed on 21 July 2025.

Coward, Mike, *Cricket Beyond the Bazaar*, Allen & Unwin, Sydney, 1990.

'CSK & RR Owners Suspended for Two Years', *ESPNcricinfo*, 14 July 2015, https://tinyurl.com/y65zszdj. Accessed on 21 July 2025.

Das, Ranit, 'Kohli's India Can Be the Best Travelling Side in the World: Ravi Shastri', *India Today*, 22 August 2018, https://tinyurl.com/fcw5mj28. Accessed on 21 July 2025.

Dev, Romi, *Kapil Dev: Triumph of the Spirit*, Allied Publishers Ltd, New Delhi, 1994.

Dikshit, Vishal, 'Virat Kohli Steps Down as India Test Captain', *ESPNcricinfo*, 15 January 2022, https://tinyurl.com/55dyn98r. Accessed on 21 July 2025.

Docker, Edward, *History of Indian Cricket*, Macmillan Company of India, Delhi, 1976.

Doshi, Dilip, *Spin Punch*, Rupa & Co., New Delhi, 1991.

'Dravid, Tendulkar and Ganguly Not in Twenty20 Probables', *ESPNcricinfo*, 7 July 2007, https://tinyurl.com/24zuvj5u. Accessed on 21 July 2025.

Engineer, Tariq, 'West Indies News: Chris Gayle Turns Down Central Contract', *ESPNcricinfo*, 29 September 2010, https://tinyurl.com/ypfd7p88. Accessed on 21 July 2025.

Evans, Colin, *Farokh: The Cricketing Cavalier*, Max Books, London, 2017.

Ezekiel, Gulu, 'On This Day in Chennai: Vinoo Mankad, Pankaj Roy Score Record 413-Run Stand', *Sportstar*, 7 January 2020, https://tinyurl.com/mr3am449. Accessed on 21 July 2025.

Ganguly, Sourav, and Gautam Bhattacharya, *A Century is Not Enough: My Roller-coaster Ride to Success*, Juggernaut Books, New Delhi, 2018.

Ghosh, Akash, 'India's Long List of Injuries on the Australian Tour of 2020–21', *CricTracker*, 12 January 2021, https://tinyurl.com/3z3ua8jj. Accessed on 21 July 2025.

Gollapudi, Nagraj, 'Anil Kumble Appointed India Head Coach', *ESPNcricinfo*, 23 June 2016, https://tinyurl.com/nse7z456. Accessed on 21 July 2025.

Gollapudi, Nagraj, 'Anil Kumble Resigns as Partnership With Virat Kohli Becomes Untenable', *ESPNcricinfo*, 20 June 2017, https://tinyurl.com/4hvdcs9p. Accessed on 21 July 2025.

Gollapudi, Nagraj, 'Supreme Court Names Administrators to Supervise BCCI', *ESPNcricinfo*, 30 January 2017, https://tinyurl.com/4wdk66nj. Accessed on 21 July 2025.

Guha, Ramachandra, *A Corner of a Foreign Field: The Indian History of a British Sport*, Pan Macmillan, London, 2002.

Guha, Ramachandra, *The States of Indian Cricket*, Permanent Black, Delhi, 2008.

Gupta, Shekhar, 'After a Debacle, New Indian Cricket Team Captain Dilip Vengsarkar Is on Probation', *India Today*, 15 December 1987, https://tinyurl.com/2yj3evwj. Accessed on 21 July 2025.

'Gupte: Kumble's Experience Should Have Been Utilised', *ESPNcricinfo*, 28 April 2002, https://tinyurl.com/3bjevk95. Accessed on 21 July 2025.

Hazare, Vijay, and V.K. Naik, *A Long Innings*, Rupa & Co., New Delhi, 1981.

Hazare, Vijay, and V.K. Naik, *Cricket Replayed*, Rupa & Co., Calcutta, 1974.

'History of ICC', *International Cricket Council*, https://tinyurl.com/yc64y3vb. Accessed on 21 July 2025.

Jagnam, Ashwin, 'A Glance Into the History of National Cricket Academy, Bengaluru', *StayFeatured*, 9 April 2023, https://tinyurl.com/yrmfaz24. Accessed on 21 July 2025.

Jaishankar, Vedam, *Casting a Spell: The Story of Karnataka Cricket*, UBSPD, New Delhi, 2005.

Jonathan Rice (ed.), *Wisden on India: An Anthology*, Bloomsbury Publishing, New Delhi, 2011.

Kamath, Vivek, 'How Mark Mascarenhas Redefined Celebrity Management', *Forbes India*, 26 December 2013, https://tinyurl.com/mvky6xxk. Accessed on 21 July 2025

Khan, Imran, *All Round View*, Chatto & Windus, London, 1988.

Krishnakumar, Sreedev, 'India and Pakistan: How the Two Countries Have Fared Since Partition', *Moneycontrol*, 14 August 2023, https://tinyurl.com/4a2ppzfx. Accessed on 21 July 2025.

Laxman, V.V.S., and R. Kaushik, *281 and Beyond*, Westland Sport, Chennai, 2018.

Lele, J.Y., *I Was There: Memoirs of a Cricket Administrator*, Marine Sports, Mumbai, 2011.

Lokapally, Vijay, and G. Krishnan, *The Hitman: The Rohit Sharma Story*, Bloomsbury India, New Delhi, 2021.

Lokapally, Vijay, *Driven: The Virat Kohli Story*, Bloomsbury India, New Delhi, 2023.

Majumdar, Boria, *Eleven Gods and a Billion Indians: The On and Off the Field Story of Cricket in India and Beyond*, Simon & Schuster India, New Delhi, 2018.

Majumdar, Boria, *Once Upon a Furore: Lost Pages of Indian Cricket*, Yoda Press, New Delhi, 2004.

'Marylebone Cricket Club', *Kiddle Kids Encyclopedia*, https://tinyurl.com/munfn43j. Accessed on 21 July 2025.

Mathur, Amrit, 'The World Cup Leaves England', *ESPNcricinfo*, 22 December 2014, https://tinyurl.com/2wpzdw82. Accessed on 21 July 2025.

'Meet Bunty Sajdeh: The Man Behind Virat Kohli's Multimillion-Dollar Empire', India Times Worth, 2 April 2024, https://tinyurl.com/bdh74tst. Accessed on 21 July 2025.

Menon, Suresh, 'Virat Kohli: Why Quitting Was the Only Option for "Cornered" Captain', *BBC News*, 17 January 2022, https://tinyurl.com/nhj8wknz. Accessed on 21 July 2025.

Menon, Suresh, *Bishan: Portrait of a Cricketer*, Penguin Books India, New Delhi, 2011.

Mukherjee, Abhishek, and Joy Bhattacharjya, *The Great Indian Cricket Circus: Amazing Facts, Stats and Everything in Between*, HarperCollins India, New Delhi, 2023.

Mukherjee, Abhishek, 'Gogumal Kishenchand: Lost in Don Bradman's Moment of Glory', CricketCountry, 14 April 2014, https://tinyurl.com/3v3f8x9b. Accessed on 21 July 2025.

Mukherjee, Abhishek, 'Indian Captaincy: A Farcical Musical Chairs—Six Captains in Seven Tests', *CricketCountry*, 6 February 2013, https://tinyurl.com/2yh6n2ae. Accessed on 21 July 2025.

Mukherjee, Abhishek, 'The 1990s Television Revolution of Indian Cricket and BCCI's Rise to Riches', *Moneycontrol*, 25 June 2023, https://tinyurl.com/434dtaaf. Accessed on 21 July 2025.

Mukherjee, Abhishek, *Caught Yapping – A History of Cricket in 100 Quotes*, Penguin Random House, 2025.

'Srinivasan: I Exercised All My Authority as BCCI President to Save MS Dhoni's Captaincy in 2011', *ESPNcricinfo*, 11 August 2020, https://tinyurl.com/4xnjpvv3. Accessed on 21 July 2025.

Narang, Rishav, 'When Rohit Sharma Wasn't Ready to Become India's Captain, Forcing Sourav Ganguly to Issue Ultimatum', *Times Now News*, 8 July 2024, https://tinyurl.com/74r5byde. Accessed on 21 July 2025.

Pandya, Haresh, 'BCCI: Backroom Blues', *Rediff India*, 7 May 2007, https://tinyurl.com/29d9x4mx. Accessed on 21 July 2025.

Pataudi, M.A.K, *Tiger's Tale: The Nawab of Pataudi*, Hind Pocket Books, Delhi, 1969.

Prabhudesai, Devendra, *Hero*, Rupa Publications India, New Delhi, 2017.

Prabhudesai, Devendra, *SMG: A Biography of Sunil Manohar Gavaskar*, Rupa Publications India, New Delhi, 2009.

Prabhudesai, Devendra, *The Nice Guy Who Finished First*, Rupa Publications India, New Delhi, 2019.

Prasanna, E.A.S., *One More Over*, Rupa & Co., 1977.

PTI, 'Srini Says Lorgat Not Reason Behind Not Finalizing SA's Tour', *The Times of India*, 10 October 2013, https://tinyurl.com/5yt7xzy4. Accessed on 18 July 2025.

Ramaswami, N.S., *From Porbandar to Wadekar*, Abhinav Publications, New Delhi, 1975.

Ramchand, Partab, 'Mankad–Roy May Be Dead, but Their 413 Lives On', *ESPNcricinfo*, 4 February 2001, https://tinyurl.com/mvsx2w5s. Accessed on 21 July 2025.

Ramchand, Partab, 'NCA Doors Closed for Expelled Trio', *ESPNcricinfo*, 23 July 2000, https://tinyurl.com/4a32zfv5. Accessed on 21 July 2025.

Rodrigues, Mario, *Batting for the Empire: A Political Biography of Ranjitsinhji*, Penguin Books India, New Delhi, 2008.

Sandhu, Balwinder Singh, *The Devil's Pack*, Rupa Publications India, New Delhi, 2011.

Santhosh, S., 'This Week, Last Year: NCA and the Lessons to Be Learned', *ESPNcricinfo*, 18 May 2001, https://tinyurl.com/5n8scp48. Accessed on 21 July 2025.

Sen, Rohan, 'Gautam Gambhir, MS Dhoni & CB Series Australia Tri Series', *India Today*, 8 December 2018, https://tinyurl.com/4hhpntak. Accessed on 21 July 2025.

Sen, Rohan, 'You Don't Decide If India Is Best Travelling Side in the World: COA Tells Ravi Shastri', *India Today*, 8 November 2018, https://tinyurl.com/3knbpeyz. Accessed on 21 July 2025.

Sengupta, Arunabha, 'The Many Feuds of Sunil Gavaskar', *Cricmash*, 24 January 2015, https://tinyurl.com/66exefv7. Accessed on 21 July 2025.

Shariff, Faisal, 'Harbhajan Singh: Harbhajan's Heartbreak at Being Left Out', *Rediff.com*, 20 March 2001, https://tinyurl.com/3esrefj9. Accessed on 21 July 2025.

Shetty, Ratnakar, *ON BOARD: My Years in BCCI*, Rupa Publications India, New Delhi, 2022.

Sridhar, Ramakrishnan, and R. Kaushik, *Coaching Beyond: My Days with the Indian Cricket Team*, Rupa, New Delhi, 2023.

'Supreme Court Recommends That Srinivasan Step Down', *ESPNcricinfo*, 25 March 2014, https://tinyurl.com/3y7x2smc. Accessed on 21 July 2025.

'The Committees Investigate the IPL Spot Fixing Scandal', *ESPNcricinfo*, 13 July 2015, https://tinyurl.com/5cy9f4db. Accessed on 21 July 2025.

'This Is How Much the Valuation of IPL Teams Has Increased Since 2008', *OfficeChai*, 26 May 2023, https://tinyurl.com/yt83jmxf. Accessed on 21 July 2025.

'Timeline: IPL Spot Fixing Controversy', *The Times of India*, 19 August 2015, https://tinyurl.com/4d9my7xp. Accessed on 21 July 2025.

Venugopal, Arun, 'How India Got Fast', *The Cricket Monthly*, 4 September 2017, https://tinyurl.com/p4yf2t3j. Accessed on 21 July 2025.

Vishwanath, Gundappa, *Wrist Assured*, Rupa Publications India, New Delhi, 2022.

Viswanath, Gundappa, 'Neil Harvey's scintillating 140 at Brabourne, six decades ago', *Sportstar*, 13 February 2017, https://tinyurl.com/yeanx8fp. Accessed on 18 July 2025.

Wadekar, Ajit, and K.N. Prabhu, *My Cricketing Years*, Vikas Publishing House, 1973.

Warne, Shane, *No Spin*, Ebury Publishing, London, 2019.

'Watch: Harbhajan Singh on How His Father's Wish and Tendulkar's Advice Kept His India Dream Alive', *Scroll.in*, 12 June 2020, https://tinyurl.com/hpy4p92v. Accessed on 21 July 2025.

Wright, John, *John Wright's Indian Summers*, Penguin Books India, New Delhi, 2006.

'WSG, Sony Bag IPL Broadcast Rights for ₹9.18 Mn', *Economic Times*, 15 January 2008, https://tinyurl.com/mtv6j2bw. Accessed on 21 July 2025.

INDEX

Abbas, Zaheer, 121, 133, 147, 216
Adelaide, 44, 82, 135, 138, 141, 169, 172, 188, 189, 236, 238, 258, 267, 276, 284, 285
Adhikari, Hemu, 51, 56, 61, 88, 99
Adhikari, Sudhakar, 92
Agarkar, Ajit, 220
Ahmedabad, 91, 143, 157, 175, 206, 256, 260, 265, 279, 286, 291
Ahmed, Ghulam, 31, 47, 51, 54, 58, 60, 70, 152
Akram, Wasim, 41, 185, 216, 217, 232
Alexander, Gerry, 111
Ali, Syed Mushtaq, 25, 26, 35, 36, 43, 121, 128, 133, 210, 216, 247
Altaf, Saleem, 121
Amarnath, Lala, 43, 44, 56, 104, 133, 136, 146, 208, 294
Amarnath, Mohinder, xi, xii, 19, 81, 87, 113, 115, 116, 120, 130, 146, 147, 149, 150, 151, 152, 153, 154, 158, 159, 164, 178, 180, 181, 182, 241, 268
Amarnath, Surinder, 81, 113, 122, 146
Amre, Pravin, 191
Apte, Madhav, 54, 92

Ashes, 8, 15, 22, 59, 99, 101, 142, 276
Ashwin, Ravichandran, xiii, 270, 277, 279, 285, 286, 290, 291, 296
Australia, ix, x, xi, xii, xiii, xiv, xvi, 1, 16, 18, 22, 41, 43, 44, 46, 50, 59, 63, 64, 65, 75, 76, 82, 83, 84, 85, 86, 87, 88, 89, 99, 101, 102, 113, 114, 115, 120, 121, 126, 130, 131, 135, 136, 138, 139, 141, 149, 152, 153, 159, 162, 163, 164, 165, 166, 168, 169, 170, 171, 172, 173, 174, 177, 178, 186, 188, 189, 190, 191, 202, 204, 206, 210, 211, 212, 213, 215, 216, 217, 220, 221, 223, 224, 225, 226, 227, 231, 232, 235, 236, 239, 240, 247, 248, 249, 251, 255, 257, 258, 259, 260, 261, 262, 263, 265, 267, 268, 269, 270, 276, 278, 280, 283, 284, 285, 288, 290, 291, 292, 295, 296, 297, 298
Azad, Kirti, 152
Azharuddin, Mohammad, 160, 161, 163, 164, 167, 168, 174, 181, 185, 186, 187, 188, 189, 191, 192, 202, 204, 205, 207, 208, 209, 211, 215, 216

Bahutule, Sairaj, 93, 211, 227
Baig, Abbas Ali, 62, 65, 99
Baloo, Palwankar, 3
Banerjee, Shute, 36, 45
Bengaluru (also Bangalore), 105, 109, 119, 125, 129, 131, 142, 145, 156, 157, 175, 190, 202, 212, 216, 221, 239, 252, 253, 262, 264, 278, 279, 280, 295
Bangar, Sanjay, 234, 276
Bangladesh, 50, 101, 180, 213, 221, 239, 240, 245, 246, 247, 248, 257, 263, 265, 268, 275, 278, 283, 285, 291, 295
BCCI, 5, 11, 13, 14, 16, 17, 18, 20, 21, 22, 23, 24, 27, 28, 29, 30, 33, 37, 39, 43, 46, 48, 49, 52, 54, 55, 59, 60, 65, 71, 76, 87, 88, 90, 91, 101, 102, 104, 105, 112, 118, 126, 128, 132, 155, 156, 161, 162, 171, 177, 178, 179, 181, 182, 187, 193, 197, 198, 199, 200, 203, 204, 207, 208, 209, 215, 218, 219, 221, 228, 229, 240, 241, 245, 246, 247, 248, 250, 251, 252, 253, 255, 257, 262, 268, 269, 271, 273, 274, 275, 280, 281, 288, 296, 299, 300
Bedi, Bishan, x, xi, xii, 79, 81, 84, 87, 98, 100, 102, 103, 106, 109, 110, 111, 112, 113, 114, 115, 116, 118, 119, 120, 122, 123, 124, 126, 129, 134, 141, 149, 152, 168, 182, 187, 192
Bhosle, Vijay, 94
Bijl, Vincent van der, 140

Binny, Roger, 131
Birmingham, 81, 127, 171, 205
Bombay Gymkhana, 2, 3, 7, 8, 9, 10, 19, 32
Borde, Chandrakant, 61, 64, 67, 68, 71, 74, 75, 76, 77, 78, 82, 83, 86, 87, 88, 89, 94, 95, 152, 160, 246
Brabourne, 27, 28, 32, 34, 35, 51, 59, 75, 88, 101, 104, 252, 260
Bridgetown, 70, 98, 114, 150, 207, 229, 292
Broad, Stuart, 249
Bumrah, Jasprit, xiii, 42, 196, 279, 281, 282, 284, 286, 289, 291, 292, 296

Central Zone, 87, 91
Champions Trophy, 174, 239, 243, 251, 262, 273, 281, 298
Chandrasekhar, Bhagwat, xii, 72, 75, 76, 78, 79, 81, 83, 93, 99, 100, 103, 105, 107, 109, 110, 113, 116, 120, 124, 126, 129, 192
Chauhan, Chetan, 85, 120, 128, 134, 141
Chauhan, Rajesh, 192, 210
Chennai (also Madras), 18, 20, 21, 23, 28, 29, 30, 36, 37, 45, 47, 48, 52, 58, 59, 60, 61, 65, 67, 72, 75, 76, 78, 79, 83, 87, 104, 105, 110, 118, 119, 120, 125, 129, 132, 135, 143, 144, 158, 161, 168, 172, 173, 179, 192, 196, 197, 252

Chopra, Akash, 237
Contractor, Nari, 62, 63, 64, 65, 66, 67, 69, 70, 71
Cummins, Pat, xiv

Daniel, Wayne, 115, 140
Dasgupta, Deep, 228
Das, Shiv Sunder, 225, 228, 234
David, Noel, 208
De Mello, Anthony, 3, 4, 5, 10, 16, 20, 27, 28, 29, 30, 35, 39, 43, 44, 45, 46, 50
Deodhar, D.B., 32, 112
Desai, Ramakant, 60, 61, 62, 65, 67, 73, 82, 84, 92, 94, 106
Dhawan, Shikhar, 270, 273, 274, 279, 281, 284, 289
Dhoni, Mahendra Singh, 240, 241, 246, 247, 248, 249, 253, 254, 258, 259, 260, 265, 266, 267, 268, 270, 273, 274, 275, 276, 279, 280, 284, 285
Dighe, Sameer, 227
Digvijaysinhji, 29, 33, 46
Doshi, Dilip, 129, 137, 139, 141
Dravid, Rahul, 41, 204, 205, 206, 207, 214, 215, 217, 219, 220, 221, 224, 225, 226, 227, 229, 230, 232, 234, 235, 236, 237, 239, 241, 242, 245, 246, 247, 248, 253, 256, 257, 258, 259, 260, 262, 264, 268, 269, 270, 271, 289, 293
Duleepsinhji, K.S., 12, 15, 36, 38, 71
Duleep Trophy, 89, 120, 145, 146

Durani, Salim, 65, 74, 89
Durban, 191, 207, 247, 264

East Zone, 71, 88, 204
Eden Gardens, 78, 156, 175, 201, 202, 226
Engineer, Farokh, 65, 78, 80
England, x, 1, 2, 3, 5, 6, 8, 9, 11, 12, 13, 14, 15, 16, 17, 18, 19, 20, 22, 23, 24, 26, 28, 29, 30, 34, 36, 37, 38, 39, 40, 43, 46, 47, 48, 49, 50, 52, 56, 59, 61, 62, 63, 65, 66, 67, 71, 72, 77, 80, 81, 83, 89, 91, 99, 100, 101, 102, 103, 104, 105, 106, 107, 109, 111, 112, 113, 115, 118, 119, 120, 123, 126, 127, 128, 129, 130, 132, 133, 141, 142, 143, 144, 149, 151, 153, 154, 155, 159, 160, 161, 162, 163, 164, 165, 168, 169, 170, 171, 174, 176, 177, 178, 182, 185, 186, 187, 188, 190, 191, 192, 200, 202, 203, 204, 205, 210, 220, 229, 230, 231, 232, 234, 242, 245, 246, 247, 248, 249, 251, 256, 257, 259, 260, 261, 262, 265, 268, 269, 270, 273, 275, 279, 280, 282, 284, 286, 289, 290, 291, 298

Gadkari, Chandrashekhar, 54
Gaekwad, Aunshuman, 110, 114, 149, 156, 212, 215
Gaekwad, Datta, 54, 61
Gaekwad, Fatehsinghrao, 15, 61, 148

Gambhir, Gautam, 249, 256, 259, 260, 266, 267, 268, 269, 279
Gandotra, Ashok, 85
Ganguly, 214
Ganguly, Sourav, 204, 205, 206, 209, 211, 214, 217, 219, 220, 222, 223, 224, 225, 226, 227, 228, 229, 230, 231, 232, 234, 235, 237, 238, 239, 240, 241, 242, 243, 247, 253, 256, 257, 258, 259, 266, 288, 289
Gavaskar, Sunil, ix, xi, xii, 39, 41, 85, 89, 93, 96, 97, 98, 99, 100, 102, 105, 107, 109, 111, 112, 113, 114, 115, 116, 119, 120, 121, 122, 124, 125, 126, 127, 128, 129, 130, 131, 132, 133, 135, 136, 137, 138, 139, 140, 141, 142, 143, 144, 145, 147, 148, 149, 150, 151, 152, 153, 154, 157, 158, 159, 160, 161, 162, 163, 164, 165, 166, 168, 169, 170, 171, 173, 174, 175, 176, 178, 179, 180, 186, 187, 188, 197, 200, 206, 226, 236, 242, 246, 259, 275, 290, 298
Ghavri, Karsan, 110, 141
Gilchrist, Adam, 60, 61, 71, 224, 226
Gilligan, Arthur, 3, 7
Gill, Shubman, xiv, xv, 291, 298, 299
Goel, Rajinder, 109
Govan, Grant, 3
Govindraj, D., 89, 126

Greig, Tony, x, 104, 119
Gupte, Subhash, 51, 54, 58, 62, 66, 180

Haldipur, Nikhil, 222
Hardikar, Manohar, 93
Hayden, Matthew, 224, 226
Hazare, Vijay, 29, 32, 33, 40, 44, 52, 63
Hindlekar, Dattaram, 25
Hirwani, Narendra, 179, 180, 189, 206
Hogg, Rodney, 130, 135
Holder, Vanburn, 110, 115, 124
Holding, Michael, 114, 115, 116, 124, 154
Hyderabad, xiii, 21, 24, 31, 58, 65, 71, 77, 82, 83, 85, 86, 89, 91, 92, 129, 147, 160, 198, 206, 208, 215, 224, 252, 253, 262, 279, 294

ICC, x, 4, 5, 10, 27, 42, 101, 105, 115, 127, 144, 151, 168, 177, 190, 197, 199, 213, 220, 228, 231, 247, 251, 260, 261, 262, 263, 264, 269, 281, 284, 290, 291, 297, 298
Indian Premier League, xiii, 3, 42, 208, 248, 252, 253, 254, 255, 260, 261, 262, 263, 268, 272, 275, 279, 281, 285, 287, 289, 294, 296, 299
Indrajitsinhji, 75
Irani Cup, 65, 87, 113, 146, 184, 190, 235
Ismail, Abdul, 94

Index

Jadeja, Ravindra, xiii, 67, 270, 273, 279, 284, 290, 291, 298
Jaffer, Wasim, 34, 234, 259
Jai, L.P., 7, 19, 21, 60, 294
Jaisimha, M.L., 65, 68, 74, 77, 82, 83, 85, 87, 89, 97, 99, 199
Jaiswal, Yashaswi, 291
Jamshedji, R., 19
Jayantilal, Kenia, 89
Jayasuriya, Sanath, 202
Jayawardene, Mahela, 40, 265
Johannesburg, 207, 243, 249, 274, 282
Joshi, P.G., 55
Julien, Bernard, 115
Jurel, Dhruv, 291

Kallicharran, Alvin, 110, 124, 125
Kaluwitharana, Romesh, 202
Kambli, Vinod, 184, 191, 192, 194, 195, 203, 204, 209
Kanitkar, Hrishikesh, 211
Karim, Saba, 70, 209
Kartik, Murali, 222, 239
Khan, Iftikar Ali, 12, 15, 16, 22, 23, 37, 38, 40, 67
Khan, Imran, 41, 121, 123, 130, 131, 147, 148, 156, 163, 165, 166, 185, 216
Khan, Mansoor Ali, 67, 68, 71, 72, 73, 74, 75, 76, 77, 80, 81, 82, 83, 84, 86, 87, 88, 89, 96, 99, 104, 106, 108, 109, 110, 111, 121, 246, 269
Khan, Sarfaraz, 291, 295
Khan, Zaheer, 197, 220, 227, 232, 243, 246, 264, 265, 266, 279

Kolkata, 76, 252
Kolkata (also Calcutta), iv, 18, 20, 23, 30, 35, 36, 39, 43, 45, 46, 52, 59, 60, 67, 76, 78, 79, 86, 87, 94, 104, 105, 110, 119, 125, 130, 132, 157, 161, 175, 178, 179, 180, 192, 201, 202, 204, 207, 208, 212, 214, 218, 224, 236, 238, 241, 252, 253, 263, 271, 275, 290, 305
Kuruvilla, Abey, 207

Lal, Arun, 149, 179, 181, 182
Lal, Madan, xii, 106, 110, 116, 134, 141, 142, 147, 152, 153, 154, 156, 164, 170, 215
Langer, Justin, 224
Laxman, V. V. S., 146, 206, 215, 223, 224, 225, 226, 227, 229, 236, 237, 243, 244, 253, 261, 263, 264, 269, 270, 271
Leeds, 49, 80, 127, 170, 234, 238, 286
Lloyd, Clive, 78, 97, 109, 124
Lord's, 13, 25, 38, 50, 62, 80, 81, 99, 100, 107, 127, 132, 143, 144, 154, 170, 171, 176, 186, 187, 205, 230, 246, 275, 276, 286

Manchester, 25, 62, 100, 107, 144, 151, 152, 186, 246
Manjrekar, Sanjay, 180, 185, 188, 190, 191, 194, 205
Manjrekar, Vijay, 49, 54, 57, 60, 61, 62, 65, 67, 70, 74, 75, 76, 82
Mankad, Ashok, xii, 85, 98, 103, 120

Mankad, Vinoo, 41, 44, 48, 56, 85
Mantri, Madhav, 49
MCC, 3, 4, 7, 8, 9, 13, 18, 19, 27, 46, 78, 81, 155, 176, 183, 187
Melbourne, xiii, 44, 82, 136, 137, 163, 165, 169, 215, 236, 257, 276, 284, 285
Merchant, Vijay, 8, 11, 19, 25, 26, 28, 29, 32, 33, 34, 35, 36, 37, 38, 39, 40, 43, 46, 52, 64, 66, 85, 86, 87, 88, 99, 124, 128, 237, 294, 299
Miller, Colin, 227
Mishra, Amit, 277
Mohali, 194, 242, 252, 253, 259, 263, 265
Mohammed, Mushtaq, 121
Mohanty, Debasis, 209
Mongia, Nayan, 193, 206
More, Kiran, 168
MRF Pace Foundation, 185, 197
Mukherjea, J.C., 46
Mumbai (also Bombay), xiv, 1, 2, 3, 7, 8, 9, 10, 11, 14, 18, 19, 21, 22, 23, 24, 27, 28, 29, 30, 32, 33, 34, 36, 37, 38, 39, 41, 44, 45, 47, 48, 49, 51, 52, 54, 55, 57, 58, 59, 60, 61, 64, 65, 66, 67, 71, 72, 76, 77, 78, 79, 81, 85, 86, 87, 89, 90, 91, 92, 93, 94, 95, 96, 98, 101, 103, 104, 105, 106, 108, 109, 110, 111, 112, 113, 117, 119, 124, 125, 128, 130, 131, 132, 134, 135, 139, 141, 142, 149, 152, 157, 158, 159, 160, 161, 165, 166, 173, 174, 178, 179, 180, 184, 187,
188, 192, 194, 196, 197, 203, 207, 208, 211, 216, 220, 224, 235, 239, 241, 242, 250, 252, 253, 259, 260, 261, 263, 271, 272, 274, 279, 289, 290, 291, 293, 295, 300, 303, 305
Muralitharan, Muttiah, 229, 258, 263, 266, 296

Nadar, Rameshchandra, 67
Naik, Ajit, 81
Nair, Karun, 279
Natarajan, Thangarasu, xiii
Nayudu, C.K., 7, 12, 13, 17, 19, 25, 35, 49, 112, 294
Nehra, Ashish, 232, 266
New Zealand, 10, 58, 59, 76, 77, 82, 83, 84, 85, 88, 112, 113, 114, 118, 127, 135, 136, 139, 141, 143, 164, 169, 170, 177, 178, 180, 185, 186, 187, 189, 193, 194, 208, 212, 213, 215, 220, 221, 231, 232, 235, 247, 249, 259, 262, 264, 269, 270, 274, 279, 284, 285, 287, 289, 290, 291, 295, 296, 298
Nikhil, Haldipur, 222
Nissar, Mohammed, 12, 14, 19, 294, 296
North Zone, 71, 112, 120, 134, 145, 166

Ogilvie, David, xi

Pakistan, x, 2, 15, 31, 41, 42, 50, 51, 52, 53, 56, 57, 58, 59, 80, 92, 101, 121, 122, 123, 124,

126, 130, 131, 132, 133, 135,
143, 145, 146, 147, 148, 149,
152, 154, 155, 156, 157, 158,
159, 163, 165, 166, 167, 168,
170, 174, 175, 176, 177, 178,
181, 182, 183, 184, 185, 186,
187, 188, 189, 193, 194, 197,
202, 206, 208, 209, 210, 211,
213, 214, 215, 216, 218, 227,
232, 236, 237, 238, 240, 241,
242, 247, 248, 249, 255, 256,
257, 262, 264, 265, 268, 278,
281, 287, 290, 291, 298
Pandit, Chandrakant, 55, 173
Pandya, Hardik, 279, 282, 292
Pant, Rishabh, xv, xvi, 284, 286, 289, 291, 292
Parkar, Ghulam, 149, 159
Parker, Ramnath, 94, 103
Pascoe, Len, 135
Patel, Jasu, 60, 61, 63
Patel, Parthiv, 237
Pathan, Irfan, 197, 240, 242
Pathan, Yusuf, 249
Patil, Sandeep, 55, 135, 140, 141, 204
Perth, 83, 121, 141, 188, 189, 257, 267, 284, 296
Phadkar, Dattu, 44, 45, 49, 56, 106
Pietersen, Kevin, 270
Ponting, Ricky, 224, 226, 257, 258, 272
Port Elizabeth, 118, 191, 229
Port of Spain, 71, 97, 100, 114, 115, 117, 132, 173, 229
Prabhakar, Manoj, 159, 171, 185, 188, 191, 218, 219

Prasanna, Erapalli, xii, 67, 79, 81, 84, 85, 87, 93, 96, 97, 103, 104, 105, 106, 108, 111, 113, 120, 124, 162, 192
Pujara, Cheteshwar, xv, xvi, 264, 270, 274, 277, 284, 286, 291
Pune, 41, 91, 280, 281, 295

Quadrangular, 2, 3, 9, 10, 12, 18, 22, 32, 194

Rahane, Ajinkya, xv, xvii, 274, 276, 277, 280, 282, 285, 291
Raina, Suresh, 264, 265
Ramchand, Gulabrai, 54, 63
Ramesh, Sadagoppan, 224
Ramji, L., 19
Ranji Trophy, 21, 29, 30, 31, 32, 33, 34, 37, 40, 46, 49, 55, 61, 65, 90, 91, 92, 93, 94, 95, 108, 109, 134, 141, 164, 166, 184, 187, 203, 208, 224, 261, 279, 289
Ranjitsinhji, Kumar Sri, 3, 8, 9, 11, 12, 20, 264
Rathour, Vikram, 289
Razdan, Vivek, ix, 184, 197
Reddy, Bharat, 126
Rege, Milind, 94
Richards, Vivian, 110, 114, 124, 149, 154, 179
Roy, Ambar, 85
Roy, Pankaj, 47, 54, 58, 62, 149, 152
Roy, Pranab, 149

Saha, Wriddhiman, 261, 279
Saldanha, Nicky, 94

Salgaonkar, Pandurang, 106, 109, 126
Sampat, Mahesh, 94
Sandhu, Balwinder Singh, 148, 152, 154
Sangakkara, Kumar, 40, 265, 266
Sehwag, Virender, 228, 229, 230, 232, 233, 235, 236, 237, 239, 242, 244, 249, 253, 256, 257, 258, 259, 260, 265, 266, 267, 270, 279
Sengupta, A.K., 60
Shami, Mohammed, xiii, 274, 282, 284, 286, 291
Sharjah, 159, 166, 167, 168, 170, 174, 180, 181, 188, 191, 194, 210, 212, 213, 218, 220
Sharma, Chetan, 159, 167, 170, 173, 178
Sharma, Joginder, 249
Sharma, Parthasarathy, 114
Sharma, Rohit, xiv, 249, 260, 261, 271, 272, 273, 281, 283, 284, 285, 286, 288, 289, 291, 292, 297, 298
Sharma, Yashpal, 129, 140, 147, 268
Shastri, Ravi, 93, 149, 160, 166, 173, 176, 179, 245, 246, 276, 281, 283
Shivalkar, Padmakar, 94, 112
Singh, Bhupinder, 3, 4, 5, 10, 12, 13, 14, 17, 19, 20, 21, 22, 23, 27, 28, 29, 30, 294
Singh, Hanumant, 80, 104, 160, 221, 222
Singh, Harbhajan, 222, 223, 224, 226, 227, 228, 230, 234, 239, 240, 249, 257, 258, 264, 266, 272
Singh, Maninder, 146, 149, 173, 174, 175, 178, 182, 183
Singh, Robin, 209, 245
Singh, R.P., 249
Singh, Yuvraj, 220, 249, 253, 266, 281
Solkar, Eknath, 85
South Africa, x, 5, 28, 40, 101, 118, 142, 168, 176, 188, 190, 191, 192, 199, 201, 202, 203, 206, 207, 210, 215, 216, 218, 220, 225, 228, 229, 231, 236, 239, 241, 243, 246, 247, 258, 261, 262, 263, 264, 265, 273, 274, 277, 282, 285, 289, 290, 292
South Africans, 292
South Zone, 71, 77, 81, 87, 88, 89, 104
Sportstar, 59, 127, 138, 158, 189, 212
Sportsweek, 160
Srikkanth, Krishnamachari, 141, 145, 149, 152, 154, 163, 164, 165, 169, 170, 181, 182, 184, 185, 202, 268
Sri Lanka, 35, 105, 106, 112, 127, 145, 151, 159, 160, 167, 168, 169, 170, 174, 175, 180, 183, 187, 193, 194, 201, 202, 203, 205, 208, 209, 213, 214, 218, 220, 221, 229, 230, 231, 232, 241, 242, 243, 245, 247, 258, 259, 260, 262, 263, 265,

267, 268, 275, 277, 281, 289, 290
Srinath, Javagal, 191, 192, 194, 197, 203, 206, 207, 208, 214, 217, 219, 220, 231, 232, 297, 298
Starc, Mitchell, xiv, xv, xvi
Sundar, Washington, xiii, xvi
Surti, Rusi, 82
Sydney, xi, 16, 44, 83, 135, 163, 164, 165, 169, 188, 189, 215, 236, 240, 257, 276, 283, 284, 286, 297
Symonds, Andrew, 257, 258, 272
Syed, Kirmani, xii, 113, 116, 125, 126, 127, 130, 137, 139, 152, 153, 156, 163, 168

Tamhane, Naren, 57, 184
Tendulkar, Sachin, 10, 41, 184, 185, 186, 188, 189, 191, 194, 197, 201, 202, 205, 206, 207, 208, 209, 210, 211, 212, 213, 214, 215, 216, 217, 219, 220, 222, 224, 225, 226, 227, 228, 229, 230, 231, 232, 233, 234, 235, 236, 237, 238, 239, 242, 243, 244, 245, 247, 253, 256, 257, 258, 259, 262, 263, 264, 265, 266, 267, 268, 270, 271, 272, 274
Thakur, Shardul, xiv, 286
The Oval, 26, 39, 50, 100, 102, 103, 127, 144, 173, 235, 246, 269, 281, 286
Toohey, Peter, xi
Trueman, Frederick, 49

Umesh, Kulkarni, 106
Umesh, Yadav, xiii
Umrigar, Polly, 47, 54, 56, 92, 115
Uthappa, Robin, 249

Valson, Sunil, 152
Vengsarkar, Dilip, xi, xii, 113, 114, 125, 127, 128, 131, 138, 143, 144, 147, 150, 152, 158, 163, 164, 165, 170, 171, 173, 174, 179, 180, 181, 182, 186, 188, 240, 247
Venkataraghavan, Srinivasaraghavan, 76, 77, 79, 81, 86, 87, 89, 93, 96, 100, 102, 103, 106, 108, 109, 110, 112, 113, 116, 124, 125, 126, 127, 128, 149, 156, 221
Vijay, Murali, 270, 276, 279
Viswanath, Gundappa, xi, xii, 59, 86, 87, 93, 100, 104, 105, 107, 110, 111, 115, 116, 119, 120, 121, 122, 125, 126, 127, 128, 132, 133, 135, 136, 137, 143, 144, 149, 160, 163, 165, 168, 183, 191
Viswanath, Sadanand, 160, 183

Wadekar, Ajit, 58, 77, 78, 79, 80, 84, 87, 88, 89, 90, 92, 93, 96, 97, 98, 99, 100, 102, 103, 104, 105, 106, 108, 190, 191, 192, 204, 215
Wankhede, Sheshrao, 105
Wankhede Stadium, 111, 133, 252, 265, 266, 271, 293

Waugh, Steve, 224, 226
Weekes, Everton, 54
Wessels, Kepler, 190
West Indies, x, 10, 28, 44, 45,
    46, 52, 54, 55, 60, 61, 66, 67,
    71, 77, 78, 79, 83, 87, 88, 89,
    93, 96, 97, 98, 99, 101, 102,
    109, 110, 111, 113, 114, 116,
    117, 124, 125, 126, 127, 132,
    133, 149, 150, 151, 152, 153,
    154, 156, 157, 158, 159, 168,
    169, 174, 178, 179, 180, 181,
    194, 199, 201, 203, 207, 208,
    209, 210, 213, 226, 229, 230,
    231, 235, 243, 255, 265, 268,
    269, 271, 273, 274, 283, 291
West Zone, 60, 71, 81, 87, 88,
    91, 92, 94, 108, 145, 184
World Cup, 5, 53, 112, 113, 114,
    115, 127, 129, 151, 152, 155,
    157, 165, 170, 174, 176, 177,
    178, 183, 185, 189, 193, 194,
    195, 198, 201, 202, 203, 204,
    208, 214, 215, 216, 217, 218,
    220, 221, 222, 223, 230, 231,
    235, 236, 243, 244, 245, 247,
    248, 249, 255, 257, 258, 260,
    262, 263, 264, 265, 266, 267,
    269, 275, 276, 278, 281, 284,
    287, 288, 289, 290, 291, 292,
    293, 295, 297, 298
World Series Cricket, x, 120,
    127, 129
WSC, x, xi, 121, 124, 126, 127,
    141

Yadav, Kuldeep, 280, 291, 298
Younis, Waqar, 185, 216, 232